THE VELVET
UNDERGROUND

Icons of Pop Music
Jill Halstead and Dave Laing, eds.

Books in this series, designed for undergraduates and the general reader, offer a critical profile of a key figure or group in twentieth-century pop music. These short paperback volumes will focus on the work rather than on biography, and emphasize critical interpretation.

Forthcoming in the series

Elton John
Dave Laing

Bob Dylan
Keith Negus

Joni Mitchell
Jill Halstead

Björk
Nicola Dibben

THE VELVET
UNDERGROUND

RICHARD WITTS

INDIANA
University Press
Bloomington & Indianapolis

First published in Great Britain in 2006 by

Equinox Publishing Ltd
Unit 6, The Village
101 Amies St
London, SW11 2JW

www.equinoxpub.com

Published in North America by

Indiana University Press
601 North Morton Street
Bloomington, Indiana 47404-3797 USA

http://iupress.indiana.edu

Telephone orders	800-842-6796
Fax orders	812-855-7931
Orders by e-mail	iuporder@indiana.edu

A catalogue record for this book is available from the British Library.

ISBN 1 904768 27 X (paperback)

Cataloging information is available from the Library of Congress.

ISBN 0 253 21832 2 (pbk.)

1 2 3 4 5 11 10 09 08 07 06

Typeset by CA Typesetting, www.sheffieldtypesetting.com
Printed and bound in Great Britain by Antony Rowe, Chippenham, Wiltshire

To Kate Lister
une femme pas fatale

Contents

Acknowledgements

The author would like to express his gratitude to the following:

- Bloomsbury Press for permission to reprint extracts from *What's Welsh for Zen?* by Victor Bockris and John Cale (1999).
- The Random House Group Ltd for permission to reprint extracts from *Lou Reed: The Biography* by Victor Bockris (1994).
- Harvard University Press for permission to reprint extracts from *Blows Like A Horn: Beat Writing, Jazz, Style, and Markets in the Transformation of U. S. Culture* by Preston Whiley Jr. Copyright 2004 by the President and Fellows of Harvard College.
- Rutgers University Press for permission to reprint an extract from Hendricks, ed., *Critical Mass: Happenings, Fluxus, Performance, Intermedia and Rutgers University 1958–72* (2003).
- Cambridge University Press for permission to reprint an extract from Keith Potter, *Four Musical Minimalists* (2000).
- Alan Hall for permission to use interview extracts from the radio documentary *Strange Brew* (1993).
- The Random House Group Ltd for permission to reprint an extract from Robert Hughes, *American Visions* (Harvill Press, 1997).
- "Batman and Robin" print (1967) courtesy of Globe Photos.

The author has made every reasonable effort to contact holders of copyright in all quoted material. Any omission of copyright acknowledgement is unintentional, and the publishers will, if notified, correct any such omission in subsequent editions.

1 New York City

New York is the greatest city in the world – and everything
is wrong with it.

New York Herald, January 25th, 1965

That was The Velvet Underground, a very New York sound.
Let's hope it stays there.

American radio DJ, 1967[1]

Although New York is not the capital of the United States, it is without
doubt the capital of America's broken rules. And it's by far the largest city in
the land, the nation's focus for finance, fashion and freakery. Many heart-
land Americans resent the place. They see New York City as a spot solely for
making money and throwing it around. Others consider it a shred of old
Europe that drifted over the Atlantic ocean and got stuck around the mouth
of the Hudson River, an island full of churlish misfits. Nevertheless, these
critics concede – even admire – the productive, adrenalin energy and the
kinetic vigour to be found in "the city that never sleeps". Perhaps, as Jean
Baudrillard argues, "There is no human reason to be here, except for the
sheer ecstasy of being crowded together."[2] The Velvet Underground's chief
songwriter Lou Reed describes it as a place where you must "Run run run
run run" just to keep yourself in drugs.

A reason put forward for this ant-like intensity is that a lot of pushy people live cheek by jowl in these cramped acres. When The Velvet Underground
(henceforth, when it suits, "the Velvets") was formed in 1965 the population
of New York City measured 7.8 million.[3] They endured an extreme density of
25,000 people per square mile (the density of Los Angeles – determined at
the time to become New York's cultural rival – was one-fifth of that, at 5,000
per square mile[4]). It's due to such compression that this otherwise flat city
shoots up in the air. Its iconic verticality – the monumental needles or slabs
of cement and glass we call skyscrapers jostling for attention on Manhattan
island – overshadows the antique stoops and blocks, the tenement buildings
and warehouses (nowadays converted into homely "lofts") already considered "immensely tall" by the Russian composer Tchaikovsky when he visited
New York in 1891. He couldn't understand even then how so many people

could live "on top of each other".[5] This peculiar, physical "pressure" is often used to explain away the intensity of certain New York art, especially that of the Velvets, as we'll hear.

Another explanation commonly offered for its manic virulence is that New York City is built for business. Its main district, Manhattan, is constructed for the most part as a transport grid of 12 numbered avenues (north–south) and 220 numbered streets (east–west). Only the old American Indian dust track called Broadway, running through them at an angle, offers variety to this rational scheme. Connecting the avenues and streets underground is the subway train system, each line duly numbered and lettered. It's this subway that provides a primal reference point to the music of a band that pointedly has "underground" in its name.

While New York is divided into five large administrative "boroughs", only two of these need concern us here: the central island of (uptown/mid-town/downtown) Manhattan, and the suburban district of Queens. It was in Queens on Long Island where Lou Reed grew up and in 1970 stumbled back, weighed down by the total failure of the Velvets, to work as a typist for his father's accounting firm. These five boroughs are then split into 38 "neighbourhoods", from Battery Park to Yorktown.

The Velvet Underground was a pioneer "downtown" band, associated as such with the neighbourhood known as the Lower East Side. Being south of central Manhattan, the quarter was literally "down-town" on the subway maps, but also "down" in its degenerate, mongrel contrast to the diamond-studded "uptown" lifestyle of fine wines and string quartets. Known for many generations to be the quintessential American "melting pot" spot for immigrant communities, the Lower East Side was commonly the first dis-trict in which the poor would stay after disembarking from transatlantic ships that docked nearby. Wave upon wave of migrancy can be detected from the remains of Jewish, Italian, and Chinese settlements still sheltering there. By the 1960s Puerto Ricans had become the majority ethnic group in the Lower East Side (before many dispersed north to Spanish or East Har-lem, "El Barrio"). There were 650,000 on Manhattan island in 1965 (a total Hispanic émigré rise from 70,000 in 1940 to 1.4 million in 1970).[6]

Lower East Side was always considered less of a place to live in than to endure and, in due time, quit. During the 1960s the area was registered as comprising no less than 43,000 cockroach-troubled tenements, "dark, smelly, hovels" according to one observer.[7] It was in one of these "hovels" at 56 Ludlow Street that the Velvets first lived together, rehearsed and formed their identity. And it was one of those 650,000 Puerto Ricans who would become "The Man", the mysterious man in the big straw hat and fence-climber shoes for whom Lou Reed waited on 125th Street in El Barrio, "twenty-six dollars in my hand".[8]

The Velvets were themselves immigrants to the downtown scene. Not one of the nine principals involved in the band between 1965 and 1970 came from the area. They had migrated there with the same motive that many other young, creative men and women moved to the neighbourhood – it was considered cheap(er), communal and artistic, with hundreds of like minds scrimping around for work, cash and drugs. As artist Frank Stella said, "You start at the bottom in New York, and the bottom is pretty bottom-like in New York."[9]

Nevertheless the East Side was a district that was being carved up for gentrification by estate agents at the very time, around 1965, that the group came into existence. This socio-geographic re-figuration reflected, in bricks and boundaries, the shifts of cultural power taking place in the city at the time. For example, the modern art market moved downtown away from the commercial midtown galleries originally located around the Museum of Modern Art. In early 1964, artist Andy Warhol initially established his "Silver" Factory midtown at 47th Street, but in early 1968 he moved it south to become part of the East Village locale at Union Square.

The northern section of Lower East Side came to be called the East Village, really to sanction rent rises and underscore the groovy, "happening" scene there. At the centre of it were the Velvets, in the guise of Andy Warhol's resident band at the Dom hall on St Mark's Place in early 1966. Guitarist Sterling Morrison later claimed: "It really sickens me still when I go to St. Mark's Place because more than anyone we invented that street."[10]

"East *Greenwich* Village" was the implication of this rebranding, at the same time marking it off culturally, racially, and economically from the Lower East Side. A physical frontier between East Village and Lower East Side was fixed by Houston Street (pronounced "How-ston"), which had also set the southern limit for Greenwich Village to the west. Below it – "South of Houston" – a similar district was abridged in name to SoHo and bolted on to the Village to undergo the same estate agent alchemy.

Greenwich Village itself was where the Velvets first played New York in December 1965, at the Café Bizarre, 106 West 3rd Street.[11] Coincidentally the neighbourhood was home to Lou Reed's hero Bob Dylan,[12] whose song "Positively 4th Street" and 1963 album cover shot for *The Freewheelin' Bob Dylan* paraded his Village affinities. This rather demure district lay at the bottom of the imposed grid pattern of Manhattan streets and avenues. Besides its low-numbered streets (from 1st to 14th) it also possessed its own criss-cross of named byways, disclosing its early nineteenth-century origins. From the start of the twentieth century onwards, when the increasingly affluent residents had moved uptown to live by the verdant bliss of Central Park, artists took advantage of cheap rents and moved in. Greenwich Village, hosting new music in bars and poetry readings in cafés, became a centre of creative, progressive bohemianism, which to a reduced degree it has maintained (both Cale and Reed of the Velvets live there now). So, for an artist to live in the Lower East Side in the 1950s or East Village in the 1960s betrayed a desire to associate oneself with the aesthetic radicalism of the area long established to the West.

Of course, it was equally an economic choice to do so. The East Village and SoHo had once housed a number of busy light-industry plants and cast-iron warehouses. But, as these closed down during the 1950s and 1960s, they freed up space for visual artists of all kinds to take on. Musicians like the Velvets would thus find themselves within a set of lively experimental arts communities, and this factor within their domestic location would influence the band momentously, at least in its first, most famous years. Yet the handing-over of workshops by engineers to artists was more consequential than this. The shift, chiefly between 1960 and 1965 when 227 large manufacturing companies left the city,[13] marked the economic decline of New York, one that would lead to its sensational bankruptcy ten years later in 1975. In terms of failure and decay, the link between The Velvet Underground and its city will become a nagging theme in this book.

The East Village was also a refuge for those who wished to reclaim radicalism, both political and artistic, for their time. Such an attitude as this was energized in the watershed year, 1963, that John Cale arrived in New York. Rebel spirits rose in response to the US government's escalation of military manoeuvres in the Asian country of South Vietnam, as well as the growing awareness of the value of civil disobedience, such as boycotts and sit-ins, informed by the black civil rights campaigns. On August 28th, 1963, over 200,000 people (including Bob Dylan) demonstrated in the nation's capital of Washington DC, where Martin Luther King gave his "I have a dream" speech.

But the main detonator was the assassination of the youngish president, John F. Kennedy, in Dallas on November 22nd of that year. These events galvanized a drive for radical social protest and change, to be expressed through political performance as well as explored and displayed through artistic action. There were many different activist currents in politics and the creative arts at the time, as we'll discover, but The Velvet Underground's very existence was motivated by these trends fermenting around it.

While this cultural reawakening was induced by dramatic events, there were two other factors we might note – one national and one local. At the national – even international – level, birth statistics show how a large generation of young adults were growing up from the "baby boom" era around World War II (1942–5 in the case of the USA).[14] Having experienced a conservative, conformist childhood of the post-war Republican era under President Eisenhower (1953–61), to be followed by a traumatically curtailed period of unfulfilled hope under the Democrat leader Kennedy (1961–3), an urge fuelled these "baby boomers" to freshen up society, challenge conventions and test notions of liberty. As Phil Lesh, bass guitarist of the Velvets' Californian competitor The Grateful Dead, put it in conversation:

> The 1950s in the United States was a very uptight kind of period. My parents used to describe Eisenhower as "a fine man". I'm sure he was a fine man but that doesn't mean he was a great president. I couldn't see how he could be a role model. Some people like to look back on the 1950s with nostalgia, because that's when they were growing up, but to me the 1950s were a cage. You know, some kids can't wait to grow up and get the hell out of it, and that was me.
>
> After the Kennedy assassination there was a feeling that the whole world had fallen apart. There had to be something new. Nobody knew what it was, but we wanted to be together to work out what it was. It was probably a very subconscious thing, but the timing was perfect for the music to break out and for the scene to break out, to throw off the chains, the shackles, of the fifties.[15]

Lesh emphasizes how "we wanted to be together", a phrase that highlights the novel notion at the time of the "group", of cooperative action and collective performance, a subject I'll return to. Historian Alice Echols endorses, in a more formal style, Lesh's general view about reacting to the 1950s:

Both the New Left and the women's liberation movement
can be understood as part of a gendered generational revolt
against the ultra-domesticity of that aberrant decade, the
1950s. The white radicals who participated in these movements were in flight from the nuclear family and the domes-
ticated versions of masculinity and femininity that prevailed
in post-war America. Sixties radicals, white and black, were
also responding to the hegemonic position of liberalism and
its promotion of government expansion both at home and
abroad – the welfare/warfare state.[16]

A second significant factor concerned the arts scene around Greenwich
Village. The reason why the early Velvets wanted to be a part of the Village
circle was that artists who lived, worked or socialized there (painters, writers,
musicians, dancers, and later film-makers) dealt with truly new art forms
and concepts, yet – instead of courting failure in terms of sales and public
interest – some were astoundingly successful in terms of fame or finance,
or both.[17] This extraordinary situation had started at the end of World War
II, when the United States emerged the capitalist victor and governor of the
global economy, but remained a nation ill at ease. The omnipotent government of the late 1940s was fixated with the threat of thermo-nuclear
war, and made its citizens terrified of subversion by the communist "enemy
within". Between 1950 and 1953 US forces fought a tense war against the
Chinese People's Republic's army in the Asian country of Korea, one half
of which each super-state was occupying to no great purpose. So, on the
sunny side of culture it was "Oklahoma!" and "Fanfare for the Common
Man", while on the other "film noir" and Senator McCarthy's anti-Left cull
of artists and entertainers.

It was as though the country had to turn its back in shame on the way
it had spent the 1930s, when the immense economic slump following the
Wall Street Crash of 1929 was contested by President Roosevelt's Demo-
crats pumping government aid into grand communal schemes to get people
working together again. Hailed as the "New Deal", his federal programmes
supported unemployed artists on big public projects such as wall murals,
street theatre and community orchestras. But after the war the inclusive
turned exclusive. In a big shift from social reform to proprietary liberalism,
the Republicans moved away from notions of collective trust towards those
of private responsibility, turning 1930s comrades into 1950s consumers. This
was the first stage in the post-war linking-together of two separate social

processes – representational democracy and the free market – as a globalizing project on the American model.

The progressive (mostly male) post-war artists of New York critically reflected these concerns in a climate of conformity. They did so first of all by adopting the old-time patriotic characteristics of "Americanism" – of the artist as a pioneering individual, free to express his personality, a hunter, quick on the draw. In this way they could project their most subjective traits as trailblazing quests. Secondly, in order to make sense of themselves in such a bewildering world after a global war,[18] several of these artists explored personal growth through cultish, unorthodox belief systems such as the new fad then of Scientology. While painter Jackson Pollock took up Jungian psychoanalytic spiritualism, his colleagues Barnett Newman and Mark Rothko studied Kabbalistic theosophy, and so forth through the back alleys of faith.

Cale's hero, composer John Cage,[19] cruised swiftly from anarchism (1945) through Hinduism (1948) to Zen Buddhism (1951). These were private routes taken in order to determine a personal "authenticity". In public these ultra-modern talents presented their authentic selves as enterprising American frontiersmen – these brave Manhattan cowboys – boldly defined through their startling artistic inventions. Europeans marvelled at how this new American work could be so "basic". In Cage's case it was so basic it led in 1952[20] to a work of 4 minutes and 33 seconds of "silence".

Projecting American-ness was central to the project, even though, or perhaps because, Rothko was born in Latvia and De Kooning in Holland (Rothko said, "We have wiped the slate clean. We start anew. A new land"[21]). A self-conscious and militant campaign was undertaken to make New York City the post-war centre of the artistic world in place of Paris. There's an irony in this. A blend of voguish philosophical positions influential at the time was known as existentialism. This attitude – crudely that the world is indifferent and we're each abandoned to make our own practical choices on how to become individual yet social – underpinned the all-American image of the brazen loner that was taken up in Village life by artists and writers.

Such ideas were coming from Europe, however – from Denmark (Kierkegaard),[22] Germany (Heidegger) and Paris itself through Jean-Paul Sartre and Simone de Beauvoir. Sartre even provided the characteristic existentialist pose of the all-smoking all-drinking, pensive writer hunched in a café jotting notes and arguing moodily against convention; this image was carried into fifties Hollywood by Marlon Brando and James Dean, then into music through Bob Dylan and, in turn, Lou Reed. They added, however, one crucial feature to make this portrait a truly American one – sunglasses.

New York School existentialism could be found in the work as well in the man. Painter Clyfford Still wrote typically in 1950 that, "My work is [as] equally independent [as me]... not proven by a continuum. I am myself, – not just the sum of my ancestors, and I know myself best by my gestures... not through a study of my family tree."[23] Fellow artist Barnett Newman even compared the viewer of his paintings to a cave dweller, a primordial being: "Original man, shouting his consonants, did so in yells of awe and anger at his tragic state, at his own self-awareness, and at his own helplessness before the void."[24]

If this intellectual framework served to give fat-headed confidence to these Tarzans of the cultural jungle in the immediate post-war New York arts scene, it was the buoyant imperialist economy of the United States that crated the art market over from old Europe to New York. Through World War II the USA had already drawn the United Kingdom into an arrangement named Lend–Lease whereby money and weapons to fight Nazi Germany would be loaned to Britain and paid back over many years and, in return – it was expected – the British Isles would be converted readily into a cultural colony of America (the final Lend–Lease payment was made as recently as 2001). In 1947 the States added the rest of Western Europe to a massive support scheme of grants, rather than loans, called the Marshall Plan.

General Marshall, its architect, intended it to build a strong Western European economy, one that would grow in alliance with the USA against the Soviet Union's claims on Eastern Europe.[25] This hegemony, this ability to exercise control with the carrot not the stick, enabled the USA to move the cultural market in its favour, especially with regard to consumption and mediation – fast food and drink, film, television and popular music. Not only that, the expanded traffic of goods into Europe benefited States-side businesses so that by the mid 1950s conditions allowed for a local luxury market in works of art to be established in New York City, one that understandably favoured new, all-American goods.

Such art had already been fortunate in grabbing spectacular media attention from the late 1940s onwards. This, however, proved to be the doing of the Central Intelligence Agency as much as culturally minded reporters. Articles in popular magazines like *Life* championed these artists,[26] who found themselves being used in "Cold War" propaganda against the Soviet Union. The Russians, limited by economic circumstance to promoting only their cultural assets, used their artists – composers like Prokofiev and companies such as the Bolshoi – to advocate "socialist realist" qualities. In response the American media seized on the Greenwich Village avant-garde as audacious models of free will and creative adventure. If realism expressed repression, then abstraction embodied liberty. America was "with it", Russia without it. This game would end in October 1957 when the USSR futuristically launched the *Sputnik* satellite and then sent the first cosmonaut into space, leading to the Soviet–American "space race" of the 1960s when art's job was taken up by science.

In particular, the American press made a star of Jackson Pollock, who placed large canvases on the floor and worked over them, sploshing and smearing paint; reporters dubbed him "Jack the Dripper".[27] His paintings were large because they were his one-man version of the 1930s collective murals. Pollock's dynamic, gestural acts, concerned with the direct physicality of paint and painting, defined a new style, swiftly marketed out of the city as "abstract expressionism" ("AbEx") or the "New York School". Mark Rothko's "fuzzy doors" (mystical blocks which hovered over coloured grounds) and Willem de Kooning's violent cartoon abstractions formed the bookends of this stylistic rack.

Although the "AbEx" painters worked in disparate studios around town, they gathered to eat, drink and quarrel at the Cedar Tavern in the Village's University Place, where they mixed with colleagues in the literary, music, performance and film scenes.[28] In this regard even the most singular of artists found intellectual need in New York for a communal forum between disciplines, in order to discuss common demands and trends. It was through their leisure time, not their work, that they found their workmates.

But soon, as critic Edward Lucie-Smith points out, "This least academic of styles made an astonishingly rapid descent into academicism. The art boom of the middle and late 1950s created a spate of bubble-reputations."[29] In a belated defence of abstract expressionism, the commentator Donald Kuspit called it "the last modern American art we had which deals significantly with the question of individuation in the megalopolis of New York".[30] In so far as "AbEx" related to lonely-guy stuff, to matters of existentialist authenticity, this is plausible, but other styles quickly emerged linked with the urban condition of being in New York, one of which launched Andy Warhol's amazing ascendancy in the mid 1960s to a point where Warhol could give up painting to run a rock group and yet maintain the degree of media attention previously devoted to Jack the Dripper.

At least two creative reactions emerged out of the 1950s "AbEx" scene. One set of artists simply dumped the "expressionism" and carefully lined in colour fields and strips, named in style "post-painterly abstraction" or "hard-edged art". Its coolness and play of surface influenced its successor, the "pop art" most associated, through Warhol, with The Velvet Underground. The other, more essential to our story, took its cue from the physical, "living" actions and spontaneity of Jackson Pollock. One of the key artists here, Allan Kaprow, wrote in 1958:

> Pollock as I see him, left us at the point where we must become preoccupied with and even dazzled by the space and objects of our everyday life, either our bodies, clothes, rooms, or, if need be, the vastness of 42nd Street. Not satisfied with the suggestion through paint of our other senses, we shall utilise the specific substances of sight, sound, movements, people, odours, touch.[31]

Kaprow meant by this a "Happening", a mixed-up, multi-media, live-now-in-time-and-space event first explored by the composer John Cage and his friends at Black Mountain College in 1952.[32] Kaprow presented the first such affair in New York, "18 Happenings in 6 Parts", at a gallery late in 1959.[33] It led to similar downtown events which relate so directly to the origins of The Velvet Underground that I'll examine them in a separate chapter. But this shift from painting to performance was influenced by the very act of living in Greenwich Village. As Kaprow put it at the time of his first Happening:

> The everyday world is the most astonishing inspiration conceivable. A walk down 14th Street is more amazing than any masterpiece in art. If reality makes any sense at all, it is here. Endless, unpredictable, infinitely rich. It proclaims THE MOMENT as man's sole means of grasping the nature of ALL TIME.[34]

A walk down 14th Street, at the top end of Greenwich Village, might have led to the door of Marcel Duchamp (1887–1968), once a controversial leader of the anti-art "Dada" movement around the time of World War I, who now lived as a cultural sage at 220 West 14th Street. In 1916 he and his American friends had declared Greenwich Village "a Free Republic, Independent of Uptown".[35]

While Jackson Pollock and his colleagues had been affected by Surrealism's automatic-writing exercises of the 1920s and 1930s, the younger Kaprow and others of his kind (Robert Rauschenberg, Claes Oldenburg, Jim Dine among them) took a step further back to Dada. But now, in Duchamp's view, this new generation was far too pro-art to be Dada. While in 1917 Duchamp had attempted to display in New York a urinal (titled *Fountain*) as an art object – in order to question what art was – Rauschenberg as a neo-Dadaist had sent a telegram stating, "This is a portrait of Iris Clert if I say so", which is more a questioning of the artist's authority.

Two elements of the old Dadaist tendency especially took the neo-Dadaists' interest. Firstly they liked its use of everyday objects, such as Duchamp's "ready-mades" and combinations of materials. When the Texan Rauschenberg rented a sequence of downtown studios in the 1950s, he took up discarded objects that he'd found on the streets around the Bowery and fixed them to his canvases, or made indescribable sculptures out of them (such as his *Coca Cola Plan* of 1958 combining Coke bottles and angels' wings). Most famously, he stuck an old tyre around the torso of a stuffed goat;[36] "I wanted to see if I could integrate an object as exotic as that", he explained.[37] Curator Richard Koshalek saw these works as a link between "AbEx" and its upcoming antithesis in realism: "Bob painted himself into the picture, much as Velásquez did. The difference is that 'himself' is what he happened to have around him at the moment."[38]

Rauschenberg's successful devising of these "combines" led to such an interest in this field that in 1961 New York's Museum of Modern Art ran an exhibition titled *The Art of Assemblage*. Its curator, William C. Seitz, wrote that, "The method of juxtaposition is a vehicle for feelings of disenchantment with the slick international idiom that loosely articulated abstraction has tended to become, and the social values that this situation reflects."[39] This mirrors John Cale's concerns about the comparative abstraction of the experimental world he was in around 1965 and the grittier realism of rock music that beckoned through Lou Reed; Cale desired to combine the two into epic forms. Some artists certainly considered Rauschenberg's "combines" a move back to reality after the all-too-transcendent abstractions of the New York School. New York was now finding itself physically in, and on, art.[40]

The second element of Dadaism that attracted the neo-Dadaists concerned acts of spontaneous performance (the happening, the moment). They liked the idea that a work of art is lived in, as though the artist is active in the studio making the composition in three dimensions. Here was a transition away from the ideology of the private to that of the shared. Performers made independent actions, unrelated to their neighbours, but together they were in the same work. The viewer could gaze, even step around the studio, from the particular to the whole. Onto this, composer John Cage had added the use of games of chance, because he didn't like improvisation, which he thought merely allowed participants to be indulgent and rework favourite stunts. Warhol, who followed these movements and schools with a kind of "Gee! Wow!" regard, would make his own "rock" version of a Happening, the Exploding Plastic Inevitable "experience" at the Dom on St Mark's Place (and elsewhere around the States in 1966) with The Velvet Underground at its core.

In sum so far, then, the New York post-war visual arts scene worked through and played out a number of concerns that The Velvet Underground would take up – freely breathe in out of the downtown air – during the middle 1960s. There were other direct artistic influences to be wrought from the town, most especially in music and literature, but they will be dealt with later in the book by scrutinizing the artists most associated with these: sound and John Cale, songs and Lou Reed.

2 The Band

In his clever backwards-history book about genes, *The Ancestor's Tale*, Richard Dawkins writes that:

> Biological evolution has no privileged line of descent and no designated end. Evolution has reached many millions of interim ends (the number of surviving species at the time of observation), and there is no reason other than vanity – human vanity as it happens, since we are doing the talking – to designate any one as more privileged or climactic than any other.[1]

As well as "interim", Dawkins uses terms such as "convergence", "rendezvous", and "confluence" to illustrate how, in what contingent and fragile ways, different life forms develop and disappear. His words are helpful to the history of popular music, too, to depict how groups come about as perpetually "interim" assemblies of artists, and they are especially welcome in the case of The Velvet Underground. Strictly speaking, the band existed in name for eight years, from the summer of 1965 until 1973. However, its most "famous" members played together for only three years, between 1965 and 1968. To complicate matters, some had worked together before that time under three other quickly discarded names. Not even in its busiest period, between January 1966 and August 1970, could it be said to be a full-time outfit in the manner of The Rolling Stones. There have been 13 players in it at various times, but never more than five on stage in any one show, even though the band was actually a quartet (see Figure 1). In other words, The Velvet Underground has always been a bit of a mess.

There were four "famous" members of the Velvets in the significant 1965–8 period: (in alphabetical order) John Cale (bass guitar/viola/keyboards), Sterling Morrison (guitar/bass guitar), Lou Reed (vocals/guitar), and drummer Maureen (Moe) Tucker.[2] There was a fifth performer who was never formally a member but was still "famous" for being a part of it – the German "chanteuse" Nico who was added by Andy Warhol (actually, by his manager Paul Morrissey) and who served only during the time while

Figure 1: Group memberships 1963–1973

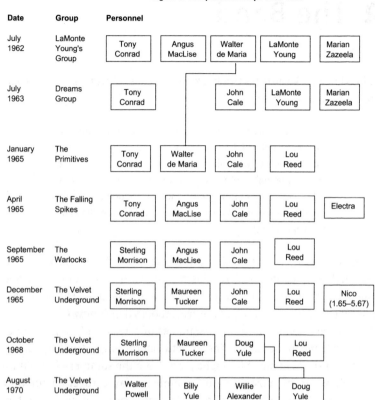

Date	Group	Personnel				
July 1962	LaMonte Young's Group	Tony Conrad	Angus MacLise	Walter de Maria	LaMonte Young	Marian Zazeela
July 1963	Dreams Group	Tony Conrad		John Cale	LaMonte Young	Marian Zazeela
January 1965	The Primitives	Tony Conrad	Walter de Maria	John Cale	Lou Reed	
April 1965	The Falling Spikes	Tony Conrad	Angus MacLise	John Cale	Lou Reed	Electra
September 1965	The Warlocks	Sterling Morrison	Angus MacLise	John Cale	Lou Reed	
December 1965	The Velvet Underground	Sterling Morrison	Maureen Tucker	John Cale	Lou Reed	Nico (1.65–5.67)
October 1968	The Velvet Underground	Sterling Morrison	Maureen Tucker	Doug Yule	Lou Reed	
August 1970	The Velvet Underground	Walter Powell	Billy Yule	Willie Alexander	Doug Yule	

Warhol was the band's manager (18 months – January 1966 to July 1967). At that latter date Lou Reed sacked Warhol (and Morrissey) to replace him with Boston-based promoter Steven Sesnick. That The Velvet Underground needs to be defined in terms of its management only goes to show how odd its biography is. To summarize, there have been four basic incarnations of the "famous" Velvets:

(i)   The Velvet Underground before Warhol: *circa* April–December 1965
(ii) The Warhol Velvet Underground: January 1966–July 1967
(iii) The Sesnick Velvet Underground: July 1967–September 1968
(iv) The Sesnick Velvet Underground without Cale: September 1968–August 1970

On August 23rd, 1970 Lou Reed quit the band. His look-alike and sound-alike alter-ego Doug Yule took over the sporadic engagements until the middle of 1973 when Yule's project fizzled out entirely. As the group often worked in a part-time way, it's difficult to determine exactly when people joined and left, but here is an attempt. It assumes that The Velvet Underground project began as The Primitives, the name given to a "scratch" band (that is, a group made up on the spur of the moment of freelance musicians) created to exploit a novelty record by Lou Reed titled 'Do The Ostrich':

Name	Time frame	Length of service
John Cale	January 1965–September 1968	3 years 8 months
Sterling Morrison	April 1965–August 1971	6 years 4 months
Nico	January 1966–May 1967	1 year 5 months
Lou Reed	January 1965–August 1970	5 years 8 months
Maureen Tucker	December 1965–September 1971	6 years 5 months

The other performers associated with The Velvet Underground in the total period of 1965 to 1973 are as follows, also in alphabetical order:

Willie Alexander (bass guitar)	1970–1972	2 years
Tony Conrad (guitar)	January 1965–April 1965	4 months
Electra (guitar)	June–August (?) 1965	3 months (?)
Angus MacLise (hand drums)	April–December 1965 + July 1966	9 months
Walter de Maria (percussion)	January–April 1965	4 months
Walter Powell (guitar)	1970–1972	2 years
Billy Yule (drums)	1970–1972	2 years
Doug Yule (vocals/guitar)	September 1968–1973	5 years

Naturally this book is most interested in the "famous" five because they created the most interesting music, but it is also keen to record the contribution of the early musicians – Tony Conrad (b. 1940), Angus MacLise (1938–71) and Walter de Maria (b. 1935) – who helped to form the band's unique sound. To borrow another term from Richard Dawkins, the "concestor" or common ancestor to four of these members – but also to much of the band's soundworld – was the avant-garde composer LaMonte Young (b. 1935), who ran an ensemble with Conrad, MacLise and De Maria, joined by John Cale for two and a quarter years, between September 1963 and December 1965, at which point The Velvet Underground gained – and soon lost – its first residency, at the Café Bizarre.

The Velvet Underground and Nico, 1967
Left to right, Nico, Maureen Tucker, Sterling Morrison, Lou Reed, John Cale

As to the five protagonists, it's notable how close the three men were in age. John Cale and Lou Reed were born within a week of each other, in March 1942. Guitarist Sterling Morrison was born five months later. They are framed in age by the two females – singer Nico from 1938 (although she wouldn't thank you for noticing that she was the oldest among them) and drummer Moe Tucker of 1945. In terms of births the five are typical wartime "baby boomers", and they can be placed in a popular music context of birthdays thus:

Year	Birth of artist (alphabetical order)
1938	Eddie Cochran, Duane Eddy, <u>Nico</u>
1939	Bobby Darin, Dion (DiMucci), Connie Francis, Neil Sedaka
1940	John Lennon, Smokey Robinson, Frank Zappa
1941	Joan Baez, David Crosby, Bob Dylan, Tim Hardin, Gene Pitney, Buffy Sainte-Marie
1942	<u>John Cale</u>, Aretha Franklin, Jerry Garcia, Jimi Hendrix, Brian Jones, Carole King, Curtis Mayfield, Paul McCartney, <u>Sterling Morrison</u>, <u>Lou Reed</u>
1943	George Harrison, Mick Jagger, Janis Joplin, Joni Mitchell, Jim Morrison, Keith Richards
1944	Jeff Beck, Roger Daltrey, Jimmy Page, Diana Ross
1945	Eric Clapton, Bob Marley, Van Morrison, Pete Townshend, <u>Maureen Tucker</u>

More significantly, this was a group that was formed by chance encounters (many groups are, of course). Its key players arrived from dissimilar backgrounds and even different countries. With one exception it was in New York City that they first came across each other. Yet there is little of a thread as to how they landed there, apart from the point already made that they hungered to be in a place, as Nico called it, which was "a city of now, a city that is always now, also where yesterday can be now too".[3] (English was her fourth language, in case you're wondering.) The following is an attempt to record how they each arrived in this "city of now".

Lou Reed

The most local of the Velvets was Lou Reed, who was born Lewis Reed in Brooklyn, across the East River from Manhattan, on March 2nd, 1942. The Reed family, however, quickly moved to Freeport on nearby Long Island, a mainly middle-class environment of around 40,000 suburbanites. His father was an accountant, his mother a housewife and apparently a former beauty queen.[4] Their surname had earlier been anglicized from the Jewish family name Rabinowitz. Lou Reed's upbringing was bourgeois but more New York State than New York City and more out-of-town than downtown. According to his biographer Victor Bockris, it was at the age of 13 that Reed discovered he was gay, and, although his subsequent behaviour has been that of a scrupulous bisexual,[5] the family's concerns for his "feelings" – considered a sickness at that time – led him, at the age of 17, to undergo 24 electro-shock treatments at the Creedmore State Psychiatric Hospital.

At any rate this is the reason Reed has put forward through his biographer. Yet Cale has referred obliquely to Reed's schizophrenia[6] ("split from reality"), intimated when he first met him in early 1965. Cale went on to mention both Reed's ongoing depression and his addiction to Placidyl at this time. But Placidyl is a sedative to cure insomnia, not an antidepressant,[7] and, as Reed was still living with his parents "who kept him on a tight rein", the drug was probably a replacement, prescribed by the psychiatrist he was still seeing, for the heroin he'd taken at university. It appears that, despite assumptions, rock stars are not necessarily the best people to pass on to us what's wrong with them, nor to explain away their drugs, prescribed or not. Ultimately, although homosexuality was in those days diagnosed as a disorder in need of treatment, what the doctors of the Creedmore institute encountered in the teenage Reed may have been far more complex than we've been led to believe.

Nonetheless, Bockris makes an interesting link in pointing out that this traumatic Creedmore episode took place in 1959 concurrent with the abrupt death of the rock'n'roll era,[8] suggesting perhaps that Reed the rock performer was subsequently attempting to recapture the rebellious musical spirit of the time before this constraining ordeal. He adds that Reed was attracted from the age of 12 to rhythm & blues. Reed probably started on the guitar around this time. He claims he had only one lesson, wherein he learned five basic chord shapes (I, ii, IV, V, vi in E). From the age of 15 Reed formed school groups, one called The Shades (later The Jades), which he in his maturity described as a "typical teenage hoodlum band".[9] However, Reed has also claimed that his favourite popular music at the time was doo-wop, songs about romance by close-harmony groups such as The Diablos and the Solitaires.[10] In 1958 he recorded his first and only songs with The Jades, 'So Blue' and 'Leave Her (For Me)',[11] the latter of which was undoubtedly doo-wop.

A radical change of musical taste took place when Reed, at the customary age of 18 in the autumn of 1959, enrolled at the Bronx (that is, north-eastern) campus of New York University. He often travelled to downtown Manhattan at nights, he recounts, to hear the latest style of jazz improvisation known as "free jazz" at the Five-Spot Club, which was then still an abstract-expressionist hangout.[12] Reed often stood outside while "the music drifted out to the street, as he didn't always have enough money to get in".[13] He said he heard there saxophonists Ornette Coleman (b. 1930) and John Coltrane (1926–67) as well as the radical black, gay pianist and poet Cecil Taylor (b. 1929) who "pound[ed] the piano until it sound[ed] like something no longer black and white but kaleidoscope".[14] Although these influential downtown excursions lasted a short period, less than a year, it is notable that Reed associated the trips with modernist improvisation, the musical avant-garde, and the sound (if not the countenance) of black pioneers.

Reed went to university for five consecutive years (September 1959 to June 1964), but after the first year in New York he moved instead to Syracuse, a north-west upstate university town about 120 miles by road from Manhattan. It was here in late 1960 that he ran a weekly radio music programme on the WAER FM campus station entitled *Excursions on a Wobbly Rail*, named after a Cecil Taylor recording. On this show it's said that Reed would mix modern jazz with doo-wop and rockabilly, giving much airtime to recorded jazz improvisations by the likes of Coleman and Taylor, Don Cherry and Archie Shepp.[15] Later, in 1962, he published with other students two issues of a home-made literary magazine, *Lonely Woman Quarterly*, named after the well-known composition by Ornette Coleman.

Although Reed's passion for modern jazz was at the time a fashionable and flaunted "beatnik" sign of cultural distinction (of which more will be made later), his sincere interest in instrumental improvisation, and knowledge of it, clearly fed into the early years of the Velvets who often improvised on stage, and which was not instead – as some have assumed – wholly a motivation of John Cale's.

Reed's move away from New York City may have been as much induced by the post-trauma therapy sessions he had to undertake there at the Payne Whitney Clinic as by a need to explore independence well away from his family. However, in Syracuse – where he formally studied literature, philosophy and music appreciation – this relative freedom soon motivated him to indulge in illicit drugs,[16] from cannabis in 1961, which Reed sold on campus, to heavier psychedelics (LSD was legal until late 1966), a not untypical path of the time. In late 1963 he started on heroin, perhaps the most addictive and potent drug commonly in use ("You are beautiful and you have no stresses and you are wrapped in fur" Nico claimed for its attractions).[17] According to Bockris, Reed was a heroin dealer before becoming a user, which is possible although it is much more commonly the other way around.[18] By all accounts Reed was a heroin user from this moment on, throughout his time with the Velvets. Yet it seems he was one of those lucky types who could stay somewhat in control of its destructive pleasures.

It had been at Syracuse in late 1960 that Reed first came across Sterling Morrison, future guitarist of the Velvets. Morrison was then a student not signed up at Syracuse but visiting his friend Jim Tucker, who lived in the same dormitory block as Reed (Morrison would spend the entire autumn of 1961 there). Tucker was the brother of Maureen, the Velvet's future drummer. As Morrison considered himself "an inconsiderate rock'n'roller", it's rather surprising that he got on so well with this jazz aficionado, and even more so given what Reed did next.

In 1961 he joined a "loosely formed" folk group, strumming an acoustic guitar and singing in the mutualist, sing-along style typical of progressive bohemians. Just at the time that Reed entered this woolly-jumper-and-jeans world, Bob Dylan arrived in Greenwich Village to work the coffee houses there. Throughout America and Western Europe the revival of interest in folk music in the late 1950s is now considered one of the first manifestations of the counter-cultural "protest" movement that peaked in the mid 1960s. It gained strength soon after the formal censure by the US Senate in 1954 of Senator Joseph McCarthy's "witch hunt" against Leftists,[19] allowing for a re-emerged interest in "the music of the people" to advance. During the post-war period this ideological regard for "roots" culture had been associated up to then with the Soviet Union and Sovietized Eastern Europe, and while it therefore carried counter-cultural credentials in the United States, it was nevertheless also considered somewhat patriotic in its rediscovery of residual songs – especially ballads – while likewise constructing others in their style.

This revival was kick-started by the popular "raise-your-voice" group The Weavers, who, blacklisted by McCarthy, reformed in 1955 after his fall from grace. But what really swept this alternative folk revival along was the opportunity it gave for teenage baby boomers to *make* music. Many of them formed amateur, communal groups mixing acoustic instruments and voices to perform in local bars and folk clubs; the songs most enjoyed were therefore those that were the simplest to play and sing. It was this sort of group that Reed joined. However, the folk revival scene was readily commercialized and professionalized in the American free-market fashion. This transition was accelerated by the annual Newport Folk Festival begun in June 1959, together with the success of The Kingston Trio (1959) and Joan Baez (1960) in the singles and albums market.

As Reed had spent his first university year as an individualist, esoteric modern jazz fan and opened his second as a communal, affirming "folkie", it shouldn't surprise us that he soon turned to a third genre, that of rock'n'roll, by now a "retro" good-times style flecked with irony and a moody discontent with the present in favour of the "lost" past. He joined friends on the campus in setting up around late 1961 a band called "LA and the Eldorados" (the "L" for Lewis as lead vocalist) which played mainly Chuck Berry covers as well as nascent versions of Reed's own mature songs such as "Coney Island Baby".[20] A local success, it's said that the band earned good fees playing up to three or four times a week for parties. A fellow student had taken up the band's management while another became its agent. However, one of the Eldorados claims that Reed was so obnoxious and contrary in his behaviour[21] that they went out sometimes as "Pasha and the Prophets" or other titles because they'd been barred under the other name from venues thanks to him.

What altered Reed's subcultural affinities yet again was the debut album of Bob Dylan, released in March 1962. Although there are only two of his original songs on it, Dylan presented a persona with which Reed could directly engage – that of the intelligent, young adult, existentialist Jewish rebel. Reed's girlfriend of the time recalled that in the summer of 1962 he bought a harmonica with a neck harness and learned to play it, but soon discarded the contraption because its use was so obviously connected to Dylan. Yet it wasn't until March 1963 that Dylan's first self-penned album came out, and it was this – with the Greenwich Village cover – that had the truly galvanizing impact of a new male image, one "that inspired countless young men to hunch their shoulders, look distant and let the girl do the clinging", according to writer Janet Maslin.[22] Reed first heard Dylan play live at Syracuse in the autumn of 1963, and the way that Reed almost slavishly copies Dylan's voice in a fledgling Velvet Underground rehearsal tape of July 1965[23] exposes the strength of the folk singer's influence so much so that one wonders if Reed's diffident stance and his habit of lurking in the shadows of the stage in the early Velvet years was because he had not yet constructed a persona – even by 1966 – to replace his rendering of Dylan's.

While he discovered that Dylan's image granted a peerless figure on which to trace a charismatic identity, Reed shifted shrewdly away from Dylan's imagery – his songwriting style, with its surreal slants and opaque images. Reed invested his identity in explicit verse. He valued simplicity, neat observation and description of character, and in that sense remained in technique a throwback to the Beat era with its use of vernacular and to the concision and clarity of 1940s thriller writers. To paraphrase Truman Capote, if Dylan's style was "writing", Reed's was "typing". But more about this later.

In the summer of 1964 Reed walked out of Syracuse a graduate and walked into the Vietnam War. No single event had created this incomprehensible and pernicious invasion. Following the Korean War, the USA involved itself in South-East Asia from 1955, backing the nationalist South Vietnam against the communist North. But President Kennedy in the early 1960s, and his Democrat successor Lyndon B. Johnson, increased the USA's military involvement to the point where conscription of American civilians was thought necessary. On August 3rd, 1964, North Vietnamese patrol boats were provoked by US gunships and in turn they "attacked" the Americans in the northern Gulf of Tonkin. This gave President Johnson the excuse he needed to seek Congressional approval to invade Vietnam and enlist conscripts, a process known as the "draft". Called up in August 1964, Reed, having just overcome a bout of hepatitis from sharing a heroin needle, attended his draft board interview after ingesting Placidyl, a sleeping pill. Thanks to this, his hepatitis and his record as a mental patient, "I was pronounced mentally unfit and given a classification that meant I'd only be called up if we went to war with China. It was the one thing my shock treatments were good for."[24] So, while others opposed the war or burned their draft cards in defiance of the war, Reed was excused it.

Instead he found a job through the former manager of The Eldorados, who had a social contact with Pickwick International and persuaded the record company to hire Reed as one of its songwriters. A tawdry entrepreneurial company on Long Island, Pickwick specialized in records that looked and sounded all too cannily like other people's records. Aside from producing discs that cashed in on crazes and genre fads,[25] it gained income through licensing, say, a hit single for use on one of its thematic compilation discs while filling the remainder with hastily written numbers by its backroom team.[26] As the royalties from each of these numbers equalled that of the borrowed track, Pickwick made fair money by that means.

Over the nine months he worked there, until February 1965, it's estimated that Reed helped to write 15 published songs, including his one near-hit, 'Do The Ostrich', supposedly by The Primitives. Emerging as a skit on a spate of novelty dance crazes in 1964, such as the Twist, it's often claimed that Reed's lyrics ask the dancers to place their heads on the floor to enable their partners to stamp on them.[27] However, it simply asks them to stick their head between their knees (and then "You do just about anything you please!"). Its music is based entirely on Phil Spector's main riff for 'Then He Kissed Me'[28] which fits the rhythm of the title line, 'Do the Ostrich', and comprises only two chords, the tonic and the subdominant (I and IV),[29] the eventual chords of choice of The Velvet Underground. As a pointer to future mannerisms it's also an early example of Reed's tendency to use "master of ceremony"-style verbal fill-ins, such as "Now c'mon, yeah" and "Go, go, go".

One of the in-vogue television teen-beat dance shows[30] phoned up Pickwick asking to book The Primitives for an appearance. As there was no such band, a Pickwick employee hastily sought some suitably modish-looking backing musicians for Reed. He struck lucky at a Manhattan party where he met by chance the long-haired John Cale and Tony Conrad, who were then working with composer LaMonte Young. They, as supposed guitarists, brought along their fellow Young performer, Walter de Maria, to play drums, and thus Reed, Cale, Conrad and De Maria became The Primitives, playing at various promotions for the few weeks that 'Do The Ostrich' had a life.

Reed mentioned to them that he'd written songs he liked but which Pickwick declined to record (as they weren't novelties or genre remakes). The other Primitives offered their services to work on the material in a casual fashion. In this random way The Velvet Underground was conceived in January 1965, though not in name. Reed gave up his Pickwick job the next month and soon moved in with John Cale at 56 Ludlow Street, Lower East Side. Reed would be jobless until December, when The "famous" Velvet Underground started to play in public.

John Cale

Cale was born in the Welsh coal-mining town of Garnant in South Wales, March 9th, 1942. His father was a miner, his mother a primary school teacher who taught her son to play the piano. In Cale's move from a provincial upbringing to a university college in London, he followed a course envisaged for working-class children in the government's wartime Education Act of 1944. Winston Churchill, prime minister at the time of Cale's birth, had told the boys at his privileged *alma mater* that, "after the war the advantages of the Public Schools must be extended on a far wider basis".[31] In response a Ministry of Education official, alluding to the Greek philosopher Plato, divided children into "golden" (gifted), "silver" (technically minded) and "iron" ("couldn't handle ideas").[32] Golden children went to the post-war grammar schools which were modelled on the fee-paying academy where Churchill had forewarned of change. Cale grew up a "golden" child and gleaned the rewards of post-war liberal education, such as it was.

Various post-war education schemes ornamented the basic system. One such was music peripatetic teaching, by which professional players were hired to travel around schools teaching children how to play instruments. County-wide (that is, regional) stores held assorted collections of instruments for schoolkids to take home and use, and there were county youth orchestras for trained youngsters to participate in. This is how Cale became a viola player, a beneficiary of state cultural provision, although he emphasized how it was doled out to him by chance. As a string instrument that falls between the high violin and the lowish cello, the viola tends to fill out the middle of a texture and doesn't therefore often have very interesting parts to perform. That Cale would end up in adult life playing drones on his viola isn't so surprising, then. That these drones were often open strings wouldn't astonish other string players either, who tend to think of viola players, rather unfairly, as the village idiots of the concert stage.

While Cale as a teenager sat at the front desk of the violas in the Welsh National Youth Orchestra, he said he developed a rebellious interest in "teddy boy" culture. Considered the first of the post-war subcultural British trends displaying discontent through style, it was a curious, racist referral to the final period of British imperialism at the turn of the twentieth century (during the reign of Edward VII – hence "teddy" and "teds"). First associated with conventional pop music,[33] teds only later switched to rockabilly when the first American white-artist records made an impact from 1955 onwards.[34] Cale, like many working-class young men around the country, would have adopted the stylistic features of a quiffed and slicked hairstyle with a long jacket as a sign of alienated social distinction.[35] That he was inclined to evince this urban trend within a conservative rural community, displays the degree that he was willing to dissent as an individual through his appearance.

By his early adult life he had become a tall, lithe and unconventionally handsome bohemian, once described as an "elongated Dustin Hoffman". From October 1960 (at the same time that Reed started at Syracuse) until the summer of 1963, Cale was a student on a teachers' training course at Goldsmiths College in south-east London. It's clear from his own accounts that he developed an interest in contemporary music by living composers. Such an environment was developing in Britain at this very time, where musicians were trying to catch up with – or evade – adventurist shifts on mainland Europe. The old neo-classical scene, which in the 1920s and 1930s (through composers such as Stravinsky and Kurt Weill) had taken a direct interest in popular dance music and "hot" jazz, was confronted after World War II with an elite modernism absorbed exclusively with unprecedented sound worlds and structures. While 1950s Britain was still drinking in the dregs of neo-classicism, avant-garde music scores of extreme virtuosity were written by composers like Pierre Boulez (b. 1925) in France, while Karlheinz Stockhausen (b. 1928) in Germany, who also made complex instrumental works, explored synthetic sounds constructed by electronic means.

A young British composer with the distinctive name of Cornelius Cardew (1936–81),[36] who worked between 1961 and 1963 as a liberal studies tutor at Goldsmiths' art department, was interested in both composers, so much so that he learnt to play a fiendish guitar part in order to perform in the British première of Boulez's formidable song cycle "Le marteau sans maître".[37] The fact that he couldn't play the guitar didn't discourage him.

Cardew had previously worked in Cologne for Stockhausen as an assistant throughout 1958. But now, back in London, he was interested in modernist improvisation and acts of spontaneous performance. Most probably in late 1962, in Cale's final year there, Cale the student came across Cardew the tutor at Goldsmiths. What brought them together in action was Fluxus.

Cardew and Cale were independently aware of the international Fluxus movement, or possibly Cale discovered it through Cardew. Fluxus was known as a new avant-garde fine art movement which engaged with performance and sound, and so it would have interested a musician working in relation to an art department, as Cardew was. Evolving in the USA from Allan Kaprow's "happenings" mentioned in the previous chapter, activists noted that neo-Dada events were taking place in Europe too, independently of Americans but in communication with them. As regards his own evangelism, Kaprow has written:

> I implicitly questioned the specialisation prevalent in theoretical discussions around the vanguard arts at that time, namely "pure" painting, "pure" music, "pure" poetry, etc... As an antidote, I recommended a collage of bits and pieces of everyday phenomena. This would, I believed, provide the rich totality totally missing in much reductionist art... In my Notes (of 1958) I wrote that the model for a total art was everyday life, not the other art.[38]

Fluxus artists considered that the role of their art − and it had a directly social role − was to criticize conventions and assumptions, and to do so by playing on the absurdity of situations. Fluxus and neo-Dada were a humorous reaction to the high seriousness of 1950s modernism. In Germany in the early 1960s the composers Mauricio Kagel (b. 1931) and György Ligeti (b. 1923) created droll works that scrutinized the conventions of concerts, while Ben Vautier and others in France made comical art pieces and wild theatrical gestures in everyday settings. There was even an emerging scene in England, and it seems that Cardew and Cale were a part of it for at least one concert (one that they appear to have co-organized) which took place at the very end of Cale's stay at Goldsmiths, in the college's Great Hall on July 6th, 1963 − "A Little Festival of New Music".[39]

a little festival

of new

music

program 6d

University of London
Goldsmiths' College
New Cross   SE 14
July 6   2 30 and 7 00

Festival Piece

The audience is invited to bring with them any inaudible (not Public) sound or combination of sounds to which they may refer during the proceedings.

CONCERT 1

John Cage
Music of Changes   Book IV
First British Performance
Fred Turner   piano

Griffith Rose
Ennead II
Griffith Rose   piano

Cornelius Cardew
Autumn '60 for orchestra
Cornelius Cardew   conductor

John Cage
Concert for piano and orchestra with Aria
First British Performance
Michael Garrett   Piano
Enid Hartle   Voice
Robin Page   assistant
John Cale   conductor

CONCERT 2

George Maciunas
Solo for violin
First British Performance
Robin Page   soloist
Fluxus Copyright

Edwin Mason
Torture Music
First British Performance
Edwin Mason   soloist

La Monte Young
Piano Piece for David Tudor   no.2
First British Performance
Cornelius Cardew   soloist
Fluxus Copyright

George Brecht
Two Pieces for String Quartet
First British Performance
George Maciunas   Thomas Schmitt
Emmett Williams   John Cale   soloists
Fluxus Copyright

Richard Watts
Two Inches
First British Performance
Tomas Schmitt   soloist
Fluxus copyright

Emmett Williams
Counting Song
First British Performance
Fluxus copyright

John Cale
Piano Piece   (unsequel music 212b)
First British Performance
Michael Garrett   piano

Nam June Paik
One for violin
First British Performance
George Maciunas   soloist
Fluxus copyright

Tomas Schmitt
Piano Piece for George Maciunas
First British Performance
Fluxus copyright

La Monte Young
For Henry Flynt
First British Performance
John Cale   piano
Fluxus copyright

Robin Page
Plant Piece
First British Performance
Robin Page   soloist

La Monte Young
Composition 1960 no.3
First British Performance
George Maciunas   soloist
Fluxus copyright

Yet Cale does not seem to have endeared himself at this time to his Fluxus peers. George Maciunas (1931–78), Fluxus luminary in the USA, wrote to Tomas Schmit in Germany, probably about this concert: "But who is this John Cale?? I have never met him. Seems to have funny attitudes about changing programmes – very stuffy."[40] Nevertheless Cale had two small scores printed in the journal *Fluxus Preview Review* of July 1963, and in 1966 – while in The Velvet Underground – he'd make a "Fluxfilm" (a Fluxus film) titled *Police Car* lasting one minute and described as an "underexposed sequence of blinking lights on a police car".[41]

It was at the time of the concert that he finished his teacher's training course, although it seems he did not pass. It's claimed that for one of his exams (possibly composition) he placed a painting of a reclining nude on the piano stand and proceeded to "interpret" the picture to the consternation of his examiners. Aside from Cale, there is no one left alive to confirm the story and, while it's conceivable, it sounds like the sort of thing a student would do who knew he'd already failed. It's possible that Cale was asked to re-sit an exam or two to get his education degree, but he flew to America instead.

If Cale's connection to Fluxus was brief and tangential, the next stage in his musical career as an avant-garde musician would prove influential and momentous. He had applied in late 1962 for a Bernstein scholarship to attend the 1963 Tanglewood Summer School in Lenox,[42] Massachusetts, near to Boston. These international scholarships were set up by the glamorous American conductor Leonard Bernstein (1918–90) to enable young composers to attend workshops given by their eminent elders. A trustee of this awards scheme was the veteran American neo-classical composer Aaron Copland (1900–90). When he visited London in May 1963,[43] Copland invited Cale, as one of several applicants, for lunch. This was more or less the limit of Cale's involvement with Copland and Bernstein despite what he has implied, and from that what journalists have subsequently written. Cale was accepted for the course, and so, in August 1963 he went to Tanglewood, supposedly on a short one-off visit.

Iannis Xenakis (1922–2001) was the workshop teacher, a Greek-born French resident who, influenced by modernist architecture, composed with militant clusters and streaks of sound charged with energy. Cale, still a Fluxist, remained fixed on performance and critical action. Instead of writing a score, he said that he wanted to smash an axe into a table. Xenakis, who had been a socialist resistance fighter in World War II and had an eye shot out by the British, would have had little sympathy for absurdist games of mock violence. Cale decided after a short while there to abandon Tanglewood for New York City, American home of the Fluxus movement. A contact on the course told him that work might be found at the Orientalia bookshop in Greenwich Village.[44] Thus Cale's arrival in New York came about in this unprepared way.

It must be said that Cale's time at Goldsmiths – and the entire career following it – has been subject to a breathtaking measure of mythologizing. Reed, Nico and Cale have each enjoyed a propensity to be discrete with facts, but for different reasons – Reed to hide his suburban upbringing, Nico to protect her mother and son, and Cale to underwrite his musical status.

Much of what he claims in his autobiography of 1999, *What's Welsh for Zen?*, cannot be verified. While many factual mistakes make his assertions improbable, formal or informal encounters with people are aggrandized into significant attachments. For example, his supposed creative relationship with the celebrated American composer John Cage is unlikely. The 51-year-old Cage, on meeting Cale in September 1963, would have taken delight in the consanguinity of their names, and Cage surely gave him advice on how to survive in New York, just as he gave advice to many others, proposing he contact LaMonte Young.[45] But that's about it. The photograph from that time of Cage taking over from Cale at the piano in an all-night recital of Erik Satie's 'Vexations' is a moment of coincidence.[46] Cale never studied with Cage, Cage doesn't mention him in his diaries, and they worked in different fields – Cage firmly rejected the improvisation that was an essential feature of Cale's method. As to Cale's understanding of Cage, a sample sentence from his autobiography is telling: "I was convinced that John Cage was at that moment performing a rendition of his silent '4' 33" ' (from Preludes and Interludes, which came out in 1954)."[47] 4' 33" (from 1952) has little to do with *Sonatas and Interludes* (from 1948); only someone who knows next to nothing of Cage's work could think that it did.

Nevertheless, Cale the immigrant did encounter, and work among, an assortment of stimulating experimental artists between his arrival in downtown New York City in September 1963 and the debut of the Velvets in December 1965. Most important among them was the composer LaMonte Young (b. 1935), six years older than Cale, with Young's constant partner, the artist Marian Zazeela.[48] The pair had just married[49] and begun to observe a 27-hour day, which they considered a more natural time frame than that imposed on the rest of us. This 27-hour day soon turned into an elastic 28–36-hour day. How anyone like Cale knew when to drop in on them remains a mystery; Young and Zazeela enjoy even now their limousine-stretched "days" and "nights".

Young's innovations in music and performance, and their effect on The Velvet Underground, will be dealt with in a subsequent chapter. Here is an overview: LaMonte Young had come to New York from California in 1960 on a scholarship[50] with a team of experimental artists. He quickly became associated with the Fluxus movement, organizing a series of provocative yet influential concerts for Yoko Ono in her downtown loft[51] during the first half of 1961. Young soon moved on from Fluxus, though, to focus directly on music through a reworking of the blues, using its repetitive chord sequences as a basis for jazz-inflected improvisations ("I am wildly interested in repetition, because I think it demonstrates control", Young has said[52]). Around the same time, he worked in clubs and bars improvising on pianos to accompany one of his fellow Californian migrants, Terry Jennings, who played alto sax meditations on modes[53] not unlike John Coltrane (who was also living and playing in New York at this time). It was Jennings who took on Cale as a flatmate for his Lispenard Street loft when the Welshman first arrived in New York from Tanglewood.

Young was quite the entrepreneur. He established a performing group from among his Californian fellow travellers – Terry Jennings was one of them – and it was this ensemble that Cale joined as a viola player in September 1963. Young has admitted that the group used drugs of various kinds as a "consciousness-expanding tool" – "We got high for every concert: the whole group".[54] Cale has claimed that Young "was the highest-quality dope dealer in the avant-garde movement".[55] Fellow artist Walter de Maria said of Young that, "He was sort of like a criminal, a dope dealer, you know, which is also interesting."[56] Young used Cale as a drugs courier on occasion,[57] for which Cale earned an income. Cale recounts that the reason he eventually left Terry Jennings' flat to live with Tony Conrad on Ludlow Street was because he, Cale, feared that the police had got wind of his drugs storage system at Lispenard Street.

Use of cannabis (also opium and heroin) was certainly common in the modern jazz scene, and such habits influenced in turn the cross-related experimentalists who were searching for the same sort of enhanced atmosphere in which to encourage creative spontaneity. Young's supplies assisted three related ensembles – a duo, a quartet which Cale calls The Dream Syndicate[58] (Cale, Conrad, Young, Zazeela), and roughly an octet called The Theatre of Eternal Music (Cale, Conrad, Young, Zazeela, with – at different times – mathematician Dennis Johnson, drummer/poet Angus MacLise and composer of "In C" Terry Riley). The last group was formed to realize Young's composition *The Four Dreams Of China* which combined very long sustained tones with improvisation. So, for 15 months Cale made his living somewhere between the Orientalia, the quartet project and the Theatre of Eternal Music, no doubt scurrying between them with someone's drugs in his pocket.

When he first met Lou Reed at Pickwick Records in January 1965, Cale was glad to earn extra cash for playing a simple-tuned guitar as one of The Primitives in the promotion of 'Do The Ostrich'. He was already thinking of "getting a band going" and Reed had mentioned that he had written a number of songs that Pickwick wouldn't record. "We got together and started playing the songs for fun... We improvised and I showed him what LaMonte could do with one-note chords and de-tuning."[59] By this time Cale had moved into Tony Conrad's flat at 56 Ludlow Street. In March, Conrad left to allow Reed to move in. Down the corridor lived the periodic Young associate Angus MacLise who played hand drums and joined in on the Reed song rehearsals. In April, Reed's old university friend Sterling Morrison had turned up on guitar to replace Conrad, and by now Cale's hopes for a rock band project was turning into a possibility.

As Reed had no job he and Cale began to look for bar gigs and also to busk on pavements, which they once did quite successfully – after failing a club audition – at the corner of Broadway and 125th Street, at the west end of that spot where Reed in his lyrics waited "for the man". Selling their blood and posing for trashy magazines as murderers were said to be other ways they earned cash. Along with Angus MacLise they took part in providing improvised sound for a number of experimental film shows organized by the New York Cinematheque in various locations. Tony Conrad was one such film-maker interested in sound, and they worked for his colleagues such as Piero Heliczer (1937–93) and Jack Smith (1932–89). As Andy Warhol went to these screenings, it's certain that he first encountered Cale and crew there, but in the guise of avant-garde musicians rather than as a rock band. At the end of the year, CBS News would record a small mainstream news feature about a Cinematheque performance of a Heliczer film, in which the early Velvets could be seen and heard as subjects.

Jack Smith had bought a professional tape recorder to enable Conrad to splice music for some of his experimental films.[60] In July 1965 Reed, Cale and Morrison borrowed it to make a demonstration tape ("demo") of Reed's songs, including 'Heroin' and 'Venus In Furs' (the title of a film by Heliczer). Cale took these tapes to London over the summer in an attempt to get managers and record companies interested[61] (Cale says he had a "green card" visa allowing him to work in the United States and travel freely from there, thanks to the invitation from Tanglewood). Instead of finding support, he returned with the latest records of British groups such as The Kinks and The Who, alarmed that they were already putting onto disc elements of the sound world he envisaged for his band, such as loose ensemble playing, textural intensity and sonoral feedback (its first use on record was in the opening of 'I Feel Fine' by The Beatles in 1964[62]).

That Cale was not only British but had the ability to make contact with the music business scene there must have given him a degree of kudos among his New York associates. A so-called "British Invasion" of the USA had begun on February 9th, 1964 when The Beatles made their American television debut on the popular *Ed Sullivan Show* (watched that night in 23 million households, a record figure then[63]) while their latest single 'I Want To Hold Your Hand' had just headed the Cashbox charts.[64] While The Beatles' early songs fitted in to the prevalent pop song style favoured in the US, other British bands such as The Rolling Stones and The Animals brought back to white America's attention the heritage within it of rhythm & blues and blues itself. It seems, however, at this time that the nascent Velvets were not interested in the blues; any member who played a blues "lick" was fined.

Although Reed eventually left Ludlow Street to move in with Morrison to a fifth-floor Grand Street flat, Cale called these few months with Reed their "intellectual puberty". He started taking heroin with Reed, sharing needles: "This was magic for two guys as uptight and distanced from their surroundings as Lou and I. It opened a channel between us and created the conspiratorial us-against-them attitude which would become a hallmark of our band."[65] This may be why they first chose for their group the name The Falling Spikes. They soon changed it to The Warlocks, but they would have discovered another band with a record out under that name. At the same time a third Warlocks dropped their name in favour of The Grateful Dead.[66] Why Warlocks? War was clearly in the (Vietnam) air, paganism too. It was only in October or early November that Tony Conrad fell upon a cheap paperback novel about sado-masochism titled *The Velvet Underground* and suggested that the others appropriate the novel's name. Differing reports claim that he found it in a gutter, on the pavement, or in the subway – all of these are emblems of the Velvet "underground" mythology, of which more later.

Soon after, Al Aronowitz, a journalist attempting to enter the management arena, saw Cale and his colleagues playing at a Cinematheque event. It is said that he took guitarist Robbie Robertson (later of Dylan's backing group The Band) to this or a subsequent show for a second opinion. Robertson dismissed them, saying of Reed's guitar playing, "He ain't nothin'".[67] Nevertheless, Aronowitz offered them a support slot for his band The Myddle Class. The Velvets agreed. On December 11th The Velvet Underground made its debut under this name at the Summit High School, Summit, New Jersey, where the band was contracted to play just three songs. According to Sterling Morrison, the audience gave "a roar of disbelief once we started to play 'Venus' [In Furs] and swelled to a mighty howl of outrage and bewilderment by the end of 'Heroin'".[68] Cale had finally consummated the effect of smashing an axe through a table simply by playing his viola in a high school. Five days later, thanks again to Aronowitz, Cale found himself playing the first Velvet show of a six-week residency at the Café Bizarre, although it hardly lasted six nights.

Sterling Morrison

The youngest male in the band by all of five months, Holmes Sterling Morrison, was born on August 29th, 1942 and brought up in East Meadow[69] on Long Island, a small town not far from Lou Reed's Freeport. As he admitted, "I stepped in and out of a scholarly life, back and forth, like someone pacing irritably between the library and the stage."[70] A conventional middle-class upbringing led him to receive, just in time for his 18th birthday in 1960, the same undergraduate scholarship as his friend Jim Tucker. Although Morrison had decided to follow Tucker to the upstate University of Syracuse, instead he enrolled at the University of Illinois to study physics. He left after only two semesters (terms). According to Morrison, his dissolute undergraduate life was led as follows:

Dates	Duration	Institution
September 1960–April 1961	2 terms	University of Illinois (Physics)
April 1961	2 weeks	City College, New York City
September–December 1961	1 year	Living at Syracuse with Jim Tucker (not enrolled)
January 1962		Supposed to start at Syracuse, but didn't
September 1962–July 1965	3 years	City College, New York City (English Lit)

Morrison graduated in English at the end of his course and joined The Warlocks. He carried on in The Velvet Underground after Lou Reed quit in August 1970 but left a year later after registering for his doctorate (in medieval studies) and relatedly landing a lecturing job in English literature, both opportunities offered concurrently by the University of Texas at Austin. At this point he called himself Holmes Morrison and for three years he made no mention of his previous rock career until he started to play guitar informally with a local Austin band.[71] Around 1982 (perhaps earlier), when he received his doctorate, he became a tugboat captain on the Houston Ship Channel. He joined in the short-lived 1990 and 1993 revival of the Velvets, and later toured with Moe Tucker's own band. He died in Poughkeepsie, New York State, of non-Hodgkin's lymphoma (a lymphatic cancer) two days after his 53rd birthday in 1995.

It was while Morrison was visiting Jim Tucker at Syracuse in late 1960 that he first came across student Lewis Reed, a fellow guitarist and dissident: "That's how we met, in college dining halls", Morrison recalled.[72] He considered himself a recreant, justifying his stand as follows:

> In the early 1960s, on college campuses, you went one of two ways. Either you were a very sensitive young person who cared about air pollution and civil rights and anti-Vietnam, or you were a very insensitive young person, who didn't care about civil rights because all the blacks he knew were playing in his band or in his audience. I was a very insensitive young person and played very insensitive, uncaring music... Anybody who needs Bob Dylan to tell him which way the wind is blowing is a serious mental defective.[73]

As a teenager Morrison enjoyed most of all rock'n'roll. As its embers dimmed in the early 1960s he kept it alive in his lifestyle, dressing "in a rock'n'roll way", a style typical of beatniks who were turning towards rock in a studied move to the anti-intellectual stand of the "punk". He had taken up the guitar as part of this image and his playing was at first restricted to chord shapes. In contrast to his course in English literature, he treated rock as anti-literature: "If you're going to rock music to learn something verbally rather than physically or viscerally, then you're in a sad shape, baby."[74] These comments make it all the more surprising that Morrison continued in the Velvets after Cale left in 1967, when Reed made the band serve his lyrics with a more "folksy" sound. Morrison, however, did admit that, "I enjoy the life backstage, the after-hours feel of everything, and the groupies",[75] which may explain his tenacity for the Velvets project even after Reed quit in 1970.

Just as curious is his remark about black musicians and audiences, seeing as the bands he played in were white. As it happens, Reed's university group LA and The Eldorados sometimes played – to a mixed audience at the 800 Club in Syracuse[76] – with singers called The Three Screaming Niggers; this is hardly a dazzling justification, though, for Morrison's lack of concern over civil rights. Morrison joined in on guitar with The Eldorados so long as his travels and courses permitted, which became limited to the less frequent vacation breaks once he had started at City College, and which must have ceased entirely, given that Reed was surprised to come across him in New York in 1965.

It seems that Morrison entered the Velvets in the same myth-laden way that Conrad found the book – on the pavement, in the gutter, down the subway. Morrison agreed that he met his old friend Reed by chance while he was in a subway train ("on the D Train at the 7th Avenue stop or thereabouts"[77]), but, while Reed claimed Morrison was "barefoot" at the time, Morrison thought this to be an idiotic assertion, especially in a dirt-strewn city like New York, but also because he resented the notion that he had to be "looked after" by the others. This chance meeting possibly took place in February or March 1965 and led to Morrison taking over from Conrad, working with Cale and Reed at the downtown flat from April onwards and taking part in the Ludlow Tapes over the summer.

In looks and stature he was not unlike Cale, though taller. They framed the smaller Reed, like sentries. Yet Morrison was unlike Cale in his relation to Reed. Morrison and Reed came from the same suburban setting. Through a mutual friend they had developed a rapport between them just at the same time that they'd left their families. They developed a friendship at college around a music scene rather than through a music profession. Morrison easily accepted Reed's bisexuality, only worrying that Reed would waste his time with "some really flabby effete fairy".[78] He also had less at stake than the other two; after all, he was on holiday from an academic career, not tied to music. Finally, Morrison could bypass the competitive streak that lay between Reed and Cale. As Morrison often said, he was the one who was "in it for the fun".

When they made their debut at the Café Bizarre for five dollars a night each, the only fun they had was "pissing [off] the owners by playing 'The Black Angel's Death Song' more times than they could bear".[79]

Maureen (Moe) Tucker

> I never had any problem. I was just playing drums, it wasn't a campaign or a statement. I just like playing drums and why shouldn't I? I don't even remember anyone either in the band or in the audience saying, "Why are you playing drums? You're a girl!"[80]

Clearly Maureen Tucker had forgotten the moment in December 1965 when she was about to join The Velvet Underground and overheard Cale declaring, "No chicks in the band. No chicks". But Tucker was hardly a "chick". She looked like a tomboy at that time, small and lithe with little or no make-up, thick laddish hair combed over. Her gender-vague nickname of "Moe" suited not only her persona then, but it also fed into the modish androgyny with which the group became associated through Warhol. When she compared herself to the six-feet tall Nico, she said, "She was worldly, gorgeous and guarded. I was the schlep from Levittown wearing T-shirts and dungarees, having no self-confidence whatsoever, trying not to be seen."[81] In turn Nico said of Maureen, "She was the most normal in the group and also the most strange. Andy [Warhol] didn't know if she was a boy or a girl just by seeing her, and that is funny, as he knew so many girls who were really boys. But Moe was not a diva – unlike Lou."[82]

Maureen Tucker was born in 1945 and brought up in Levittown on western Long Island, near the childhood homes of both Morrison and Reed. She knew Morrison from the age of 12[83] because he was her brother Jim's friend. Tucker claims that she took up drumming as a teenager because a drum seemed quicker to learn than a guitar (and it was cheaper to buy a snare drum than a Gretsch). She played very simple patterns, and so – as she had little time for virtuosity – she had little to learn. Tucker played alone at home on Long Island for her own pleasure, drumming along to the pulse of Bo Diddley records as well as a cult LP, *Drums Of Passion*, by the Nigerian drummer Babatunde Olatunji (1927–2003). His record of spiritual drumming in praise of the Yoruba religion (an influence on voodoo) had been released in 1960. From 1963 onwards Tucker had a job as a key-presser for rudimentary computers. Apparently her mental and physical coordination was extraordinary. Morrison said that, "She worked for a temping agency. They would call her at noon and she'd work the afternoon but they'd pay her for a full day... She could do more in an afternoon than most people could manage in three days."[84]

Tucker certainly had a rational approach to her drumming as well as acutely specific values. In a very fine interview in Karen O'Brien's survey of women musicians, *Hymn to Her*, Tucker states: "I consciously, purposely, didn't learn more about drums because I didn't want to sound like anybody else... What I liked about the drumming was that the person was just in the background, playing drums, keeping the tempo and not ever taking over the song. I like Charlie Watts [of The Rolling Stones] for instance; he's just there, he's perfect, he never overtakes a song... I can't stand drum solos. I just hate them! I can't stand really fancy drummers who are thrashing around... And also I can't stand songs where all you hear is that bass drum throughout the whole song, it begins to drive me crazy!"[85]

What is most remarkable about Tucker – aside from her eventual role as the first famous female drummer in rock – is that she was thoroughly idiosyncratic in her approach, as much from reasons of logic as ideology. She didn't like cymbals (she apparently had one but it was so clanky that it was beyond use). Her kit comprised a standard four-piece set of snare, two tomtoms and a bass drum (no hi-hat cymbals), but Tucker liked to use the snare drum as a high tom-tom, and she didn't use the bass drum with a foot pedal but instead laid it on its side to strike it with her hand-held beaters. As she had no foot pedals to control, instead of sitting on a drum stool, she stood.

Tucker would play in this manner with The Velvet Underground from December 1965 to late 1971. In 1970 she became pregnant with the first of her five children, and Doug Yule's brother Billy took over as drummer for a period, a role he retained when she quit in 1971 following Morrison's departure. She moved with her husband to Phoenix, Arizona. Having neglected music for a decade, in 1982 she released her solo debut of cover versions, with a further record of her own songs following in 1986. Now separated from her husband, she moved to Douglas, Georgia, working for Wal-Mart. Another Tucker album was released in 1989, financed by one of the celebrated Penn and Teller magic entertainers, Penn Jellete. It included contributions from Lou Reed and The Velvet Underground-influenced post-punk band Sonic Youth.[86] She toured venues around Europe with Morrison and her sons in 1994. Like Cale and Reed, she is still active as a creative musician – but, unlike them, a grandmother.

Tucker entered the world of The Velvet Underground just two days before its first appearance at Summit High School on December 11th, 1965. Up to that point the nascent Velvets had benefited from two different drummers, Walter de Maria (January–April) and then Angus MacLise. De Maria (b. 1935) is now one of the world's leading sculptors, a founder of the late 1960s Earthworks movement, and famed for his New Mexico site-piece *The Lighting Field* (1977). Yet he started out in California as a trained drummer, having studied as a teenager with a percussionist from the San Francisco Philharmonic Orchestra. He became interested in free jazz and, when he arrived in New York in 1960 as part of the LaMonte Young invasion, he played a few sessions with trumpeter Don Cherry. His colleague Tony Conrad asked him to help out in January 1965 as the drummer of The Primitives with their crazy song, 'Do The Ostrich', and then on into the emerging world of the Velvets.

However, this dramatically led the 29-year-old De Maria to face a crisis and a change of creative focus, from music to art. As he put it, "When I was with the Velvets, here was a real choice... Do I want to go to rehearsal every day and every night, you know, take all these drugs?[87] Do I really want to keep playing these rhythms, is that going to be enough?... No, I'm not going to haul those drums to another place and I just can't keep playing these songs."[88]

Astonishingly, in the very next flat to Cale's there was another professionally trained Californian progressive drummer to take over. An exceptional figure on the downtown experimental scene as a poet, composer and organizer of multimedia events throughout the 1960s, Angus MacLise had in his youth enjoyed a formidable education in various styles of drumming,[89] including jazz at the Buddy Rich School (Rich was a celebrity swing band drummer), orchestral percussion and Latin American techniques. In 1964 he travelled to Morocco to learn something of North African drumming traditions, and when he returned in early 1965 he put what he'd learnt at the disposal of LaMonte Young and also his Ludlow Street house neighbours, Conrad and Cale. MacLise used his collection of free-standing, ethnic drums of various sizes including some from North Africa, India and the Middle East. In comparison to the traditional rock drummer on a coordinated drum set of snare drum, tom-toms, bass drum and cymbals, MacLise was utterly extraordinary.

Unique he was, too, in his treatment of time. In line with Young and Zazeela's dilation of days and nights, MacLise had invented a new calendar, the Universal Solar Calendar, with new names for each day of the year, a practice of classifying which he and other artists observed in their writings.[90] MacLise had so little sense of clock time, according to Cale, that it was difficult to arrange rehearsals with him, and he would play along only if he felt it right to him to do so. When Aronowitz announced the first Velvets gigs in December 1965, MacLise was said to have complained, "You mean we start when they tell us to and we have to end when they tell us to? I can't work that way." And he left.[91]

Desperate for a replacement in order to play at Summit High School, Morrison suggested his friend Jim's 19-year-old sister. According to

Maureen, "Lou came to my house to see if I could actually keep time, and I passed the audition. It was just supposed to be for that one show, just three songs. From that show they immediately got another job two nights later [actually five] but they weren't allowed to play drums in [Café Bizarre] because it was too noisy. So they said, 'Come and play the tambourine'. So, from there I was in the band." In the band she was, despite Cale's rule of "no chicks".

Nico (Christa Päffgen)

Nico was born in Budapest in 1944. Or Berlin in 1943; Cologne, 1942; Poland, 1938. Her parents were Russian; or, half Russian and half Turkish; a quarter Russian and Polish and German and Turkish; or, ingeniously, "Russians who happened to be passing through Germany". She lied so often about almost everything to do with her identity that she managed through it to turn herself into a mythic being. Nico lied to hide from her son, Ari (b. 1962), that he was the illegitimate child of an illegitimate mother.

Christa Päffgen was born in Cologne a year before the start of World War II, in October 1938. She was the illegitimate daughter of a member of the powerful Päffgen brewery firm in the city. Her working-class mother took her baby to Berlin and then, when the war started, to a town of shelter in eastern Germany where Christa's grandfather was the signalman for an important railway junction. When Nico (as we'll from now on call Christa) told Lou Reed that she saw Jews being transported in cattle trucks by trains to Poland, she was probably telling the truth.

After the war her mother took her back to an utterly ruined Berlin, where Nico grew up among the rebuilding programmes of the American quarter. She later declared that they should have left it alone: "It would make a marvellous museum now. The National Museum of Destruction. That would be fun, wouldn't it?"[92] Nevertheless, she grew up out of severe poverty into an increasingly prosperous post-war locale, where she decided at the age of 15 that she wanted to be "discovered". Nico hung around the doors of Berlin's grandest department store, the KaDeWe, trying to look like the gamine Audrey Hepburn out of the 1953 hit film *Roman Holiday*. The leading German couturier of the day was Heinz Oestergaard and one of his assistants spotted Nico, giving her a job as a KaDeWe mannequin where she showed off Oestergaard's gowns to customers. She was "discovered".

Christa Päffgen, Berlin, 1955, photographed by Herbert Tobias

A local gay fashion photographer became her best friend (Nico wanted to be him, and he wanted to be her, she said), put her face in German fashion magazines, and took her to Paris where Willy Maywald, one of the chief fashion photographers of the 1950s, took her up as a cover girl. While working in Paris she heard of a celebrated nightclub owner, producer of a banned film by Jean Genet,[93] and husband to the stunning French film star Anouk Aimée. He was called Nico Papatakis. Christa liked his first name so much that she stole it for herself, the androgyny of a male name on a tall, flawless paragon like Nico being a characteristic choice. Eventually by chance (Nico preferred to call this fate) the two Nicos met at a Harper's Bazaar dinner party and "fell in love".[94] He flew her to New York now and again when he had business there (they became a part of the archetypal "jet set"), while she continued her work as a photographers' model in Paris, eventually earning enough to buy a villa for her mother on the Spanish island of Ibiza. Meanwhile, Nico met the young French film star Alain Delon and had a child by him, Ari, whom Delon declined to recognize as his son.[95]

Among the many "beau monde" encounters and adventures around this time, Nico managed to appear in one of the most controversial and emblematic films of the early 1960s, Federico Fellini's *La Dolce Vita*, where her character was called Nico. This appearance became her passport for the next decade, as many viewers of the film could remember the scene where Marcello Mastroianni calls out "Nico!" on Via Veneto and, instead of a man, a sensational woman appears. But she also relished the infamy of the film, traduced at the time as a "nihilist parade of depraved and idle scum".[96]

In May 1964 she met Bob Dylan in Paris, had a short affair with him, and he wrote a song or two for her, including 'I'll Keep It With Mine' possibly about Ari (although Nico said she couldn't understand what Dylan sang to her. "Twing, twang, twing, twang, baybee: that's how it went", she complained). When London took over as the chic place to be, around 1964, Nico started to hang out there where, among so many others, she had a quick but effective affair with Brian Jones of The Rolling Stones. He arranged for Nico to record a Gordon Lightfoot song, 'I'm Not Sayin'', which was released as a single in August 1965.

On this record Nico's naturally low voice is raised and lightened a little, revealing a fragile vibrato (too much like that of another Rolling Stone girlfriend-singer, Marianne Faithfull). But the stronger, liquid, subterranean timbre and the diction that would define Nico in later years is already perceptible. She based her vocal style entirely on that of the post-war German film star Hildegard Knef, whose songs were popular when Nico was growing up. Knef in turn based hers on the Nazi pin-up Zarah Leander, who was heavily promoted as the pro-Nazi version of the anti-Hitler Marlene Dietrich. In all cases these voice were maternal, a phenomenon of the 1940s (Vera Lynn in Britain, Edith Piaf in France, Dinah Shore in America, for example), and it may be no coincidence that Nico took up singing only after the birth of Ari. Therefore, when critics claim that Nico based her voice on Dietrich's, they are only three times removed from the truth.

Although Nico's single was not a chart success, she later remembered an aged record company man at a London party telling her, "Singles are history. Each year people buy less and less. And girl singers only account for 20 per cent of the sales... There is a future – a future for groups and a future for albums. And I'll tell you what – a girl leading a group, that would be a winner!"

While in Paris she had met Andy Warhol and his assistant Gerard Malanga, who invited her to visit Warhol's midtown studio The "Silver" Factory next time she was in New York. As her London contacts, including photographer David Bailey and Beatle Paul McCartney, began to tire of Nico's loitering presence, her thoughts turned to New York. Armed with a copy of her single, she flew there in November, where she found a little modelling work to keep her going (she was now a venerable 27 years old). The Rolling Stones were touring the States then, and so Brian Jones took Nico to visit The Factory, which she was disappointed to discover was merely the fourth floor of a warehouse, covered in silver baking foil.

Warhol immediately gave her a "screen test", which every intriguing visitor had to endure, and she in turn gave him her copy of 'I'm Not Sayin'', which the Warhol crew promptly played and "sort of liked". A few days later Warhol invited her to appear in one of the fixed-camera two-reel films he was making at The Factory. Called *The Closet* (the gay subtext of which was lost on her), Nico lived in a cupboard with gay boy Randy Borscheidt for 70 minutes of non-adventure. She would eventually appear in six Warhol films, including a leading part in his most famous, *Chelsea Girls*.

Warhol and his team, led by his manager Paul Morrissey, went along to see The Velvet Underground perform, somewhere around the 19th of December, during its curtailed residency at the Café Bizarre. While Morrissey was interested in the band, he equally had a problem with it, and he believed that the solution would be Nico. "I turned to Andy and said, 'Andy, the problem is these people have no singer. There's a guy who sings [Reed] but he's got no personality and nobody pays the slightest attention to him. They need someone with a bit of charisma.' Andy nodded. So I suggested Nico but I can't remember if we got her to see the band."[97] Nico said that she did once see the band at the Café.

Morrissey went on to recount how he offered the band a management deal with money for the band to live on, to cover their rent and buy some equipment. "But", he added uneasily, "you need a singer...and, er, we know this singer, and er, what if she sang with your group?" They listened to Nico's record. Morrissey watched their reaction: "Right away that sour little Lou Reed bristled. He was hostile to Nico from the start. I told them I thought that Nico could be part of The Velvet Underground and just fit in there under that name. Lou replied, 'Let's keep Nico separate in this. The Velvet Underground – and Nico'." As Nico observed on how she was placed last, "That's because I was the girl".

The Velvet Underground – and Nico – was finally formed, though hardly primed, for the next stage of its highly erratic life.

3 Reed

Three supreme rocksong writers have turned the ordinary into the extraordinary. They are Chuck Berry (b. 1926), Ray Davies of The Kinks (b. 1944), and Lou Reed. In his pre-Velvet years Reed played Berry songs in public such as 'No Particular Place To Go', 'Johnny B. Goode', 'School Day', 'Carol', 'Memphis, Tennessee' and 'Rock And Roll Music'. The Beatles, The Rolling Stones and The Animals played these, too; John Lennon said, "If you were trying to give rock & roll another name, you might call it Chuck Berry."[1]

When the Velvets first performed publicly in late 1965, and even during 1966, they often covered such songs, initially because they didn't have enough of their own, but also to offset the more experimental improvisations they offered. The improvisations told the audience where the Velvets "were at", while the Berry songs make it clear where they came from. Berry's simple but slyly witty songs, mainly about the frustrations of teenage life, at once evoked a 1950s world left behind by the Velvets' audiences.

In Britain The Kinks had also begun with Berry numbers, in 1962, and their early albums mixed rhythm & blues standards with Ray Davies's first songs such as 'You Really Got Me' and 'All Day And All Of The Night'. When John Cale returned from London in the late summer of 1965 with the *Kinda Kinks* album, he and Reed realized that they faced pressing competition in their aim to expand the subject matter and the sound world of rock. Two Kinks' songs in particular must have raised an alarm. 'Tired Of Waiting For You' is almost – almost – a heroin song, and 'See My Friends' runs mainly on a drone. However, Reed had no need to chase Davies. Their careers ran a remarkable, parallel course. While Reed's songs always dealt through subtle wit with social observation, Davies moved only gradually to satire, starting in 1966 with 'Dedicated Follower Of Fashion' and following it with 'Sunny Afternoon', about the new phenomenon then of whinging rock stars. By 1970, however, it is as though Reed and Davies had interfused in the latter's "Lola", an account of meeting, in "a club down in old Soho", Lola who "walked like a woman and talked like a man". There is an irony that this immensely successful song of Davies's, comprising just three adjacent pitches, would appear at the very time that Reed quit not only The Velvet Underground but the music business entirely. Three years later Reed would live with Rachel, formerly known as Tommy.

This chapter, though, concerns Reed the consummate songwriter. His lyrics are considered by many to be exceptional, and the reasons given are summarized as follows. Reed's songs:

(1) observe and describe characters in situations;

(2) use simple words to convey rich thoughts;

(3) deal frankly with those people otherwise dispossessed of song;

(4) carry a hint of the subconscious at play, of shrewd implications about personal identity and social anxieties;

(5) possess a dry humour, finely balanced between satire and cynicism.

To take these in turn:

(1) Observation

Reed's songs are often about people who are characterized. That is, they are identified, through words, by distinguishing features or qualities. These characters are described, given an account of. Sometimes they have names ("Severin awaits you" in 'Venus In Furs'; "Teenage Mary said to Uncle Dave" in "Run Run Run") but other times not ("Here she comes, you better watch your step" in 'Femme Fatale'). We the listeners are often given roles, too. We are "You" in 'Sunday Morning', 'Femme Fatale', and the "Your" in 'I'll Be Your Mirror'; we are "my friend" in 'There She Goes Again'. In other words, we too are assigned a status within the situation wherein the characters operate. In most cases Reed is the narrator, describing a scene or warning us of our position in it ("Watch out, the world's behind you" in 'Sunday Morning'), but, to add a disconcerting insecurity in order to enrich the account, he often switches between narrator, subject, and character. For example, 'Sunday Morning' shifts between "I" and "you"; 'I'm Waiting For The Man' also moves between "I" and "you" – "You gotta wait, I'm waiting for my man", while Reed plays a third character who shouts "Hey, white boy...", and finally describes "my dear, dear friend" the dealer, "he".

Reed has often commented on the way he likes to be other people, to embody a character but at the same time to stress that this character isn't him: "Put all the characters together and it's certainly an autobiography. It's just not necessarily mine."[2] He has also implied that, as he is the singer throughout the second and third albums, this consistency provides a narrative unity. By this means the main character of the third album (1969) is apparently the girlfriend of the junkie narrator of the first two[3] (released 1967, 1968). There is actually very little to link the songs together in any of those albums, and this may simply be an unconvincing claim to connect these Velvets records with the vogue for the "concept" album current in the late 1960s. On other occasions he's suggested that the "records were letters. Real letters from me to certain people".[4] He's also compared songwriting to making films: "Some people make movies of people who interest them. Andy Warhol has been doing it for years. Actually, I do it with my songs."[5] Perhaps his most convincing explanation was made while publicizing his first solo album (*Lou Reed*, 1972), where he likened it to performance:

> Writing songs is like making a play and you give yourself the lead part. And you write yourself the best lines that you could. And you're your own director. And they're short plays. And you get to play all different kinds of characters. It's fun. I write through the eyes of somebody else. I'm always checking out people I know I'm going to write songs about. Then I become them. That's why when I'm not doing that I'm kind of empty. I don't have a personality of my own. I just pick up other people's personalities.[6]

Reed often establishes his characters in what might be the scene of a play by indicating their arrival or departure, like a stage direction – "Here he comes, he's all dressed in black" ('I'm Waiting For The Man'); "Here she comes, you better watch your step" ('Femme Fatale'); "Here they come now/see them run now" ('Chelsea Girls'); "Who's that knocking on my chamber door?" ('Sister Ray') and the song titles 'There She Goes Again', 'Here She Comes Now', among others. And certainly his attempt to project a potent visual image through words explains his reference to films and plays. He once said, "I try to give you a very visual image in very few words so that you can picture it in your mind really quickly."[7] In Reed's verses, ordinary places are transfigured by the events within them. While there is the after-hours bar where, "If you close the door, the night could last forever" ('Afterhours'), the brownstone building on 125th Street ('I'm Waiting For The Man') and the Chelsea Hotel on 23rd Street ('Chelsea Girls') serve simply as settings for the daily epiphanies of drug-taking by the characters he enjoys describing.

Biographer, novelist, letter-writer, film-maker, playwright, actor: it's not surprising that Reed himself claims adoption of these different personas in his creative operations, given the range of cultural influences he's alleged for this work, which we'll come to. But part of this need for characterization derives from his generally weak singing voice, the reason why Morrissey and Warhol wanted Nico in the band as "*the* singer". Just as Reed had "taken up" Dylan's nasal brogue in the early 1960s, these characters are surely his attempt to construct his own Dylans, in that they exist for the benefit of his voice as much as they do for his words.

(2) **Simplicity**

While admitting that "I personally think that writing something simply is the hardest thing you can do",[8] Reed confirms time and again that this is his objective. To achieve this he mostly uses words of one syllable ("And I guess that I just don't know" in 'Heroin'; "When you think the night has seen your mind" in 'I'll Be Your Mirror') or one and two syllables ("I'll be your mirror, reflect what you are" in 'I'll Be Your Mirror'; "Downy sins of streetlight fancies" in 'Venus In Furs'). The most extravagant words he tends to use are those of three syllables: "myriad", "demurely", and, for that matter, "heroin", where, in the song of that name, each syllable is smoothly savoured.[9]

Reed's economy in choice of syllables is partnered with an economy of expression, such as "Let me be your eyes" in 'I'll Be Your Mirror'. He has said elsewhere that "I always wanted to write a song called 'I Love You' and make it fresh. If I could take a phrase like that and turn it into something, then that would be a real accomplishment."[10] Above all there is the very notion of 'All Tomorrow's Parties' for which "the poor girl" sits and cries in "a hand-me-down gown". This was understandably Warhol's favourite song.

(3) **Prohibited subjects**

According to Reed "realism was the key".[11] A drug dealer, like him, and a drug user, like him, is bound to have met a range of marginalized people mired in illegality. Unorthodox and maverick, not to say desperate and deranged, some of them might almost have been as troubled as he has been. After his admittance to Andy Warhol's Factory scene, which he joined with the rest of the band in December 1965, Reed had no need to exert his imagination to find renegade characters. He recounted, "I watched Andy watching everybody. I would hear people say the most astonishing things, the craziest things, the funniest things, the saddest things. I used to write it down."[12] Paul

Morrissey considers that Reed got on so well with Warhol for this voyeuristic reason, that they were both "a little without personality so they looked around to absorb it from others".[13] Reed saw himself in a more positive light as a kind of ethnographer, reporting on the behaviour of those he came across who were dispossessed of convention, or indisposed to it.

Characters Reed lighted on tended anyway to be the most self-seeking, like the transvestite Candy Darling (James Slattery) of 'Candy Says' or the drugged Bridget Polk "all wrapped in foil" ('Chelsea Girls'). In fact, although there are in his output only a few descriptions of transgendered characters, such as Pepper in 'Chelsea Girls' who's "having fun/She think she's some man's son", it remains one of the few factors by which we can connect Reed to that project of sexual emancipation by which the 1960s has been strongly identified. In his references to gay life, for example, he said, "My gay people don't lisp. They're not any more affected than the straight world. They just are."[14]

In this regard, by the way, it is sometimes wondered whether 'I'm Waiting For The Man' has a gay subtext, as the phrase "The Man" appears only in the title. Reed sings "my man" – "I'm waiting for my man/Twenty-six dollars in my hand". The subway station rendezvous ("Lexington 125") adds a hustler touch, and the line that women are furthest from his mind aids this alternative reading, as does the "sweet taste" satisfaction once he's met "his man".

For a more direct example of candid sexual reportage, 'Sister Ray' is about "a bunch of drag queens taking a bunch of sailors home with them, shooting up on smack and having an orgy when the police appear".[15] But, while 'Chelsea Girls' is an account of real people (rather sad ones, it has to be said, some of whom we see in Warhol's corresponding film[16]), 'Sister Ray' is fiction, which may explain its more cartoon-like, exultant style. Reed has explained that it "echoes" scenes from Hubert Selby Jr's novel *Last Exit To Brooklyn* (1962).[17] Yet 'Sister Ray' may in the end be one of Reed's aberrant songs, of which there are three others of the same period – his spoken stories 'The Gift' and 'The Murder Mystery' and his experimental 'Black Angel's Death Song', which was an attempt at spontaneous writing in the style of Jack Kerouac and his fellow Beats (the Black Angel in question was a yacht tethered at the 79th Street Basin and owned by one of the former Eldorados[18]). For the most part Reed based his characters and situations on observations of those who, as Phil Lesh of The Grateful Dead said, were "breaking out".

Reed's second link to the 1960s *Zeitgeist* is that of drugs. While the West Coast rockers were advocating psychedelics, Reed was writing about heroin and amphetamine, drugs as much associated with danger as with pleasure due to the criminal scene associated with the trafficking of them. Just as 'I'm Waiting For The Man' – at least on the surface – describes how Reed scored smack in Spanish Harlem (his university girlfriend recalled driving him to buy drugs: "I remember going up to 125th Street. Really vile, nasty hallways"[19]), so 'Heroin' and 'White Light/White Heat' are songs of experience.

'Heroin' doesn't acclaim the drug or censure it. Instead an encounter is described. The effect of injecting heroin into a vein is likened through a simile to a trip on a subway train, represented by the music accelerating from a terminal and hurtling along, ecstatically faster and faster ("rushing on my run"), but ultimately, "Thank God I'm as good as dead", only for the cycle to recommence. It's probably the first song written about heroin that doesn't preach or pretend it's about something else. The religious rapture invoked in it ("And I feel just like Jesus' son") was endorsed by Nico: "It is when you use it the first thousand times that you feel like a god. Of course, I am supposed to be a goddess now and so I am bored after a million million times. But it is something he knew. It is a song of feeling, not about Lou being someone else."[20]

(4) **Latency**

When Bridget in 'Chelsea Girls' is "all wrapped in foil/You wonder if she can uncoil", this eccentric image presumably refers to the act of "chasing the dragon", of heating heroin powder on a sheet of baking foil and sucking in the resultant fumes through a foil tube. Nico's own account of the effect of heroin is that "you are wrapped in fur". Reed's metonymic image of foil for the effects of heroin, together with the triple meaning of "wrapped (up)/rapt", is one of a small number of more complex images in his output, as he otherwise prefers to be direct. Perhaps his most inferential song is 'Sunday Morning', a seemingly innocuous number that is really about the morning-after paranoia a night on drugs can release ("Watch out, the world's behind you"), which is how Nico understood it to be.[21]

In this, Reed is unlike Dylan who, from 1964 onwards, made a speciality of surreal images ("Einstein disguised as Robin Hood/With his memories in a trunk...", 'Desolation Row', 1966). The re-emergence in the 1960s of bizarre juxtapositions (of the kind we find in dreams) by which surrealism had made its name, was partly a result of the baby-boom generation finding parallels between the work of inter-war surrealist writers and artists (especially Salvador Dalí, who visited Warhol's Factory in 1966) with the images they experienced using "mind-expanding" drugs. This renewal in public reception of surrealist painting differed from the abstract expressionists' professional interest in surrealist procedures. It matched the 1960s post-abstract attraction to pictorial representation; Dalí's landscapes with melting watches and Magritte's bowler hats joined Warhol's garish Marilyns and Lichtenstein's newsprint cartoons as poster-prints on the walls of student bedrooms.

André Breton, self-appointed leader of the inter-war surrealists, had defined his movement as a new kind of reality in the way that the conscious and the (Freudian) unconscious could meet, as a sur-reality. West Coast artists were directly the most receptive to this commodified 1960s renewal; "It came out of psychedelics, of seeing what you thought you'd known [consciousness] in a less delusive light [unconsciousness]", explained Phil Lesh of The Grateful Dead.[22] Californian groups who explored this terrain included Jefferson Airplane (*Surrealistic Pillow*, 1967) and The Doors ('The Crystal Ship', 'Horse Latitudes'), two bands formed about the same time as the Velvets. Reed and Cale favoured "hard" drugs such as heroin. They derided the West Coast "hippie" culture so much so that they set their "realism" flush against it. Reed declared, "The Velvet Underground very consciously set out to put themes common to [representational] movies, plays and novels into pop-song format... At the worst we were like the antedated realists."[23]

Yet their chosen name, The Velvet Underground, is rather surreal. Even the narrative of this name's discovery, of it lying in a gutter or a subway – a chance encounter under the ground – is a typical act of surrealist mythologizing (it relates, too, to Cage's embrace of chance, which was influenced by surrealist games). This vision of tactility that the name throws, of a velvet-covered subterranean tunnel, recalls the erotic fur cup made by surrealist artist Meret Oppenheim.[24] And Reed's 'Sister Ray' is clearly next of kin to Man Ray, the American surrealist eroticist and photographer.[25] However, all this tells us is that the Velvets were to an extent embedded in this widespread resurgence. Nevertheless, they confronted surrealism with its existential nemesis. Jean-Paul Sartre had already stubbed his cigarette out on surrealism's "pretty stupid optimism".[26]

With regard to Dylan's obscure imagery, there is one early exception to Reed's careful avoidance of comparisons. This is 'European Son', the final and most cryptic track on the debut album. It was dedicated to the then senior but still living poet – barely alive, a paranoid, pill-popping alcoholic

– Delmore Schwarz. Sarcastic lines like "You spit on those under twenty-one"/"You want to make love to the scene" echo Bob Dylan's 'Like A Rolling Stone' (released in July 1965) with Dylan's recurring accusatory use of "didn't you?"[27] Reed even uses a Dylanesque voice. That he had to echo Dylan to achieve this degree of bile shows how far it helped Reed with his singing to adopt characteristics of others, however fictitious they may have been. Yet this spiteful song also brings together two of Reed's heroes, Dylan and Schwarz. It seems to show off that side of Reed described by Paul Morrissey as "sour", and by Nico who said that "Lou could spit poison when he kissed you".[28] There is more to mention on Schwarz and 'European Son'.

(5) **Humour**

It's on the second album, *White Light/White Heat*, where the "funny" songs are, in all senses. Reed has explained that the sole spoken track, 'The Gift',[29] is a story he wrote when he was a student at Syracuse. While his girlfriend was back home in the Midwest he wrote letters to her, including this narrative parodying his own situation – of a boy who posts himself as a parcel to his girlfriend only to be sliced in half as she tries to open the box with her father's sheet-metal cutter. But this is wet-blooded rather than dry humour. As a lyric it came out of the band's desire to improvise (being a spoken short story, it can be adjusted to fit any length of musical material), and also Reed's need to recycle good material from his university days when put under pressure to produce repertory. For the record, 'I'll Be Your Mirror' was apparently another song for his university sweetheart (although elsewhere Reed mentioned that he elaborated this from a phrase of Nico's when they were briefly lovers), while 'I'm Waiting For The Man' was a further undergraduate lyric.

Most well known among Reed's waggish output is his solo song 'Walk On The Wild Side' ("Shaved her legs and then he was a she") and the little comic song of 1968 sung by Maureen Tucker 'I'm Sticking With You' ("'cause I'm made out of glue"). Yet his earlier songs are also peppered with humour and irony. Take, for example, the misunderstanding in 'I'm Waiting For The Man' as to why he's in East Harlem ("Hey white boy, you chasin' our women around[?]/Oh pardon me sir, it's furthest from my mind..."), the "Don Giovanni" realization that the Femme Fatale has a book of conquests ("You're number 37, have a look"), or the whole satire of 'Venus In Furs' with its baroque inversions ("Comes in bells, your servant, don't forsake him") and the sick fun of 'Lady Godiva's Operation' from the second album, where surgery – possibly for a sex change – goes wrong. This resembles 'Venus In Furs', using again jokey inversions ("Patient it seems is not so well sleeping").

Reed cites as an influence on his lyrics the radical, Jewish, New York comic Lenny Bruce (Leonard Schneider, 1925–66). Bruce, "The Virtuoso of Shock", barked at hypocrisy and laid bare the paradoxes of Western society ("Classic paranoia is like, the Mafia is always chasing you. It'd be beautiful if we'd find out years later that the Mafia really was chasing these people. There was no paranoia at all!"[30]). But while Bruce openly used swear words in his monologues – he was arrested for obscenity five times in his career[31] – there are none in Reed's Velvets songs. Not even 'Sister Ray' has any; "cocks" refers strictly speaking to Cecil's gun, while people suck on "ding-dongs", an expression that would hardly impress Bruce. No doubt Bruce influenced Reed in his open portrayal of sex and drugs as subjects for public discourse. But Reed's humour relies on a nudge of the arm rather than Bruce's jab in the face.

In any case, the market for Bruce-style outrageous humour had been cornered by another Lower East Side group, The Fugs. Formed in 1964, this anarchic band developed like a folk-rock mirror of the Velvets, capable of adventurist experiments but also creators of catchy, elemental songs. While the Velvets appeared severe, The Fugs came across as clowns. In fact The Fugs and its offshoot The Holy Modal Rounders often supported the Velvets at the Dom, a matter of laughter before tears. With knockabout songs like 'I Couldn't Get High', 'Carpe Diem' ("Sing children sing! Death is a comin' in!") and 'Defeated' ("When I was a very little boy my mother defeated me/She would not let me play with my cock or suck on her soft titty"), The Fugs had, by the time they recorded their first album in the summer of 1965,[32] defined a territory next to which the nascent Velvets needed to define another.

Perhaps this explains the curious role of clowns in Reed's songs, who "cry behind the door" in 'All Tomorrow's Parties', who are the victims of the 'Femme Fatale', and who, in 'European Son', wave Delmore Schwarz goodbye.

At various times Reed has offered a range of literary influences to explain his approach to lyrics. There are:

(a) The "Beat" writers of the 1940s and 1950s such as Jack Kerouac (1922–69) whose "spontaneous" *On The Road* (1957) set the Beat fad for writing as reporting, William Burroughs (1914–97) whose novel *The Naked Lunch* helped to establish his notion that language is a virus and not a tool of liberation, and the poet Allen Ginsberg (1926–97), author of the angst-ridden confessional epic *Howl* (1956).

(b) Classy detective writers such as Raymond Chandler and Dashiell Hammett, as well as the novelist Hubert Selby.

(c) The pre-Beat elegance of Delmore Schwarz, who was a writer-in-residence at Syracuse University from September 1962, during Reed's last two years there.

(d) The writers of the rock'n'roll and doo-wop repertory from the 1950s with whom Reed associated himself, Chuck Berry above all.

What connects these diverse American artists are their creative contributions to those aspects of 1940s and 1950s US culture delineated in the first chapter, and their work as, or about, American "outsiders" – for example, Allen Ginsberg claimed that to be a junkie in America was like having been a Jew in Nazi Germany.[33] To take each in turn:

(a) *Beat*

In summary, the "Beat Generation" is the name given to a mainly metropolitan subculture[34] prevalent in post-war USA (main duration, 1943–63). Principally defined by literature – and so by a few key writers – it was firmly influenced by the philosophical viewpoints of existentialism in its efforts to address human detachment. There's a slight paradox, then, in the Beat writers' account of their adversarial abandonment of social norms on the one side, and their rampant desire for social fellowship on the other. It was rather "lonesome cowboy" and "live it up, lads" at one and the same time.

At the level of lifestyle,[35] a Beat follower was defined in 1960 by Elias Wilentz as "a kid with a beard, rumpled clothes, sandals, bongo drum, jazz records and a copy of *Howl*. Hints of sexual immoralities and use of drugs add a perverted glamour."[36] Lou Reed is discernible in the second sentence, if not the first. The movement to which Reed subscribed from 1958 was considered by several critics of it to be pseudo-intellectual, full of affected posturing, and to consist of young people who wished they were old, tired of life, hanging around café-bars for death to catch up with them, intemperate of those who embraced "the (capitalist) system" with its notion of working optimistically in the present for the future. This different view of time led the Beats and their associates to turn to improvisation with its "ever-present newness now".[37]

In one sense, then – that of existential despair – the Beat writers were a literary counterpart to the abstract expressionist painters. But there was an inversion of principles at play. The Beats were working in reaction to a literary clique of inter-war abstract modernism. That is, the Beats moved back to representation and aimed to deal with depictions of "real life" as they each subjectively saw it. Being bourgeois Romantics, the Beats cut out of their concerns the social conformists around them to replace them with the outlawed, the urban reprobates and the vagabonds of the street scene. In other words, the Beats were the most recent revival of the Bohemians, an early nineteenth-century youthful reaction to the development of mechanized industry, where Bohemian meant "gypsy-like" ("of Bohemia"), a subculture associated with unbridled artistic aspiration, poverty from being in advance of the market, and in consequence a connection with the disenfranchised in order to be free of conventional social responsibilities.

So, in among their subcultural selections of difference, the Beats one century on chose criminality (in 1946 William Burroughs became an apprentice pickpocket; five years he later accidently shot his wife) while in music they picked the polarizing improvisations of Dizzy Gillespie and his "hepcat" kind, with an overstated regard for black creativity that ran near to racism.[38] Down in the cellar bars of the Beats, it was all about sex and drugs and be-bop jazz.

But the "beat" in question was not the beat of jazz drummers. A self-conscious, constructed term, its original meaning was "beaten up". In 1950 Kerouac had written about "the pit and prune-juice of pure beat life itself".[39] "Beat" as a subcultural signifier really evolved after a Beat-friendly writer, James Clellon Holmes, introduced it in a *New York Times* magazine article of 1952. As "Beat" became taken up by the media, Kerouac, who had converted to Buddhism in 1955,[40] suddenly attempted to give the term a positive spin, relating it to a state of blessedness – "beatitude". As this contrived pun was hardly consistent with the miserablist, downbeat character of his writing, the former meaning stuck. It became, in fact, by this time an alternative term to another epithet put to use, from the mid 1940s onwards, to describe someone – black or white – who was into the new jazz and the style of dress, drugs and patois associated with the marking-out of this new subcultural territory – "hep".

From the West African Wolof name for savvy or smart, "hep/hip" evolved in a way that held on, throughout its use, to the notion of being aware of the new and of being confident with it. In contrast "Beat" took on the role of defining those who, although they embraced difference, did not acknowledge the progressive changes that the "hepcat" accepted. In their maturing as a boundaried, absorbed scene the Beats became easy targets for media satire. When the first Soviet satellite went into space in 1957, a journalist wrote that the Beats were as "far out" as *Sputnik*.[41] Thus the "beatnik" was launched, and the commercialization and Hollywoodization of the oversized-black-sweatered rebel image followed on.[42] As a final shift in this taming of "Beat", it would be taken up in name for cute, identically suited and hairstyled pop stars. The etymological path of both "beat" and "hip"[43] is roughly as follows:

Year	"Beat"	"Hip"
1945		Hepcat
1950	Beat ("beaten up")	Hep/Hip
1955	Beat ("beatitude")	Hipster
1958	Beatnik	
1960	The Beatles	
1965		Hippie

Reed was 16 in 1958 and he took on the lifestyle of a beatnik, just before the time that his "deviancy" was rewarded with electroconvulsive therapy at the Creedmore State Psychiatric Hospital. This truly radical act permitted by his parents and administered by the authorities should not divert us from understanding just how restrained in its own radicalism Beat subculture was. More than anything it was a backlash against the oppressively confident, positive and economically liberal nature of the dominant culture.

Given the apolitical, abstracted condition of beatnik subculture,[44] an alternative emerged from those who shared the Beats' dissatisfaction with social values but who sought change through cooperative and directly political action rather than personal non-conformism. These were the activists, especially students, who together became known as The Movement. According to student activist Casey Hayden in 1963, "the beatniks were – and are – just the Movement without altruism and energy. They are alienated by exactly the same things we are, but they just can't act on their discontent in an effective political way."[45]

A difference in musical taste distinguished them, too. Activists tended to support folk music of the kind Reed took up for a time at university (see Chapter 1), while beatniks followed modern jazz, shifting from be-bop (Dizzy Gillespie, Charlie Parker, Thelonious Monk) and hard bop, through the "cool" subgenre of the mid 1950s (Miles Davis, John Coltrane, Bill Evans) to the free jazz of the late 1950s (Don Cherry, Ornette Coleman, Cecil Taylor). Bob Dylan's success in 1963 came from his extraordinary ability to appeal simultaneously to these two subcultures, as a beatnik poet with a guitar as much as a civil rights "folkie". He was aided by the fact that around that time the free-jazz movement had become highly politicized and supportive of black consciousness campaigns, thus posing an exclusion too far for some white fans, who then switched to Dylan and the emergence of folk-rock. In sum, the contrast is as follows:

1945–60	1955–65
Jazz	*Folk*
Individualist	Activist
Esoteric	Popular ("of the people")
Instrument-based	Lyric-based
Polyphony	Homophony
Black	White[46]

By the time that The Velvet Underground started up in 1965 there were three main radical, adverserial "tribes" available for affiliation in the social life of young adults. While the Hippies and the Activists advanced towards maturity, the third grouping was a remnant of 1950s Beat ideology. It was searching for a clear stylistic position from which to differentiate itself from these formidable, utopian, progressive forces. Generally, beatniks of Lou Reed's tendency had by now manneristically taken up 1950s rock'n'roll, a musical movement concordant with the original Beat period, and with an apolitical, "good-times" feel that was now being evoked ironically (Sterling Morrison was the Velvet member most consistently plugged in to this current). Practitioners were here concerned far more with the force of the music than with finesse, and it was a move against the growing trend to virtuosity (see Maureen Tucker's comments on this in Chapter 2).

But this subculture had also shifted resolutely against intellectualism. Since the 1950s, a prominent intellectual wing associated with the Beat scene had adopted a less elitist and more radical socialist agenda, aligning itself with the growing wave of activism. In contrast, the anti-intellectual wing emerged out of the misanthropic, unsociable side of the beatnik subculture, and it gained the tentative name "punk", meaning crude or rotten, in part from a 1957 book about deviants by Leo Margulies, *The Young Punks*. Their music became described as "garage", from the domestic site where a band might work it up, a name that promoted the notion of home-grown amateurism.

In terms of ideology the differences may be listed thus:

Activists	*Hippies*	*Punks*
Protestation	Pacifism	Aggression
Revolutionary	Utopian	Apocalyptic
Socialist	Communal	Antisocial
International	Rural	Urban
Alliance	Commune	Cult

So, Lou Reed could not only claim that he was influenced by Beat writers but also that he took up their agenda one generation on, emerging from the caterpillar of the beatnik to the butterfly of the punk, a black-leather butterfly in blue jeans and dark glasses. However, we've yet to determine how he might have been attracted to the likes of Burroughs, Ginsberg and Kerouac and how they may have influenced his lyric writing. There are seven aspects:

(i) *"Crazy credentials"*[47]
In 1941 William Burroughs snipped off the end of his left-hand little finger and spent a month in the psychiatric ward of New York's Bellevue Hospital. A year later Jack Kerouac was discharged from the navy for displaying signs of schizophrenia and "ambisexuality". In 1949 Allen Ginsberg committed himself to the Columbia Psychiatric Institute in uptown Manhattan, staying there for eight months. In 1959 Reed underwent treatment at two psychiatric institutions, around the time that the work of these three writers became published – Ginsberg's *Howl* (1956), Kerouac's *On The Road* (1957) and *The Subterraneans* (1958), and Burroughs' *The Naked Lunch* (1959). *The New York Post* published a 12-part series on the Beat Generation in March 1959. *Life* magazine followed suit with "Squaresville USA versus Beatsville USA", while a B-movie *The Beat Generation* appeared in 1959 and an MGM film version of *The Subterraneans* in 1960.[48] So while Reed endured his deranged humiliations, he may have found solace in a subculture where madness is a just response to a mad world.[49]

Madness appears as a gothic malady throughout many of Burroughs' books, but Ginsberg resoundingly opens *Howl* with it ("I saw the best minds of my generation destroyed by madness") and he hammers home its presence throughout: "Epiphanies! Despair! Ten years' animal screams and suicide!"[50] The suicidal depression and incarceration in a sanatorium of his mother gave Ginsberg "an enormous empathy and tolerance for madness, neurosis and psychosis", according to his biographer Barry Miles.[51] Nico once said that,

> Lou's women in their songs are mad, you know. They are deranged in some way. Of course, Andy told me that Edie [Sedgwick] was mad, that her brothers went mad and committed suicide. And she went mad. 'Femme Fatale' is supposed to be about Edie, isn't it? It's also supposed to be about me. Maybe we are all mad to Lou. Maybe that's why he likes boys so much.[52]

(ii) *Sexuality*

One of several reasons why Ginsberg committed himself to psychiatric care in 1949 was that he wanted to be cured of his homosexuality. Told by his university professor that he must choose between "criminals and society" he sought the latter, but in the end he found the world not through the nuthouse but through his poetry where he declared his gay sexuality and celebrated it in many of his works.

Ginsberg was gay, as was Burroughs. Kerouac was bisexual, if not, as the navy claimed (and the navy would know), ambisexual. Ginsberg wrote that "Burroughs is one of the very few gay liberation minds...that has actually questioned sex at the root – not merely rebelled from heterosexual conditioning or heterosexual social/moral fixed formation – to explore love between men as he experienced it."[53] This encomium places Burroughs on a more exalted plane than his actual books might have you believe, with their down-to-earth allusions to "queers", "fruits", "fags" and "cocksuckers", but perhaps "cocksucker" is what Ginsberg meant by "sex at the root".

While Kerouac carried too much Catholic guilt to write openly about his male encounters, it was well known that the "buddy" odyssey *On The Road* was a record of his affair with fellow writer Neal Cassady. However, Ginsberg made up for any confessional reluctance by his colleague Beats in his narrative poem *Howl*, its biblical vocabulary evoked in homage to the pioneer gay poet Walt Whitman. As historian John D'Emilio has observed:

> *Howl*'s description of gay male sexuality as joyous, delight-
> ful and indeed even holy...offered gay male readers a self-
> affirming image of their sexual preference... Ginsberg served
> as a bridge between a literary avant-garde tolerant of homo-
> sexuality and an emerging form of social protest.[54]

At the time of Reed's entry to Syracuse, Paul Goodman in *Growing Up Absurd* (1960) could write – here in summary – that gays now had the opportunity to see themselves as nonconformists rather than deviants, and as rebels rather than immature, unstable personalities.[55] This must have offered some relief to Reed after his recent ordeal at the clinics. According to Morrison, Reed enjoyed a number of gay sex encounters while at Syracuse, and sought out gay bars in which to find some fun.

Reed read a eulogy at Ginsberg's memorial service in 1997.

(iii) *Words with music*
The Beats created the Jazz Poetry evening, where modern jazz musicians would improvise while simultaneously a poet read aloud a work. According to historian Preston Whaley Jr, "Local [San Francisco] poet ruth weisz[56] and musicians such as Sonny Nelson, Wil Carlson, and Jack Minger started merging poetry and jazz in 1956 at the Cellar, a North Beach [San Francisco] spot that sold beer and wine. Kenneth Rexroth and Lawrence Ferlinghetti recorded poetry and jazz for Fantasy Records in 1957."[57] Rexroth considered that its origins could be found in the talkin' blues such as those recorded by Big Bill Broonzy, where "the voice is integrally wedded to the music".[58]

An elaboration of this aural alliance came about when poets improvised as musicians. Influenced by the 1930s and 1940s "scat" singing style of Louis Armstrong and Ella Fitzgerald, poets would explore the sounds of vowels and consonants, connecting with the jazz musicians in a spontaneous manner. Without the music, this style was called "sound poetry", of which the Velvets' early drummer Angus MacLise was a practitioner. When Ginsberg became a Buddhist he would play an Indian harmonium and perform chants in public, and in 1969 he began using jazz musicians in order to realize his settings of verses by William Blake (released on record in 1970).[59]

Between 1965 and 1967 the Velvets performed a number of pieces where Reed spoke impromptu texts while the band improvised music. Of the recorded output, both 'The Gift' (1967) and 'The Murder Mystery' (1968) offer a stunted glimpse of what was attempted, while 'Melody Laughter' on the *Peel Slowly And See* album (released 1995) offers an example of the Velvets – with Nico – improvising. There is also a concert recording of an improvisatory piece called 'The Nothing Song', and Cale tells us that the Velvets would often perform 'Sister Ray no. 3' as a finale, an extended improvised version of 'Sister Ray' different from the *White Light/White Heat* recording in that "Lou would become a southern preacher man, telling stories and just inventing these fantastic characters as we played".[60] Cale commented elsewhere that:

> One of the things [Lou] did was sit down and just make up
> songs. At the drop of a hat he would be singing about how we
> would go and see Walter de Maria in his loft and so on... He
> had such an ease with language.[61]

Although his facility in improvising texts had been honed by his work for Pickwick International, Reed's interest in marrying this with improvised music incontestably arose from his experience of free-jazz performances and recordings between 1959 and 1962, when he was a young beatnik attending shows at the Five-Spot Club (see Chapter 2). Cecil Taylor, whose tracks he played on the university radio station, would often vocalize while playing the piano, and in early 1965, when the Velvets were starting up, John Coltrane's album *A Love Supreme* was released with a poem by Coltrane, which determined the structure and melodic rhythm of the final section, printed on the album sleeve.

In sum, there were many recent and current examples of the marriage between words and improvised music to be found in the modern jazz scene. That Reed managed to transfer this to rock music is an intriguing, if short-lived, achievement, and one entirely lost to account. He was supported by Cale whose original idea was "to create an orchestral chaos in which Lou could spontaneously create lyrics".[62]

There was a major difference, however, between Rexroth's "talkin' with music" and Reed's: Rexroth maintained that the sound world should be "small and comparatively quiet".

(iv) *Spontaneous text*

Jack Kerouac worked on writing paragraphs in a spontaneous – unreflexive – manner, which accounts in part for his use of simple words. He was able to write very quickly in this way, striving to record something of events as they happened to him without contemplating their significance.[63] It was this approach that led rival writer Truman Capote to make the bitchy comment accredited to him, "That's not writing. That's typing".

Kerouac's technique related to the inter-war surrealist mode of "automatic writing" which in turn influenced the painter Jackson Pollock in his "actions", and subsequently the "Happening" performers in theirs. Reed obviously used this method in 'Black Angel's Death Song' ("antiseptic remains cool goodbye/so you fly") and 'The Murder Mystery' with its double, unrelated texts (recorded on separate channels in a stereophonic mix – stereo was still a relatively new transmission system when the track was recorded in November 1968[64]).

(v) *Reality*

The Beat project came about originally in 1944 as "The New Vision", a literary pursuit made against what its protagonists saw as a tired imitation of European styles by Americans such as F. Scott Fitzgerald. They felt that they were Americans who wanted to be Americans, while the other Americans wished to be French. "Real words" and American vernacular phrases were used to make clear to readers and critics how little the Beat writers were concerned with current and, to their eyes, outmoded and elitist notions of "fine writing".

The character based on Neal Cassady declared in Kerouac's *On The Road* that, "One should write as newly as possible, as if he were the first person on earth and was humbly and sincerely putting on paper that which he saw and experienced and loved and lost." When Ginsberg first read *Howl* to a public at a gallery in San Francisco, October 1955, the poster boasted an evening of "ALL SHARP NEW STRAIGHTFORWARD WRITING".

Time and again Reed refers to the realism of his songs, which were written about people he knew in situations he'd faced (the most significant of his remarks on this appear in Chapter 2). Yet he also considered the "reality" of the genre in his desire to create lyrics capable of commanding attention by themselves and thus evading their depreciation as "words to a song". He attempted this by composing his texts with other generic forms in mind: "Instead of making a division between pop songs and a real story or a real poem, [I was] merging them so the separation didn't exist any more."[65] In 1970 he gave his first poetry reading at St Mark's Church in East Village, announcing that from now on he was a poet. He would include song lyrics in this and subsequent recitals, on which he's observed that, "I was continually struck by the different voices that emerged when the words were heard without music."[66]

In 1991 Reed organized a book of his selected verses, *Between Thought and Expression*, which included both 'The Black Angel's Death Song' and 'The Murder Mystery' as well as 'Heroin' and 'Chelsea Girls' (certain lines were repeated in print as he would have sung them). In this way, thirty years on in print, he aligned himself through the bookshop rather than the record store with the Beats' affirmation of poetry as "all sharp new straightforward writing".

(vi) *"The White Negro"*

In constructing their tribal boundaries in the mid 1940s, the Beats looked to the "sussed" subculture of the black "hepcat" with its elitist and sharply defined look, lingo and sound. "Hep" musical allegiances were tied at the more popular end to the "jive" or "jump" scene (Louis Jordan and his Tympany Five) and – at the more esoteric – to the chamber jazz known as be-bop emerging around the small basement clubs of New York City's 52nd Street, mostly associated with pianist Thelonious Monk, alto saxist Charlie Parker and trumpeter Dizzy Gillespie. Be-bop was part of an intention to forge an exclusivist black scene which, through language and performance, would prove unimpeachable to exploitative whites. Such a policy came about in reaction to the appropriation by many white musicians of the innovations by black artists in the "swing band" era of the 1930s, at that time in its final, most mannerist, phase.

The Beats, however, saw the hepcat scene as a virtually "exotic" culture, embodying everything from which white conformity was excluded, and in which therefore they, the Beats – being excluded from conformity – should be included. While in general, musical style is the leading aural delineator by which subcultural distinction is defined, music performances are themselves aural meeting points, being set in the marketplace, where subcultural values may be encountered and "auditioned", and so it's not surprising that the Beats rather self-consciously took up modern jazz at the level of performance, emphasizing its "spontaneity", its improvising traits, and its physical setting.

Cultural theorist Preston Whaley Jr sees the bigger story in this, asserting that "The Beats certainly trafficked in primitivisms".[67] He considers that this desire by artists and intellectuals to unctuously identify with black creative "spontaneity" was actually a desire to return back to the contemporary alienated personality, "what machine-age modernity had taken away – nature". However sophisticated this black subculture aspired to be, Beats saw themselves as more reflexively refined in their ability to detect its intrinsic "natural" roots. The contention of this book, in line with Whaley's thesis, is that this motive also took hold 15[68] years on at the time of the arrival of "free jazz" and the punkish revival(s) of rock'n'roll.

The degree of racism implied here (that blacks are more primitive – closer to nature – than whites), is one that Lou Reed has displayed himself falling prey to in his notorious – and to many minds blatantly racist – solo song of 1978 'I Wanna Be Black',[69] in which he wants to have "natural rhythm", a "stable of foxy little whores", and a "big prick". Add to that John Cale's clumsy belief, as reported by Paul Katz,[70] that black music has "a pronounced beat and a very strong bass line" because of the heroin that black musicians ingest, and it's most fortunate for the standing of The Velvet Underground that Maureen Tucker took an interest in the West African drumming of Olatunji for its complexities rather than any "primitivisms".

The confusion engendered here, about how an admiration toward otherness might proceed into an ingenuous racism, was cannily grasped by

New York writer Norman Mailer in 1957. In his essay of that year, "The White Negro: Superficial Reflections on the Hipster",[71] Mailer identified that: "the source of Hip is the Negro" who had lived for two centuries on "the margin between totalitarianism and democracy". In contemporary Greenwich Village, Mailer notes how "the bohemian and the juvenile delinquent came face-to-face with the Negro", the ménage-à-trois forming the hipster.

As the essay shifts ground from the "Negro" to the "White Negro" as its subject, Mailer goes on to consider the hipster as a "philosophical psychopath", the latter term used in its contemporary sense then of someone who is not actually delusive or inchoate but is nonetheless emotionally unstable, unable to form personal relationships and indifferent to social obligations. Adding the former term to the latter, though, allows that "Hip is the sophistication of the wise primitive in a giant jungle", for hipsters are conscious of their state, unlike the "ten million Americans who are more or less psychopathic" but unaware of it. He cites popular psychologist Robert Lindner whose term "rebel without a cause", to describe a psychopath, Mailer now applies to the hipster.

After considering Hip patois as a dynamic, pictorial language about change – go, beat, cool, dig, flip, creep – Mailer presciently wonders whether Hip's sexual impetus may "rebound against the anti-sexual foundation of every organized power in America" – yes, it did – and he concludes by considering whether a radically different world is truly conceived by "the hipster's desire for absolute sexual freedom" or whether this desperate outlaw is "equally a candidate for the most reactionary and most radical of movements".

In sum, Mailer's essay is all about Lou Reed the beatnik, the punk, and the writer of 'Heroin', 'Sister Ray', and 'I Wanna Be Black'.

(vii) *Intensity*
According to Thomas Newhouse, the Beats didn't care "about whether it was well-made, but about its intensity"; their mode of operation was "behavioural rather than aesthetic".[72] The Velvet Underground characterized the punk conviction that virtuosity was arid decoration. They gazed at the burning building not the curls of smoke in the air above it. It has become a cliché to write, as far too many have, that *White Light/White Heat* is the worst-recorded album in the history of music. In terms of its sound, however, it is certainly one of the most intense.

(b) *Crime novels*

Reed has picked out writer Raymond Chandler (1888–1959) as a demigod craftsman, able to provide a brilliant portrait in a few words: "I felt like an amputated leg", "His smile was stiff as a frozen fish", "She was as cute as a washtub". Reed has also mentioned Dashiell Hammett (1894–1961), similarly gifted in imagery ("The fat man moved forward until his belly stopped him"[73]), who was slightly ahead of Chandler in creating a more "realistic" crime story genre where their ethical and incorruptible private detective sees how hungrily the law and the lawless mutually feed off greed.[74] Chandler and Hammett described street life, low life and high life in diamond-hard phrases set with impeccable rhythms.

Reed clearly attempts to emulate their achievements in lines like "She can't turn out her light" ('Chelsea Girls'), "When I put a spike into my vein" ('Heroin'), or "Got my eyeballs on my knees" ('I Heard Her Call My Name'). His regard for these exquisite writers offers an alternative route in the formation of his "realistic" style from that of the Beats, and one that betrays an awareness of the counter-cultural, popular literature scene conterminous with the "fine writing" clique of the 1930s which the Beats derided.[75] Reed's interest may have been generated through his university literature course.

(c) *Schwarz*

This need not detain us long. The association between Delmore Schwarz (1913–66) and Lou Reed is a brief and exaggerated one, more material than intellectual. It may be read as a case of undergraduate hero worship aggrandized afterwards into a "buddy-buddy" coupling straight out of a Beat book. Schwarz was the first famous writer Reed had met. Before they encountered each other as drugged-up lecturer and drugged-up student in the autumn of 1962 at Syracuse, there were two links between them:

(i)   Schwarz and Reed were both Jewish and born in Brooklyn, Schwarz three decades earlier.

(ii) In 1957 Schwarz was committed to the psychiatric division of the Bellevue Hospital in Manhattan and later moved to the Payne-Whitney Clinic, where he was diagnosed a paranoid schizophrenic. In 1959 Reed attended the Payne-Whitney Clinic following his treatment at the Creedmore State Psychiatric Hospital to cure his teenage angst.

Schwarz, as an author of poems and short stories from 1938 onwards, and as editor of the anti-communist *Partisan Review*, enjoyed membership of that elitist literary clique so detested by the Beats; the modernist James Joyce was his literary hero. In turn, he called Ginsberg and company the "San Francisco Howlers" and dismissed them as "faggots", even though he conceded that they fitted into the overarching American literary project he defined as "criticism of American life".[76] He poked fun at existentialism, dousing Heidegger's formulation that "no one else can die for you" as "no one else can take a bath for you".[77]

Reed has never mentioned Schwarz's poems but four aspects of the elder's work may have vaguely influenced Reed's lyric writing:

(i)   Schwarz's work is almost wholly autobiographical. According to him, writers reveal their private lives in their work. His early story *In Dreams Begin Responsibilities* (1938), which Reed called "one of my favourite pieces of writing of all time",[78] is an account of Schwarz "seeing", four years before his birth, his mother and father projected as a film in a cinema.

(ii) Schwarz "possessed a tireless, mythologizing imagination, a genius for eliciting general laws from the particular scenes of his life"[79] according to the fine biography by James Atlas.

(iii) While his style was elegant and considered, Schwarz attempted to use "plain, direct, prose", though never as plain as the Beats.

(iv) He considered fiction to be "reality testing".[80]

By 1962 Schwarz was an alcoholic wreck addicted to Nembutal, Seconal and Dexedrine. His colleagues, including the poet Robert Lowell and the author Saul Bellow, tried to get him a university sinecure to help him out financially, which is how he ended up at Syracuse in September 1962. Asked to give some token lectures, he filled out the time in them by reading aloud plenty of James Joyce and T.S. Eliot. Reed, as an English literature undergraduate, would have attended these wretched affairs. Without a doubt he befriended, as other students did too, this desolate ruin of a writer, trying to help him face the academic days. But Schwarz ultimately rejected him and others, in his paranoia thinking them spies working for the plutocrat Rockefeller.

A peculiar aspect of the claims Reed has made about his connection to Schwarz is that he dedicated a song on the debut album to him, the final track, 'European Son (for Delmore Schwarz)'. The song was recorded in April 1966; Schwarz died, neglected, in Manhattan three months later on July 14th. Its accusatory lyric, written in the style of Bob Dylan, bids a malicious farewell to its subject ("Hey, hey, bye bye bye"). With its cryptic text of personal details ("But now your blue car's gone"/"You made your wallpapers green") it reads like little more than a song of loathing to the eminent poet, one who detested rock music. Schwarz had refused to see Reed when the former student had tried to visit the forlorn recluse, who was living out his last days in a downbeat mid-town New York hotel.

How far this song is about, rather than "for", Schwarz, it's not possible to discern, and in later pressings of the album the dedication is missing. Nevertheless, and fortunately for Schwarz, he was far better memorialized by Saul Bellow, as Schwarz – the "East River grey"-faced "hero of wretchedness" – is the Humboldt of *Humboldt's Gift* (1975) which helped Bellow win the 1976 Nobel Prize for Literature.

(d) *Rock lyrics*

Many rock'n'roll and doo-wop songwriters of the 1940s and 1950s managed to combine clear descriptions of situations with simple words composed in easily rhymed (and crucially – for the singer and listener – easily remembered) verses. Chuck Berry added ingenious wit. For example, his song 'No Particular Place To Go' describes him riding in his car with his girlfriend. His attempts to get at her body are thwarted by the safety belt that wouldn't budge. The full implication of the title becomes clear only at the end, that it's as much about a geography of body as it is of place.

In "Memphis, Tennessee" he's frantically asking the telephone operator to contact a girl, Marie ("She could not leave her number but I know who placed the call"/"Cause my uncle took the message and he wrote it on the wall"). It's only at the end that we learn this girl is his six-year-old daughter. Above all it's the novel detail of the realistic setting that made his songs so effective to its substantive, working-class audience, as in 'You Can Never Tell' where "the coolerator was crammed/with TV dinners and ginger ale."

Instead of the standard stanzas of four lines, Berry's stanzas often comprise six lines (following the form of a 12-bar blues in a rhythm & blues context, with his voice/guitar "call and response" dialogue).[81] But 'Roll Over Beethoven', for instance, is in five-line stanzas, as is Reed's 'I'm Waiting For The Man', 'I'll Be Your Mirror', and 'European Son'. Of course, variations to formulas can be found throughout the blues, rhythm & blues and the rockabilly genres. What makes Berry special is the quality of his lyrics, his avoidance of hackneyed phrases, and his ability to sustain a narrative with a witty pay-off at the close. However aware Reed was of Berry's skill, he generally avoids goal-directed narrative. He has been more concerned with situations and descriptions of characters who are paraded before us (coming and going), in a cyclic trajectory (as in 'Heroin', or differently 'Chelsea Girls' – "Here they come now").

Reed's writing is closer to an eminent pair of white, Jewish songsmiths who wanted in the 1950s to "write black", Jerry Leiber and Mike Stoller (both b. 1933). There are often varied characters in their songs like in Reed's, such as Shifty and Bugsy in 'Jailhouse Rock' of 1957. Also there is a dark, Reed-like element to some of Leiber and Stoller's lyrics (their 'Love Me' of 1954 is almost 'Venus In Furs' without the whipping). 'Dirty Dirty Feelin'' of 1960 includes a verse where, although the man's girl is off "runnin'/ pretty soon you're gonna fall", and then he'll drag her home and "chain you to the wall".

Despite Reed's several experiments in structure (from the formalism of 'I'll Be Your Mirror'[82] to the synchronism of 'The Murder Mystery'), he has kept in mind the verse, metric, and rhyming patterns of the rock'n'roll music he covered in his school group and at university with The Eldorados. Yet those formulas are used as references rather than schemes. Reed is looser, with a tendency for lines to float rather than to be metrically grounded and rhythmically articulated in the manner of Berry. Reed's distinctive success lies in the hybrid application of the different influences, from the intellectual, anti-intellectual and popular traditions, to make potent lyrics describing what until that time was taboo.

Unlike Lenny Bruce, Reed was never arrested for obscenity, because his songs were made public at exactly the time that a progressive social call took place for the opening-up of social discourse on such topics as sex and drugs. Yet he was well aware of the generational unease surrounding his output, as he had experienced the oppressive counteraction from his parents as a teenager. As he articulated it in retrospect in 1978: "They don't want their kid sitting around masturbating to some rock and roll record – probably one of mine. They don't want their kid ever to know he can snort coke or get a blow job at school or fuck his sister up the ass... I'm still dangerous to parents."[83] A remark, no doubt, still aimed at his own.

4 Cale

> I would fit the things Lou played right into my world.
>
> John Cale[1]

Cale's world comprised:

(1) The conceptual, multi-media actions of the Fluxus movement
(2) Epic performances by LaMonte Young's ensembles
(3) The "Wall of Sound" productions of Phil Spector
(4) The emerging textures of rock music

Let us take these in turn:

(1) Fluxus

When Cale co-produced "A Little Festival of New Music" at Goldsmiths College in London on July 6th, 1963, he gave the British première of *X for Henry Flynt*, composed by LaMonte Young two years earlier.[2] Composer and Goldsmiths tutor Cornelius Cardew had introduced Cale to this text composition. Cardew met Young when the American was a guest of Strockhausen's at the Darmstadt Summer School (for Modern Music) in Germany in the summer of 1959. At that time Young was still writing some pieces that used conventional notation while he was also developing an interest in giving instructions to performers through the written word – "performers" rather than "musicians", by the way, meaning that you didn't have to play an instrument or read music to take part. These instructions were conceptual in character, and Young through his Fluxus pieces became a progenitor of what became called "conceptual art".[3] Wim Mertens, in his book on minimal music,[4] divides Young's work of this time into three periods:

(i)   1955–58   Serial music/"Sustenance" (the use of sustained sounds)[5]
(ii)   1958–61   Performance art works (Fluxus)
(iii) 1962   Ensemble works

X for Henry Flynt falls into the middle period of Merten's bald summary, one that conceals the infamously seditious and controversial nature of Young's music. Its proper title is *Arabic Numeral (Any Integer) to H.F.* Flynt was a friend of Young's on the Fluxus scene. He was a mathematician, hence one of the significances of using a number. This work requires the performer to "repeat a loud, heavy sound every one or two seconds as uniformly and as regularly as possible for a long period of time".[6] At the Goldsmiths concert Cale followed the favoured way of playing it, which is by habitually thrusting both forearms – evenly spread – onto a piano keyboard, with the intention of producing exactly the same sound each time ("uniformly", "regularly"), although this is barely possible to achieve.

Cale claims that some of his fellow students in the audience had brought in dustbin lids which they proceeded to march with around the hall, in the manner of a funeral cortège, and bang to try to put Cale off his job. They probably thought they were marking the death of music[7] that Cale had brought on by playing *Flynt*, though how members of an audience could walk into a concert hall carrying dustbin lids and sticks without anyone suspecting trouble remains a mystery.[8] However, Cardew apparently leapt on stage to help Cale keep time. Some of Young's Fluxus pieces continue to provoke this kind of exorbitant reaction from their audiences, sometimes because they are considered provocatively simple, or "unmusical", or at least unprofessional. As these are critical terms that were later directed at The Velvet Underground, this is one of several aspects of performance that aligns Young's ideology with the Velvets'. Young, though, was striving for a more positive response to his work (which we'll come to). Cardew had likewise explained in writing why the piece attracted him so:

(i)   its duration, and proportional to that:

(ii) the variation within the uniform repetition;

(iii) the stress imposed on the single performer and through him [*sic*] on the audience... These elements occur rather in spite of the instructions, although naturally they are the result of them. What the listener can hear and appreciate are the errors in the interpretation. If the piece were performed by a machine this interest would disappear and with it the composition.[9]

At the time that Cale gave this British première Young was merely a name to him, one among a number associated with the Fluxus movement, centred in New York City. Cardew had considered Young to be especially interesting because he was a composer, while other Fluxus artists had joined in from visual arts or poetry backgrounds. However, the whole point of Fluxus was that it fused different art forms together. Artist George Brecht wrote that:

Individuals with something unnameable in common have simply naturally coalesced... Perhaps this common something is a feeling that the bounds of art are much wider than they have conventionally seemed, or that art and certain long-established bounds are no longer useful.[10]

But Young sought the musical in everything. He said, "Isn't it wonderful if someone listens to something he is ordinarily supposed to look at?"[11] Young's 1960 Fluxus piece *Poem for Table, Chairs, Benches etc.*, consists of a timed series of acts of dragging the named furniture across the floor. While the sounds should be "as constant and continuous as possible"[12] – like *Flynt* – the audience focuses on the inevitable imperfections. Cale would find a use for this very manoeuvre in the Velvets' debut album.

Fluxus's other artists soon emulated Young's concern for sound, and from this moment Fluxus "gave permission" for visual artists to move into music. The development in 1960s and 1970s within Britain of the art college "experimental" rock band relates to this drift, the exemplars of the flow between a visual arts background, a Fluxus commitment, and a rock music application being Yoko Ono and John Lennon (who met at a Fluxus exhibition in London[13]). But, when Cale came to New York in August 1963, he found firstly that the Fluxus scene was shifting towards what would become termed "performance art" (ultimately much more concerned with the body and the "self") and the burgeoning "underground" film scene. Secondly, when he connected with LaMonte Young, he discovered that the composer had moved on to the third period in Mertens' division of his output, that of making music with others as an ensemble.[14] In contrast to John Cage's "multiplicity" (an acceptance of different things happening at the same time), Young distinguished himself from this by turning to "singularity" (focusing on the aural riches to be found in the purity of sounds).

What Cale had taken from his brief involvement with Fluxus was:

(i)   music as performance, as action;
(ii) the use of "noise" in performance;
(iii) how variants in "noise" are perceptible, even engrossing;
(iv) long-term repetition;
(v)   how there is a technique in attaining simplicity;
(vi) that the simplest events can produce the strongest reactions in audiences.

(2) Young's ensembles

Young himself has provided a clear account of his projects at this time, which may be found on his MELA Foundation website (http://www.

melafoundation.org). Yet all is not as clear as it could be, despite the assiduous work of historian Keith Potter and composer Dave Smith in sorting out more detail.[15] At root Young created settings for the performance of music conceived by him and for which he provided the frame for improvisation to take place; he gave his performers "instructions" and "rules". In this way Young ran five main musical projects between 1962 and 1966, each of them influential in some way on The Velvet Underground. The first three of them didn't directly involve Cale, while the last two did so most powerfully:

(a) Young's Blues (1962–)

This evolved into The Forever Bad Blues Band. Starting as a duo with Cale's first New York flatmate Terry Jennings on a B-flat soprano saxophone, Young played on the piano one of the traditional harmonic formulas of the Blues (I – IV – I – V – IV - I) and slowed it down to a sequence of static drones to enable a kind of analytical improvisation to take place. Young was exploiting the connection between the blues' use of seventh chords and the modes being explored by John Coltrane (another player of the soprano saxophone) around this time.[16] As Young put it, "The concept in that style of Blues was to spend long periods of time on each chord change to emphasise the modal drone aspects of the music."[17] The subsequent Blues Band, which would employ Just Intonation (see iii below), was the closest that Young ever came to playing in a rock band.[18]

From this, Cale would first of all grasp on behalf of The Velvet Underground the fundamental relationship between the principal chords in this sequence – I and IV (tonic and subdominant; played three times in each cycle, the subdominant is heard in three different contexts: I–IV, V–IV, IV–I twice) and the ability to apply them as conjoined drones. Secondly, he would sense how to use modality and sustained drones in a rock context (most noticeably 'Venus In Furs', 'All Tomorrow's Parties').

(b) The Bowed Disc Ensemble (1963–)

Young and Marian Zazeela performed this ritualesque duo. The five-feet-diameter black steel gong ("the disc") had been created for them by the artist Robert Morris with a white bull's eye at its centre. They wore black uniforms with white gloves and black sunglasses. They would bow the gong with double-bass bows in order to extricate its constituent harmonics, usually the lower ones.

From this the Velvets developed their sense of ritual in performance, and, above all, the use of black and white costumes (the band would appear in black with sunglasses, Nico in white).

(c) *The Well-Tuned Piano (1964–)*

Young became interested in 1964 with a tuning system known as Just Intonation. In contrast the tuning system in general use since the eighteenth century in Western music is known as equal temperament. It divides the octave into twelve equal steps, or semitones. But to do this means that no interval in it, aside from the octave, is acoustically pure. Just Intonation ("Just" meaning "natural") is an alternative and older tuning system, based on the pure intervals of the fifth and the third. This ironically means that to some people nowadays a piano tuned to Just Intonation can appear "out of tune". Nevertheless, it produces pure triads, and the system is considered more amenable – more natural – to vocal singing. Moreover, Just tones are closer to the harmonics of string instruments such as Cale's viola.

Young's title *The Well-Tuned Piano* is a satirical comment on Bach's *Well-Tempered Clavier*.[19] It took many years for Young to find a means of tuning a piano this way, and so the project was not heard in public until the 1970s,[20] although he had started work on it in March 1964 when Cale was an ensemble member. Young would ingest cannabis, "get high" and improvise in a rubato, rambling way.

From this Cale would acquire a disregard for the conventions of Western tuning, and comprehend the benefits of drug use for the act of improvisation.

(d) *The Theatre of Eternal Music (1963–)*

Starting in May 1963 (three months before Cale arrived in New York City), Young formed an octet in order to realize one part of his epic and ever-expanding work *The Four Dreams of China*.[21] China for Young is an image of timelessness. The section of the work in question is titled *The Second Dream of the High-Tension Line Stepdown Transformer from the Four Dreams of China*. The high-tension transformer was an electricity generator which hummed near his childhood home (a log cabin in Idaho) when Young really was young.[22] His inclination for long stream-of-consciousness titles got more fanciful as his project developed.[23]

The eight performers each had one pitch to play, and the instruments they used were all stringed, with the ones normally plucked (like mandolas and lutes) bowed:

LaMonte Young	bowed mandola	Larry Poons	viola
Marian Zazeela	violin	Joseph Byrd	guitar
Tony Conrad	viola	Dottie Moscowitz	lute
Angus MacLise	violin	Jack Smith	mandola

While the line-up changed now and again,[24] readers will recognize three names from Chapter 2 who are linked to the early days of the Velvets – Tony Conrad, the drummer Angus MacLise, and the film director Jack Smith who had bought the tape machine on which the Velvets' Ludlow Tapes were made (Smith was also a decisive influence on Warhol's decision to make films about sex). Cale with his viola joined this ensemble around September 1963. At some point in the life of the group, MacLise moved over to his hand drums (perhaps shifting from violin when Cale joined). Without setting a regular pulse, he would play subtle rhythms and micro-patterns.[25] When he left for a time to travel to North Africa in February 1964 he was not replaced and The Theatre of Eternal Music was drumless once again. The overall sound remained throughout the combining of extensively sustained notes with silences in between, and a fair degree of improvisation.

The Theatre of Eternal Music also split into components to perform other Young-conceived improvisations. Sometimes they would take one of Young's blues, where Young would play his E-flat sopranino saxophone[26] and other times give public performances of samples of Young's repertoire. One studio recording mentioned by Potter uses MacLise's calendar[27] to describe its date: "The First Twelve Sunday Morning Blues" (that is, Sunday January 12th, 1964). Cale performs on this. The order of pieces form a symmetrical sequence as follows:

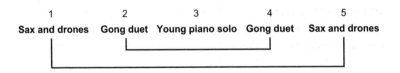

The common factor is Young who fronts all of the sections. His egoism began to irritate Cale, who then developed ambitions to run his own ensemble. Cale hadn't come all the way to New York to play one note for two years without recognition and advancement. This explains the contrary accounts of Young's next project:

(e) *The Tortoise, His Dreams and Journeys (1964–)/The Dream Syndicate (1964–)*

What seems to be agreed between Young and Cale is that they, with Zazeela and Conrad, came together as a quartet at some point after MacLise's Atlantic crossing: Young and Zazeela singing, Conrad on violin, Cale on viola (he also played an Indian – plucked – string drone instrument called the sarinda, which can also be heard on the "Ludlow Tapes"). According to Young he used the quartet to realize his new work called *The Tortoise, His Dreams and Journeys* (Young and Zazeela kept turtles). Like *The Four Dreams Of China*, it was epic in scale and composed of sections with lengthy, poetic titles. One such is *The Tortoise Droning Selected Pitches from the Holy Numbers for the Two Black Tigers, the Green Tiger and the Hermit*. Zazeela explains that the totem animals were herself and Young as the two black tigers (because they dressed alike in black), Conrad was the Green Tiger and Cale the Hermit; "If you know him he's a very interior kind of person and has a lot of secrets".[28] The Holy Numbers are the integers 2, 3 and 7 which feature a lot in Young's work. Sections were realized around a constant sine tone (60 Herz[29]) which later became the hum of the electrical motor on the turtles' tank in Young and Zazeela's loft, which they amplified.

In contrast to this version of Young's, Cale states that "Tony and I formed The Dream Syndicate... The concept of the group was to sustain notes for two hours at a time." He adds, "This was my first group experience and what an experience it was! It was so different! The tapes of it are art objects."[30] Cale seems to be describing *Tortoise* under another name (one where only the notable word "Dream" is kept) and under another leader. It seems that for Cale this project was the transitional step between The Theatre of Eternal Music and The Velvet Underground. He tantalizingly mentions tapes of the undertaking. Young taped all rehearsals of all projects that took place in his loft, and he is the owner of these tapes. But these particular tapes are not commercially available due, it's claimed, to a quarrel between the protagonists. This is a state of affairs due, so it seems, to the question of a composer's role within an already creative group dynamic, indeed to the difference between the musical work as a construction and the work as an experience.

Young has said of his compositions around this time, which are not notated,[31] that he set "rules and elements" for the performers, who worked within – or from – this concordance. Individual improvisation by its nature means that each performer makes a creative contribution to the overall work at some stage, not just in a particular performance, but – while the work is rehearsed – within its genesis.[32] As Keith Potter puts it:

> It may be asserted that Young provided the material; but others may also have had an input into this, especially at the earlier stages of such music's conceptualisation. The group clearly provided the elaboration of it, each performer being ultimately responsible for his [*sic*] own part.[33]

However, the dispute appears to run even deeper than that. It is apparently about the intellectual property[34] – the creative ownership – of the project.

Whatever subsequent disagreement there has been about this vocal/strings quartet, one aspect of its genesis in Cale's version surely rings true. On the tape of 'Sunday Morning Blues', mentioned above, Young can be heard playing a continuous, bubbling and very high-register stream of sound on his sopranino saxophone (Smith has transcribed this in his essay[35]). Cale writes that on a similar occasion he started to imitate Young's sound of this kind on his viola by using high harmonics. Young noticed this but also recognized that the viola was playing natural harmonics which were "out of tune" in the equal temperament system of his saxophone yet "in tune" with natural law. It was this that apparently led Young to turn to Just Intonation in his group improvisations.[36] He firstly adjusted his playing and tuning of the saxophone (which was invented by Adolphe Sax[37] in the nineteenth century wholly for equal temperament) to fit in with this different tuning system, but at some point in the summer of 1964 he abandoned his sax for singing. This may well have been the start of the quartet project. But this is not the only significant switch that took place. To put them in a rather arbitrary order:

(i) *Amplification*

As far as the facts currently present themselves, in order to achieve a balance in The Theatre of Eternal Music, the string instruments were amplified by being placed near acoustic microphones, or, at least, this was explored. A need to balance the sound between the string instruments and the saxophone was the cause of this experiment. Then during the quartet project Tony Conrad tried a guitar pick-up (a clip-on contact microphone[38]) on his violin, with one for Cale on his viola, which gave a far stronger sound (Cale calls it "an enormous noise"[39]). They determined a balanced sound between the violin and the viola by using a sound mixer. Young and Zazeela eventually sang through microphones in order to get a steady balance between the four performers. From this point it's correct to say that Cale played an amplified viola (but not an "electric" one, which didn't exist then and is anyway a separate sort of instrument with a solid body). This amplification didn't just make the instrument sound louder but allowed the listener to hear greater detail, especially to detect better the component harmonics, the overtones, that made up the sound, as well as the sympathetic resonance from the other strings. In contrast, a viola next to an acoustic microphone would have mainly rendered the articulation of the bowing in greater detail.

By transferring his amplified viola into the sound world of a rock band, Cale gave it sonoral parity with solid-body instruments but also with voices, as he'd learnt from Young. Reed is a rather thin-toned bass-baritone[40] and Nico a contralto. Their ranges align upwards from D at the centre of the bass stave (see Example 1), and these ranges cross those of the viola. This is why Cale often uses the higher harmonics in order to allow the voices more space to define themselves.

Cale went on to explore amplification in the Velvets by commissioning suspension speakers for his bass guitar. The experiment didn't work, but he used the band's money to pay for it and this became a key source of friction between the members. That said, Reed was also keen on new technology, and the band was always looking for sponsorship deals from companies providing them with their latest backline equipment; to do so made sense as they were operating in a period where amplification systems were being refined year on year.

(ii) *Adaptation*

According to Marian Zazeela, in order to play drones for Young's projects, "John adapted his viola. First he made a two-string drone and then [for *Tortoise/ Dream*] he filed down the [wooden] bridge to make a three-string drone, and that really was his own idea, how to get more sounds going together."[41] Filing down the bridge flattened it, in the style of a guitar, to enable the bow to pass over the strings simultaneously and evenly. This was Cale's ingenious attempt to turn a viola into a bowed guitar (four-stringed mandolins had already been used in Young's projects in this way). To add to the effect, he used metal guitar strings in place of traditional viola strings to get "a drone that sounded like a jet engine".[42] Cale endorses Zazeela's description in his account of the Dream project, of how the quartet held six pitches for two hours: "LaMonte would hold the lowest notes, I would hold the next three on my viola, his wife

Ex. 1 VOCAL RANGES

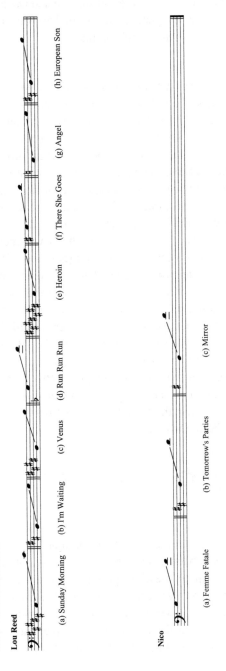

Lou Reed

(a) Sunday Morning   (b) I'm Waiting   (c) Venus   (d) Run Run Run   (e) Heroin   (f) There She Goes   (g) Angel   (h) European Son

Nico

(a) Femme Fatale   (b) Tomorrow's Parties   (c) Mirror

Marion [*sic*] would hold the next note and Tony Conrad would hold the top note." It was this filed-down, guitar-stringed, amplified viola that Cale used throughout his time in The Velvet Underground.

(iii) *Attunement*

This project was concerned with the exploration of discrete, "pure" intervals, of which the intervals of a fifth and second are prominent. Young would often use the pitches G, D, and A (two consecutive fifths, but also intervals of a fourth, a fifth and a second in aggregate, or inverted, form, D–G–A). According to Smith, "Young improvises vocally on these drone frequencies in rhythmically free fashion, sliding from note to note at varying speeds. The vocal style seems to have close associations with Indian models, but in reality stems more from his earlier work."[43] In other words, the work is concerned with non-functional harmony rather than melody.

This forms the basis of Cale's vision for The Velvet Underground. He transposes these features over to tonality and rock music. The harmonies to Reed's songs on the first two albums (that is, those on which Cale participated) are almost always restricted to the tonic and the subdominant (the songs are in different keys, although this is sometimes the result of reducing the speed of the tape on which they were recorded to make the song sound deeper and slower). For example, 'Heroin' is in C sharp major. Its two harmonies comprise the tonic triad, C#–E#–G# and the subdominant F#–A#–C# (see Example 2a). The common pitch between these two is the tonic C# (to put it in a less than elegant way: the tonic becomes the dominant of the subdominant in the second triad). The C# is thus Cale's drone,[44] to which he adds the dominant G sharp.

Ex. 2 Heroin

(a)　　　　　　(b)　　　　　　(c)

However, G sharp is only present in Triad 1. In Triad 2 it forms the interval of a second with the subdominant, a relationship (F#–C#–G#, Example 2b) which accords with Young's use of the pitch matrix G–D–A. This implies, in fact, that these were the very pitches used by Cale in 'Heroin', and the four-track recording tape was slowed down a semitone in editing onto the master tape. The track is slightly flat against the standard tuning of the period of A = 440 Herz, which supports this hypothesis. As what is on the album was a re-recording made in Los Angeles (May 1966) in a studio where concert-pitch keyboards were present, this further supports the possibility that the tape was slowed down. Yet in any case we can see how Young's practice is transferred directly to Cale's in The Velvet Underground, when the use of the interval of the second produces a different effect from its employment by Young. It enriches, turns "thicker", makes the chord more sensual by sounding two adjacent wholetones: F#–G#–A#–C# (Example 2c). This is the function it takes on in Cale's settings of Reed's songs. We find it too in 'Venus In Furs' (also in C sharp and recorded in Los Angeles but in tune with A = 440), with the added piquancy that, in the E major middle section ("I am tired, I am weary"), Cale adopts the pitch matrix D–A–E. While the guitar plays a B dominant 7th chord, Cale plays D natural against it, producing a luscious discord in the context of this simple song.[45] This discord mirrors that of the verse in C sharp where, at the end of each fourth bar, the tonal seventh B sharp is sounded against a modal (flattened) B natural.

'Venus In Furs' contains Cale's most inventive use of the viola drone. He plays C#–G# as a rapid glissando to represent the strokes of the whip. He improvises so that, although the strokes are repeated, they're unexpected. For example, the sequence in the second half of Verse 1 (over 17 seconds, from 0:26 to 0:43) runs as follows:

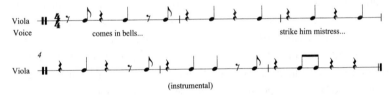

Another variant of the drone is found on 'The Black Angel's Death Song' where Cale employs C–G–D over two octaves using harmonics (these pitches are the bottom three open strings in a conventional viola tuning, making strong and easily produced harmonics).[46] Even where the viola is not present, the drone is used. 'All Tomorrow's Parties' has it on piano throughout in a relentless paradiddle[47] pattern, while the guitar naggingly opens 'Heroin' with a pulsed tonic reiterated in turn against the tonic and subdominant triads. Cale introduces an organ drone on G–D near the start of the G-major-keyed 'Sister Ray', and then reiterates it into the chaos at 7:25–8:12 (only to be followed by a contrasting chromatic episode). Later he plays a drone on the subdominant C (11:29–12:22), followed again by G–D (12:22–13:06) against which Reed sings for the only time in the song.[48]

Concerning this appropriation of methodology, Young has commented,

> Many people were coming up to us and saying [in 1966], "Oh, John's doing your thing up there"... but the one thing that was very clearly there was these long sustained drones which John then gradually introduced to the Velvets. I think that was his main thing in the concept of static form, a kind of form where the music can appear to be not changing, this kind of theory of Cale's where things are apparently the same but little tiny differences make big differences eventually.[49]

The B major/D major discord is an example of this effect in action, as well as the addition of the interval of the second in a subdominant triad.

(iv) *Apperception*

Smith observes that "Young is deeply interested in the psychological effects of his music".[50] Young has claimed that, "the artist...has the potential, if it can be preserved over time, to make statements which are much more encompassing and affect both the conscious and the unconscious in a way that is so profound and so powerful that...it can go deep within the human consciousness".[51] According to this hypothesis, drones, as the ear attunes to their nuances, induce over time a psychological state fusing consciousness and unconsciousness. Such a state is related in intent to the surrealists' aim of inducing a revelation of the latent and the hidden by holding back the intellect and instead "bringing to mind" the otherwise inaccessible. In this regard Young has pointed out the use in classical Indian music of ragas (configurations of pitches) for use at certain times of the day and night, for certain circumstances, and to produce or reflect particular moods on its meditative listeners.

Cale took on these precepts and adapted them to The Velvet Underground. He stated that "the aim of the band on the whole was to hypnotise audiences [through repetition and drones] so that their subconscious would take over",[52] and elsewhere that "it was an attempt to control the unconscious with the hypnotic".[53] However, he is no more clear than this, and Young's comments need to be added in to make some sense of what was being attempted. Any difference here surely lies between Cale's "subconscious" and Young's "unconscious". The latter is derived from Freud, to explain how we have desires of which we're not aware. What Cale's hypnotized subconscious is based on is hard to determine, except that the notion of music generating a meditative trance-like state in listeners is recognized in several cultures around the world.

At the same time, Young and Zazeela, who really were West Coast, peace-and-love-style proto-hippies,[54] embraced an agenda for social liberation which Reed and Cale, as proto-punks, had no time for. The love that the Velvets sought was for themselves. As Cale said of their hypnotizing objectives, "I think it worked because people who tell you they love the band are never able to tell you why".[55]

(v) *Ambience*

It was through Angus MacLise that in 1962 Young met Zazeela. They married in July 1963, a month before Cale began his bohemian adventure in New York. Zazeela was then a young artist. She became concerned to develop a distinct visual identity for Young's projects, which, given her success in this, are now considered Young and Zazeela's joint projects. Using ambient light, she defined a stylish visual setting for The Theatre of Eternal Music (1963–), and for the Bowed Disc Ensemble (1963) she designed the stark lighting mentioned earlier. Her most elaborate arrangement yet was devised for *The Tortoise, His Dreams and Journeys*. Although rehearsals had begun in May 1964 the public première was only given a year and a half later, on the weekend of October 30th, 1965 at the Pocket Theatre (where Cale had made his performance debut in New York when he took part in Cage's *Vexations* marathon). The long title of that improvised performance was the one previously mentioned where Cale was "the Hermit".[56]

As the quartet was by now entirely amplified, and to an acute degree so that the component partials of the pitches could be clearly heard, Young chose to place the speakers around the space so that the audience was surrounded by the sound. Working to produce a visual parallel to this, Zazeela assembled her most sophisticated visual design just in time for the largest of these opening performances, for the Film-makers' Cinematheque Festival of Expanded Cinema (in the basement of the Wurlitzer Building, of all places, on 41st Street) on 4th and 5th of December. This version of the section of *Tortoise* was titled *The Tortoise Recalling the Drone of the Holy Numbers as They were Revealed in the Dreams of the Whirlwind and the Obsidian Gong and Illuminated by the Sawmill, the Green Tooth Ocelot and the High-Tension Line Stepdown Transformer.*

There is some irony here in devising such a sophisticated light show, as it was on the night of November 9th, 1965 – in the middle of this project – that New York City faced an almighty blackout. A power station at Niagara Falls had failed, plunging the city into darkness, one of several infrastructural crises that began to affect the well-being of the city. That Young had started out three years earlier on purely acoustic projects, and then had become increasingly reliant on technology, mirrors a general shift on the music scene. Incidentally, the composer Edgard Varese, who pioneered a fusion of experimental music and technology, had died in New York City three days before the blackout.

Zazeela's visual solution might well have been suggested to her by the nature of the film festival. She lit the entire room with the complementary colours red and green. Four slide projectors threw up an artwork of hers titled *Ornamental Lightyears Tracery*, a sequence of calligraphic images which moved almost imperceptibly in and out of focus. These images were thrown onto and behind the performers, who wore black and white. As Zazeela recounts, "The idea to present lights with music, although now it seems so obvious and common, was actually new at the time. [I] developed that concept of the musicians performing with projections that slowly changed that were superimposed on the musicians as they performed."[57] Andy Warhol attended this show and a month later took up Zazeela's scheme in order to make a noteworthy visual setting for The Velvet Underground which would become known as the *Exploding Plastic Inevitable*, the title itself a three-word pop art evocation of Zazeela's own.

This performance was the last that Cale gave with Young. Three nights later he was playing in a New Jersey school hall to launch The Velvet Underground.

To summarize LaMonte Young's influence on The Velvet Underground:

(i)   *Performers*. Three players directly connected with him – John Cale, Tony Conrad, Angus MacLise; and one indirectly so – Walter De Maria – helped to form the rock band.

(ii) *Static harmonic fields*. Young's use of an extremely confined range of related tones was translated into the Velvets' employment, within tonality and modality, of the tonic and subdominant harmonies of the home key.

(iii) *Drones*. Young's governing concept, the use of an extensively sustained fundamental and its fifth, was transferred wholesale to the Velvets, with Cale playing a drone viola, physically converted for this purpose, in both ensembles. The interdependence between pitch and timbre, which Young explored in this ascetic way, was taken up by Cale but transformed into the domain of expressionism.

(iv) *Improvisation*. Young encouraged improvisation from all his members.[58] Influenced by two sources – modern jazz (in particular Coltrane) and the "happening" – the ensemble's exploration of the "eternal now" was transferred to the rock band. Lou Reed's coincidental knowledge of modern jazz eased this exceptional generic fusion of the jazz, experimental and rock fields through the Velvets' improvisation in live performance.

(v) *Amplification*. By a gradual process of balancing the sound levels of the acoustic instruments through an amplifier and speakers, and then between amplified instruments and voices (in the *Dream* quartet), the exploitation of technological resources on stage by Cale enabled him to utilize unconventional sounds (such as harmonics and clusters), balance normally dissimilar strengths of timbre, and explore "noise" in The Velvet Underground's performances.

(vi) *Ritual*. Critic on the experimental scene Richard Kostelanetz wrote that Young's and Zazeela's shows were "among the most admired works in new theatre", emphasizing their impact beyond the experimental music scene.[59] This sense of ritual circumstance and seriousness permeated the aesthetic of The Velvet Underground, which differed from the "garage band" mode in its image and stage presence (promotion of a sense of occasion, the disinclination to face the audience, the wearing of sunglasses on stage to mask contact,[60] the literal addition of theatrical actions by Warhol's troupe).

(vii) *Lighting*. Zazeela's lighting schemes, and especially the use of slide-projected images onto the stage, covering the performers dressed in black and white, were taken up by Warhol.

(viii) *Specific references*. In 'European Son', Cale drags a chair across the studio in the manner of Young's *Poem*. In 'I'm Waiting For The Man' he plays piano clusters in an amphetamine-frenzied version of *X for Henry Flynt*. In both 'Heroin' and the opening of 'The Black Angel's Death Song' he plays rapid viola harmonics in the style of Young's saxophone arpeggios on the recording of *The First Twelve Sunday Morning Blues*.

(3) Phil Spector

Born in New York City merely 15 months before Lou Reed (and thus Cale), Phil Spector made the move into professional songwriting at the age of 18, with the Teddy Bears' hit 'To Know Him Is To Love Him', a level of attainment that Reed might have envied. Yet it was Cale who most admired Spector, less for his songs than for his productions. Spector claimed invention of the expression "record producer". While records were certainly produced before Spector started up, "production" tended to mean the process that got a song tape-recorded and duplicated onto shellac or vinyl discs for packaging, distribution, and sale. There was even somebody who took responsibility for the song to be recorded on time and within budget, but a name for this task wasn't exactly necessary, as this person usually had some other managerial function in a small, maybe sole-run, operation. Spector gave this domestic endeavour a regal dimension, turning the handicraft of recording into an executive vocation (he bought a smoked-glass-windowed Rolls Royce car in 1961, at the age of 20, and employed a bodyguard,[61] which, due to his ego, he needed).

Rather than provide a dressing for a song, like an arranger, what Spector sought to define was the aura of the recording. He did have an arranger, Jack Nitzsche (1937–2001), who employed many of the finest session musicians, known as the "Wrecking Crew", and provided Spector with the successful backing tracks for hits from 1962's 'He's A Rebel' up to the 1966 chart failure of 'River Deep, Mountain High'. But Spector supervised the overall timbre which he determined through experimentation in the studio, racking up thousands of dollars in costs where just hundreds had been set aside. He was indeed a *record* producer rather than a music producer, though it was through the music – the selection of instruments and backing voices, their registers, the choice of tempi, the generic derivation of the drum pulse (often Latin) – in harness with the technical decisions he made – the degree of mechanical echo he set for each sound, the creative aspects in the process of mixing-down on tape – that he attained his sensational results. At its simplest he wanted the songs he took on to be placed inside an endless orchestra, one controlled by a mighty percussion section at the centre of operations, hammering a vigorous pulse into an infinite, echoing tunnel. The complete experience was known as Spector's "Wall of Sound". He called these records "little symphonies for the kids".

For someone like Cale, who had played in youth and local orchestras in his teens, Spector's use of traditional acoustic instruments, sometimes in novel combinations, would have been highly seductive. Although Spector's orchestration recalled the use of studio orchestras in popular songs of the 1950s,[62] the ultra-romantic size of the sound and the overstated use of reverberation took it into a domain of conspicuous production, to coin a phrase. Spector's sound was camp[63] in its self-conscious exaggeration. Yet it was also poignant as the overstated last gasp of traditional production processes in the face of two challenges – the rhythm & blues-influenced rock band[64] and the recently developed technologies of stereophonic recording (which Spector was very much against) with multi-tracking.[65]

Cale recalls how he told Reed early in 1965 that, "if he could make up lyrics and let me get the basis for the music going, we could use a Phil Spector-style orchestral back-up to create songs with a rock quartet. That combination would knock the socks off Bob Dylan, I thought."[66] While this goal was never realized, Cale took the following elements from Spector into The Velvet Underground:

(a) *Wall of Sound*

Cale adopted Spector's graphic notion of the record producing for the listener a band of solid, full-range sound across the spectrum of the speaker(s). He converted this into a perpetual stream of dense instrumental sound within which Reed's lyrics would be placed. Cale linked this to Young's idea of sustained tones.[67] His original idea was to create "an orchestral chaos" into which Reed could "spontaneously create lyrics".[68] Closest to this notion (at least on record) is 'Heroin' on the debut album between 4:58 and 6:44 with its mixture of viola *sul pont*,[69] fingered harmonics and guitar feedback behind Reed's intermittent voice, and 'Sister Ray' on the second album, where Cale improvises on an organ[70] against Morrison's and Reed's guitars (there is no bass guitar on this track) as the divisions between the verses and instrumental sections start to collapse. In 2004, on the BBC radio programme *Desert Island Discs*, Cale said that he had wanted to create "a landscape, tapestry, of sound behind simple chords. I thought we could do what Phil Spector had." Elsewhere he admitted that, "We were trying to do a Phil Spector thing with as few instruments as possible."[71]

(b) *Symphonic gigantism*

Echoing Spector, Cale said that he had aimed to "turn Lou's little pop songs into symphonies".[72] Certainly a number of the recorded songs are longer than many pop songs of the period – 'Heroin' timed at 7:10, 'All Tomorrow's Parties' at 5:58, 'European Son' at 7:47, 'The Murder Mystery' at 8:53 and 'Sister Ray' at 17:25 – this is due to the instrumental contributions between or after lyrics. Voice entries are sometimes delayed to follow extended instrumental preludes – 'Heroin' at 0:52, 'All Tomorrow's Parties' at 0:29, even 'Run Run Run' (where little happens but vamping) at 0:18.[73] As for instrumental variety, the debut album uses celesta, glockenspiel, viola, piano and tambourine as well as the expected two guitars, bass guitar and drum kit. Tambourines (often more than one) were a favourite feature of

Spector's. We learnt earlier that Maureen Tucker had to play one in place of a drum kit at the Café Bizarre. Nico was given one to play on stage when she performed with the Velvets, although Cale agreed that "it wasn't the best thing to give her given her sense of time".[74] On record the tambourine anchors, in Spector style, "'Venus In Furs', 'All Tomorrow's Parties', and 'I'll Be Your Mirror' (it also appears in 'Sunday Morning', 'Femme Fatale', and 'There She Goes Again', played with a drumstick).

(c) *Instrumental prevalence*

Spector used the voice or voices as components in the overall timbre (there are many stories about the poor treatment he directed at singers; he some-times substituted one for another without credit[75]). Cale has written that, "I thought that the abstraction of instrumental music was more power-ful than songs".[76] 'Sister Ray' comprises an uncoordinated, even competi-tive, improvised instrumental trio lasting 13 and a half minutes (from 3:56) between organ and two guitars, with six brief vocal interjections[77] against rather erratic drum kit support. 'The Murder Mystery' (on the third album, 1969) comprises two monophonic tracks of which an exclusively instrumen-tal nine-minute option can be taken by the listener.

(d) *Production*

Cale considered himself "a composer and arranger". He did not produce the two Velvets albums with which he was associated, and he would have been frustrated if he had by the economic limitations of investment placed on the recording process. For the debut album, ten tracks[78] were taken from a recording session in a poor if adequate studio in New York (April 1965). But a professional producer called Tom Wilson – of whom more later – arranged for one new track to be recorded, 'Sunday Morning', and four to be re-recorded in a better studio in Los Angeles (May 1965). They were:

  (i)   'I'm Waiting For The Man'
  (ii) 'Venus In Furs'
  (iii) 'All Tomorrow's Parties' (sung by Nico)
  (iv) 'Heroin'

It's noticeable that these tracks are superior in clarity to the New York ones, if only from Spector-sized percussion tone on 'Venus' and 'Parties'. In each case the magisterial bass drum thud on the main beat and the tambourine on the back-beat emulates Spector's sound on The Righteous

Brothers' hit 'You've Lost That Loving Feeling' (1964), for example. In the early 1960s Spector had been told of a New York studio engineer, Bill Mac-Meekin, who had placed the microphone inside the bass drum to get a "thunderclap" effect. Spector added to this an echo by placing an ancillary microphone in a stairwell.[79] When it came to the Velvets, Maureen Tucker's physical arrangement of her drums would have aided the sound their Los Angeles engineer achieved on the debut album, as the bass drum was laid horizontally like a tom-tom and hit with drumsticks.

The admitted tendency on the first two albums to reduce the speed in mixing down to the master tape and thus make the sound deeper is probably influenced by Spector too. He preferred to use deep-voiced singers, such as Bill Medley of The Righteous Brothers, or Darlene Love, and he often used instruments in low ranges, especially at the opening of numbers. It's surely this sound that the Velvets wish to emulate in 'Venus In Furs', 'All Tomorrow's Parties', and 'Heroin', among others. Further, it was in the Los Angeles studio that Cale found the celesta and the glockenspiel lying around with which, by "bouncing down" the two tracks to one, he opens 'Sunday Morning'. There is some irony here that the debut album opens "high" with these delicate, tinkling sounds from the West Coast and closes "low" with the murk of Reed's "Ostrich"[80] guitar, whistling feedback and an unfathomable rumble from the East Coast. If only in this range of recorded sound, Cale exceeded Spector.

(4) Rock textures

In an interview for the Melody Maker, February 9th, 1963 (when Cale was in his penultimate term at Goldsmiths), John Lennon said of The Beatles that, "We don't play real rhythm and blues... Our musical tastes are various – we like a little bit of classical music, a bit of modern jazz, a bit of everything." Although this might be considered the remark of someone wishing to attract a broad market, The Beatles' use of acoustic instruments in solo obbligato roles – the cello in 'Yesterday', the French horn in 'For No One', the "harpsichord" (actually a speeded-up piano) on 'In My Life', the sitar in 'Love You To', for example – displays their sincere interest in hybridizing genres rather than preserving them.[81] Even the more "bluesy" groups who led the "British Invasion" of 1964 – such as The Animals and The Rolling Stones – valued acoustic variety. Indeed, it was this marriage, of the direct sonoral novelty of the pop song with a generic affiliation to a "roots" authenticity, that revitalized the Western scene and ushered in the era of "rock" as opposed to its progenitor "rock'n'roll".

Rock and "beat" artists of the middle 1960s brought together two sets of textures: the aural dazzle of pop's gem-bright pinning and the visceral, transgressional hispidity of the blues. While rock'n'roll bands of the 1950s were like small swing bands in their variety of instruments – the saxophone, the guitar and organ of Bill Haley's Comets, for example – the rock group was quite corporate in its instrumental conformity of guitar, guitar and (bass) guitar with a drum kit behind them. Due in part to the baby-boom teenage interest in music-making, and the eager equipping of this new market by electric guitar manufacturers, the guitar band evolved in the late 1950s out of Buddy Holly's Crickets. In 1959 two guitar groups came into being almost simultaneously in Seattle (The Ventures) and London (The Shadows), supplying instrumental novelty hits between the demise of rock'n'roll in 1959 and the launch of Merseybeat in 1963. Their sound was pristine, confederate, and as uniform as their chic, identical suits.

But, thanks to the subcultural vogue at the time around Europe[82] for urban blues and "rhythm & blues" records (R&B – a liberalizing but market-constructed name replacing the term "race" records), fledgling white guitarists heard how to turn this technique "dirty", how to make the guitar a richly expressive resource through a finger-shaking vibrato, or the bending of strings, or glissandi (slides), or by stressing the shift of the hand between chord changes, or the use of devices on the strings such as a bottle neck or a metal ring, as well as exploiting the possibilities on the electric guitar of its amplification – overdriving the system, feedback and so forth. By intersecting these two guitar styles – the clean, commercially successful "white" pop style with the passionate, vocalizing "black" style of R&B, the guitar band became the customary configuration for those wishing to mix singing and playing while in control of their own resources. The alternative was to be found in the all-vocal groups, derived from 1950s doo-wop and gospel, identified with the black subgenre named soul – The Miracles, The Supremes, The Temptations – who relied on professional backing bands consisting of varied instruments in the swing band tradition.

In this sense The Velvet Underground was, in its instrumentation of two guitars (Reed, Morrison), bass guitar (Cale) and drums (Tucker), one more part of a conformative, market-driven scene. Nor was it unique in offsetting this corporate pattern by having an active multi-instrumentalist like Cale. The most commercially successful bands of this period retained a remnant of the rock'n'roll band's diversity by employing at least one multi-tasker such as Brian Jones of

The Rolling Stones, George Harrison of The Beatles, Brian Wilson of The Beach Boys. These inquisitive all-rounders didn't have to be universally proficient, but they displayed a willingness through experiment to vary the overall texture through freshness of timbre. Even Eric Clapton of Cream played the violin. John Cale fulfilled this role for the Velvets. He moved between his amplified viola, keyboards, backing vocals and bass guitar.

Cale had learnt the last especially to play in the group, and his bass guitar patterns offer an insight into his very hazy understanding of the rhythm & blues style. Morrison said of Cale that his bass pattern formulas "were strange and difficult to learn. I had to play bass guitar when John was playing something else and I hated it. Hated it!"[83] By the way, this explains why there is little or no bass guitar on numbers like 'Heroin' or 'Sister Ray', as the players were normally involved in other functions.

Morrison singled out 'I'm Waiting For The Man' as "weird". It is. Although Cale has adopted a standard bass pattern, the rise to the dominant of D major (G–G#–A) at the end of each second bar isn't justified harmonically, as the song remains in the subdominant at that point (see Example 3b). Also curious is the pattern at the end of the verse which runs chromatically up from the dominant and crashes into the tonic under a dominant chord. In both cases Cale has used stock bass patterns but which contradict their harmonic functions. In 'European Son' the bass shifts maniacally between a symmetrical arc of fourths through D–G (high)–D–A (low) with chromatic runs in between, although the harmony is grounded entirely on the tonic. The band's uncertain conflation of subdominant and dominant functions explains the unusual drift in the coda of 'I'll Be Your Mirror' in G major where the male backing vocal harmonies move from D major to C major against the bass which moves in the opposite direction from C to D.

A different kind of example is 'Femme Fatale' in C major, where the bass drops from the tonic to the subdominant, thus foreshadowing the tonic/subdominant pattern of the chorus, but does so under an A minor 7th chord (A–C–E–G); this appears to be an attempt by Cale to lock the verse into the Velvets' basic tonic/subdominant pivot, never mind how applicable.[84] In 'All Tomorrow's Parties' the bass follows the voice two octaves below in one bar and then the lead guitar for the following two bars. Presumably the more conventional bass patterns, such as that of 'Sunday Morning', are by Morrison. After Cale leaves, the bass patterns become drearily conventional or self-conscious in their desire to be interesting.

Ex. 3 (a) Sunday Morning

Ex. 3 (b) I'm Waiting For The Man

Ex. 3 (c) Femme Fatale

Ex. 3 (d) Heroin

In almost all of the tracks in which Cale appears, he takes an unconventional approach, with the sole exception of 'Sunday Morning' (celesta, glockenspiel, viola), which was the last to be written by Reed for the debut album and intended to be circulated as a single, where the viola counter-melodies (in two parts, mixed down) display from the start of the album Cale's skill in producing simple but effective figurations (see Example 3a). In fact, many of the tracks on the first two albums use counter-melodies (that is, counterpoint) and inner figuration of some sophistication, given the deliberately limited range of harmonies employed. Four examples are notated here – 'Sunday Morning', 'I'm Waiting For The Man', 'Femme Fatale', and 'Heroin' (Example 3 a–d). In each instance the keys approximate to those on record, which in the case of the debut album are rather a mess in terms of key relationships. The upward arrow indicates where the track is slightly sharp with A = 440 Herz, the downward arrow where it is slightly flat. These shifts might indicate a slowing-down or speeding-up, for the reasons mentioned earlier, when the recording tape was transferred to the master tape. More interesting are the wide variety of tempi, showing the ability of Reed to create slow-paced songs that aren't mawkish ballads. In the second album the narrower range of tempi implies the desire to be closer to the genre of garage rock. These factors are placed together below:

I. The Velvet Underground & Nico			II. White Light/White Heat		
Track	Key	Tempo (bpm[85])	Track	Key	Tempo (bpm)
1. Sunday Morning	F#↓	108	1. White Light	A♭	126 → 130 end
2. I'm Waiting...	D↑	126	2. The Gift	D	111 → 116
3. Femme Fatale	C↑	105	3. Lady Godiva...	D	115 → 118
4. Venus In Furs	C#	73	4. Here She Comes...	D	116 → 118
5. Run Run Run	D↓	146	5. I Heard Her...	F	144 → 149

6. All Tomorrow's...	D↓	86 → 93	6. Sister Ray	G	127 → 136
7. Heroin	C#↓	71 → 98 → 144			
8. There She Goes	G	128			
9. I'll...Mirror	G↑	110			
10. Black Angel's...	C↑	86			
11. European Son	D↑	156			

In terms of tempi, most impressive is 'Heroin', where the four "subway rides" hurtle out over increasing spans and yet the band manages to return each time close enough to the original slow tempo. Maureen Tucker is exemplary in setting the slow tempi, but it's Sterling Morrison's guitar that holds the accelerandi together and brings each to its limit of 144 beats per minute. Their timings and speeds are as follows:

Re. 'Heroin'	I	II	III	IV
Duration:	27 secs	33 secs	36 secs	1 min 53 secs
Track timing:	1:17–1:23–1:44	2:23–2:56	3:33–4:09	4:48–6:41
bpm:	98 → 144	104 → 144	110 → 144	103 → 144 → 150 (100)

Of the 17 songs on these two albums made during Cale's membership of The Velvet Underground, only five might be considered "standardized" as Theodor Adorno[86] defined it: that is, units of eight bars leading to a chorus of 32 bars (4 × 8) and a range of "one octave and one note". While the formal trajectory was a matter for Reed as the writer of the songs, most Velvets songs were determined by the combination of vocal and instrumental passages, in which Cale had a hand. 'Sunday Morning' would be the most conventional of all if it wasn't for the odd effect of the conspicuous reverberation added to the voice in verse two; but in formal terms it simply comprises nine cycles of eight bars each. 'White Light/White Heat', the music to 'The Gift', and 'Lady Godiva's Operation' fall into eight-bar patterns, as does the outline form of 'Sister Ray' – but not its improvised content. In the remaining 12 songs, each has something structurally peculiar in it to avoid Adorno's accusation of being "standardized".

'I'm Waiting For The Man' falls into verse sections of 12 bars followed by choruses of six bars with a "middle eight" instrumental section of 18 bars. 'Venus In Furs' is also in units of 12 bars. 'Femme Fatale' has a chorus of 10 bars. 'Run Run Run' runs along in units of 5, 8, 11, and 15 bars. Similarly 'I'll Be Your Mirror' contains odd-numbered units in verses of 17 bars (vocal element 3 + 3 + 4 + 2 + 2). The accelerating sections of 'Heroin' form units of

26 bars (I 13 + 13; II 2 + 5 + 19; III 5 + 21; IV 78). Most remarkable is Warhol's favourite song 'All Tomorrow's Parties', which not only includes at the head of each verse a bar of 6/4 followed by five bars in 4/4, but has a dramatically resolute, staccato ending.

That Cale's structural contributions are significant can be measured by his creative absence on the two subsequent albums led by Reed, *The Velvet Underground* (released USA March 1969) and *Loaded* (released USA September 1970).[87] Of the 20 songs on these albums only 'The Murder Mystery' (composed while Cale was in the band) is in units of 12 bars (and in two alternate sections: A at 126 bpm, B at 112 bpm), the whole locked on a tonic/subdominant pivot (if one accepts the key as G minor or dorian mode on G). The remainder, such as 'Candy Says', 'What Goes On', and 'Pale Blue Eyes' fall into conventional patterns of eight-bar units. Only 'Jesus', with foreshortened verse lengths and a couple of 6/4 bars in the second instrumental section (as well as the absence of drums on it) offers formal novelty.

Nevertheless, the innate tonic/subdominant matrix is discernible on both of these subsequent albums. 'Some Kinda Love' (D–G), 'Pale Blue Eyes' (F–B♭), 'Jesus' (G–C–F), 'Rock & Roll' (C–F–B♭) and 'Head Held High' (G–C) retain the garage band model in a folksier setting, while 'After Hours' (G–C–F–B♭) and 'That's The Story' (Dmin-G–C–F–B♭–E♭) extend it.[88] This is not to deny that, left to himself, Reed introduces fresh chromaticisms, such as the chord sequence in 'Candy Says' which runs D–F#min–F–B7–Emin, or, in 'Who Loves The Sun', A–G#–A–F#7–D. These are symptomatic of Reed's desire to define a guitar-chord-driven style post-Cale, but in doing so he takes the Velvets closer to the general folk-rock sound of the time and the band loses distinction thereby.

To summarize the foregoing, what distinguishes the approach of The Velvet Underground from other groups around 1966 is the way that idiosyncratic interests, training and technical constraints produce a distinctive sound world, close to three strands of nascent but rapidly developing rock sub-genres: firstly, the fledgling guitar rock style being developed at the time by, say, a theatrical band like The Who, concerned with forging a powerful energy verging on violence; secondly, the amateurish good-time verve of the garage bands such as The Kingsmen and The Sonics; thirdly, the communal, studiedly non-virtuoso anarchic satire of New York City's The Fugs.

The members of The Velvet Underground, especially Reed and Cale, were utterly capable as creative musicians. They were also serious in their intent. Yet they lacked the practical, on-the road experience of The Beatles and The Rolling Stones, or the nurturing studio environment those bands enjoyed, and they struggled creatively, socially, and economically thanks to this dearth of facility. They didn't lack ambition, but they lacked nous. They also lacked a generosity towards each other. It appears in the end that New York was simply not the place to make rock, or to make rock work, or to make rock pay.

5 The Factory

It's not what you are that counts, it's what you think you are.
Andy Warhol

The Velvets were totally insecure the whole time.
Betsey Johnson, fashion designer

Simply put, rock'n'roll trades on the act of sex while rock trades on the act of masculinity. 'Rock Around The Clock', 'Good Rockin' Tonight', 'Whole Lotta Shakin' Goin' On' and so forth celebrate the performance of Rabelaisian coupling, coded as a dance between two partners who touch each other, if only palm to palm. 'I Want To Hold Your Hand', 'I Saw Her Standing There' (1964) make a transition that reflects the dance crazes of the time – twist, jump, jerk, and even Reed's ostrich – which began a new phase because they detached dancers from each other (masturbatingly so in 'Can You Jerk Like Me?'). Meanwhile, 'It's All Over Now Baby Blue', 'Get Off Of My Cloud', 'Got To Get You Into My Life' and so many other hit songs of 1965 portray the single male gazing out to identify what serves him best, and least.

Given how McCartney joined Cale, Morrison, and Reed in reaching the age of 23 in that year, while the others on our list in Chapter 2 fell between the ages of 20 to 27 (with apologies to Nico), it's not unexpected that many of the songs, at least sung by those who were not Velvets, left teenhood for manhood,[1] forsaking sex as carnal gratification in favour of love as a perplexing, erotogenic mutuality. Of course, an interplay of this kind was mainly addressed song-wise in the form of the man as subject rather wishing he were the object. Still, it was a significant development that band members in general had by now started up songwriting partnerships to attempt a more mature and profitable, in-house, phase of production. They were inspired by the alliance of Beatles Lennon and McCartney who had begun by covering existing songs such as those by Chuck Berry previously mentioned, but gradually they had moulded their own, increasingly sophisticated, constructive methodology, a flexible one where it could not always be said that one supplied the words while the other supplied the music.[2] It took The Rolling Stones slightly longer to effect a writing partnership but Jagger and Richards eventually succeeded.[3]

Not so The Velvet Underground. Reed was the songwriter. Exceptions arose only where album tracks were the result of general improvisations, such as 'European Son', 'The Gift', 'Here She Comes Now', and 'Sister Ray'. In those cases equal credits were given to all, and therefore publishing royalties were shared. Cale was considered the arranger and had to press his claim for compositional credits on 'Sunday Morning' and 'The Black Angel's Death Song'. As Cale recalled, "Lou brought the words for 'Sunday Morning' and I assumed we were going to work on it the same way [as 'Black Angel'] but then he turned round and said, 'No, I don't think of you as the songwriter'. I was hurt because I thought this was why I was involved with him."[4] Conversely Cale supplied no lyrics for the Velvets.

Given his incontestable achievement as a songwriter, Reed's dominance was ironically one reason why The Velvet Underground did not succeed as a viable project. While other bands were conjoined with their audiences in dealing with wrenching issues of politics, social liberation and progressive relationships (between individuals and indeed between cultural formations) – although they did so from the position of the "liberated male" ("Come on, baby, light my fire"[5]) – Reed was still playing the surly teenager. He enacted this role in a fashion-conscious middle-class band where three out of its four members possessed academic degrees. As Bockris has pointed out, Reed the adult songwriter seemed to be working through the issues of his life exactly as they were before he was institutionalized at the age of 17 . He was a university graduate of 23 who wanted to act the dumb punk rebel, keen to shock the mainstream with his Beat-style fixations on sex, drugs, and "freaks". Reed claimed that, "Anybody who made love to our music wouldn't necessarily need a partner."[6]

The word "love" appears only once in the 17 songs on the first two albums. Yet it does so only in terms of drugs, to express how far he "loves to watch that stuff tip itself in".[7] Warhol had little time for love, either, he said, explaining that, "During the Sixties...people forgot what emotions were supposed to be... I never thought in terms of 'love' again."[8] This was hardly wisdom attained through maturity – although Warhol was 37 years old when he signed the Velvets – but instead what his manager Paul Morrissey called "Andy's desire to be a helpless kid, like Doris Day trying to be a virgin once again".[9] Nico said, "I think [my young son] Ari was older than Lou sometimes. Anyway, The Factory was like a kindergarten. Andy was a child too, of course. In those days they talked of people being children. But you know – flower children."[10] It would be Reed's recalcitrance that would make the band out of place in 1967's Summer of Love, but would also give it – ultimately – unprecedented cult esteem.

In terms of rock music, the central 1960s is as complex to map as its many historians have claimed, certainly so in terms of getting a grip on the genre shifts and the musical artists working in diverse markets which were at that time being constructed (folk-rock especially, and the "proto" stages of punk, hard rock, jazz-rock fusion). Cale's mentor at Goldsmiths, Cornelius Cardew, went on in the 1970s to put forward a theory[11] that, under the emergent phase of global capitalism in the early 1960s, all sorts of music was being made in a kind of "cottage industry" environment of people offering home-made goods (songs, "numbers"). The music industry systematically tried out samples of the broad range that was on offer to see what might arouse public interest. From that point, rather than markets being identified, markets were constructed to rope in the makers and the consumers of the music, to render the music useful in the ideological terms of the ruling class. He saw it as a kind of order out of chaos leading to a dead end. Cardew's trajectory is seductive, as it makes it much easier to delineate what took place by working backwards into the creative magma, but at some point a halt can be conveniently called when the going gets tough.

Still, an attempt must be made here to place The Velvet Underground in the context of other bands at the time of its entry into the public domain, when Warhol and Morrissey took them on in January 1966. Applying the categories used earlier – "activists", "hippies" and "punks" – it becomes crucial to make the point that, while some artists were activists, some were also hippies (The Grateful Dead) while other activists were punks (such as the MC5[12]). So, a basic division is attempted here between "activists" (usually, but not always, of the Left) and "non-activists", who did not align themselves directly with progressive movements or perhaps spoke against activism (some shifted ground towards such a position around this time, including Bob Dylan). These are then divided into three loose genre categories,[13] and band or artist names offered that may be identified with those divisions around 1966–7 (see over).

While the attempt here is to map the Velvets' ideological stance in relation to prevalent discourses, it also intends to place the band in relation to its competitors by positioning it transversally to its "sworn enemy",[14] The Mothers of Invention led by Frank Zappa. It also throws up the issue of how far West Coast musicians dominated the scene at the time, isolating the East Coast Velvets – even more so when The Mothers took up residence in New York City, as we'll learn.

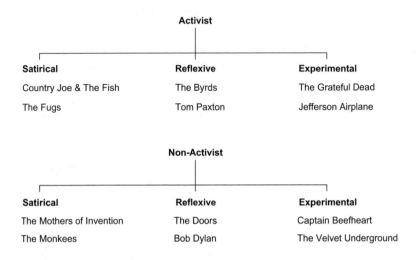

Activist		
Satirical	**Reflexive**	**Experimental**
Country Joe & The Fish	The Byrds	The Grateful Dead
The Fugs	Tom Paxton	Jefferson Airplane

Non-Activist		
Satirical	**Reflexive**	**Experimental**
The Mothers of Invention	The Doors	Captain Beefheart
The Monkees	Bob Dylan	The Velvet Underground

Yet the speed at which The Velvet Underground had itself asserted its presence in New York City was remarkable. Within a month of making its debut in a high school hall in December 1965, it found for itself a marked identity and a mediated status through its association with the celebrity of Andy Warhol, which we'll examine in this chapter. By January 1966 it had a management contract with the artist, and the members each enjoyed a monthly financial retainer to pay their rents, as well as a studio – Warhol's midtown "Silver" Factory – to rehearse in. Yet thanks to this arrangement the band was promptly considered by the media and eventually by the public to be part of the "degenerate" scene surrounding Warhol. Critic Robert Hughes has summarized in retrospect a common view of Warhol's Factory:

> [Everyone around the Factory] were all cultural space-debris, drifting fragments from a variety of sixties subcultures (transvestite, drug, S&M, rock, Poor Little Rich, criminal, street and all their permutations); talent was thin and scattered in this tiny universe.[15]

Judiciously, Hughes goes on to single out Cale and Reed as owning this scattered talent. Moreover he was writing after the event, in 1982, when a certain enlightenment[16] had by then proscribed the word most cuttingly used in the mid sixties to describe the Warhol scene: "faggots". The Velvets were seen as a "faggot" (homosexual) band,[17] which was a claim likewise directed by Americans at some British groups, especially The Rolling Stones (due to Jagger's appearance, clothes and stage mannerisms, actually copied from black American performers). Yet this is a curious claim to make of the Velvets, where their dress was puritan black and white, where their image was faceless, and all the more strange as there were exceptionally two women in the band. However, Maureen – as Moe – looked like a lad or a boyish lesbian, and Nico had the singing voice of a breathy male;[18] at six feet tall, in the dark of Warhol's stage, in her white suit and long hair, she even had the bearing of a man. She also had the name of one. But ultimately they were tarred with a big, gay brush because of Warhol.

Nico as Batman, Andy Warhol as Robin, 1967

While Reed revelled in the ambience of the "Silver" Factory where "everybody was rude to each other and nice at the same time" and "everyone looked good and terrible at the same time",[19] he and Cale were the ones who got most out of it beyond its use as a workplace. For a short time around January 1966 Cale had an affair with Warhol's first "superstar" Edie Sedgwick, an ultra-fashionable heiress whom he met at the Factory;[20] she went on to have a desultory affair with Bob Dylan and become a heroin addict in the process, from which she died of an overdose in 1971. "I felt sorry for her, but the rest of the Factory thought she was a stupid cunt", said Nico. Nico herself had a short affair with Lou Reed at the start of her professional association with the Velvets, which resulted in Reed's "pyschological" 'I'll Be Your Mirror' and 'Femme Fatale' being given to her to sing. Cale called the affair between Reed and Nico "both consummated and constipated".[21] It ended, according to Cale, when:

> We really learnt how Nico could be the mistress of the destructive one-liner. I remember one morning we had gathered at the Factory for a rehearsal. Nico came in late, as usual. Lou said "Hello" to her in a rather cold way, but just "Hello" or something. She simply stood there. You could see she was waiting to reply, in her own time. Ages later, out of the blue, came her first words: "I cannot make love to Jews any more". What a good start to the day that was![22]

So, the liaison with Warhol which gave the Velvets public life, as well as a second singer in Nico, may also have hastened its public demise and provoked the private insecurities that undermined its identity. Warhol's offer of patronage, proposed after he and his retinue had heard the band play at the Café Bizarre, was a sensational opportunity for a band not quite a year old and with barely half a dozen gigs to its name. So greatly was this offer remarkable that we must examine quite what was going on. In tracing the itinerary of the Velvets and Warhol through 1965, it becomes clear that the Café Bizarre date wasn't the first time he had encountered the musicians, nor heard the type of music they played, nor been unaware from where their special sound derived. Their circles of contact were closer than has been assumed, and what brought them in range of each other prior to the Café Bizarre performance was underground film. In order to explain Warhol's interest in this medium, his background up to this point needs to be set down.

Andrew Warhola was born in the steel manufacturing city of Pittsburgh in 1928. His parents came from the small town of Mikova in Slovakia. Warhol was therefore a first-generation American; Nico, for one, said she often heard the adult Warhol speak to his elderly mother in Czech.[23] Brought up in a working-class milieu where his father was a construction worker, the child suffered a neurological disease. While he was convalescing his mother gave him colouring books to use, rewarding him with a Hershey chocolate bar for every page he completed. In this anecdote some critics see the future artist, firstly wedding art to direct material reward and secondly observing art as a sequence of tasks (the outline and colouring-in), elements of which he would later involve others. When he was 13 his father died but left a small bequest used to enable Andy to attend the local Carnegie Institute of Technology where he studied illustration.[24] As part of his training Warhol worked on a window display at a Pittsburgh department store, an experience that would later gain him work in New York, which he moved to at the age of 21 in 1949 ("Mother, the future is New York City", his elder brother heard him say[25]). He soon sent for his mother, and they lived together in Manhattan for the rest of her life. She was devoutly Catholic, and so was he.

Throughout the 1950s Warhol gained some notice as a distinctive illustrator of articles in magazines,[26] but he wanted to be known as a "real artist" and from 1952 exhibited in shows. He was easily dismissed by the critics, who at that point were pondering over the New York phenomenon of abstract expressionism and had little time for the representational work of a commercial sketcher.[27] Furthermore AbEx had lionized painting, and Warhol would need to prove himself in that dominating medium. To fail in that would be to let slip a lack of masculinity.

Abstract expressionism was macho and virile, a visual rendition of broncobusters out a-hunting for their gods. What Warhol did was sissy stuff – window displays and drawings of shoes. With an assertive hauteur, AbEx ideology repudiated the mass-produced, the standardized, the everyday.[28] It was professionally hostile to the "aesthetic" gay culture which to AbEx eyes not only avoided the issue of a transcendent future by delighting in the material present, but also displayed a lack of duty to stylistically (and physically) propagate the genus. These dual imperatives, negative ones, were drawn from a dual need: firstly for abstract expressionism to become the first truly American art form which the outside world would hail as high-minded;[29] secondly to convince an American public that the artists associated with the movement were not at all like the cliché of degenerate nancy boys, but were incarnate Pilgrim Fathers, fit to head the artistic New World.

In contrast, Warhol was gay and a born shopper. He wrote, "Buying is much more American than thinking, and I'm American as they come."[30] With his gauche demeanour, his ultra-pale skin and scrawny frame, he moved increasingly around a gay art constituency of the 1950s that included dealers, critics and curators as well as celebrated figures such as writer Truman Capote, who characteristically thought of Warhol that, "He seemed one of those hopeless people that you just know nothing's ever going to happen to. Just a hopeless, born loser."[31] But here Warhol found an understanding community of similar "outsiders" and "losers" who sniggered like him at the oppressive posturing of the AbEx circle and who found their revenge by taking pleasure from those parts of life that the AbExes cast out – the mass-produced, Hollywood, popular music, "horror comics", the tabloid press – even life itself.[32]

Among the gay artists who were looking to undermine the authority of AbEx, Warhol ran across Robert Rauschenberg and Jasper Johns (see Chapter 1). He knew them as fellow window dressers,[33] working for the same swanky stores that he did – Bonwit Teller, Tiffany & Co. But in their otherwise modernist artwork they introduced something of real life. While Rauschenberg used objects he found in the street, Johns painted numbers, letters, and the Stars and Stripes flag, using in a sardonic manner the gestural smears and drips of abstract expressionism. Rauschenberg was given a De Kooning drawing which he rubbed out to turn it into a "Rauschenberg". In these ways they gave Warhol the confidence and the ideas to be both a "fairy" and a "real artist".[34] As critic Kenneth Silver put it, "Warhol made American blue-collar gay American art. His subjects were drawn from both the mass culture in which he grew up and the 'campy' culture he grew into."[35]

So it's not surprising that Warhol tried to turn abstract expressionism into camp. He started in 1960 by painting, in a drippy AbEx way, newspaper ads onto canvas. Like Johns, these gestural strokes and drips were his first mockings of the imperious AbEx style (one such prank of his – a Barnett Newman "zip" banana – would be done for the Velvets and would become his most well-known parody). In this mix of the common and the exclusive he also tried to paint famous comic book characters, but fellow artist Roy Lichtenstein was doing this more deftly around the same time, and so Warhol sought a substitute subject. Working on two paintings – a straight, graphic, "real" painting of two Coca-Cola bottles against an AbEx parody of the same – an art dealer friend told him to go with the graphic version (hard-edged work had become popular among the new buyers who were too late for AbEx bargains[36]). He transferred the idea to 32 Campbell's soup cans (the brand his mother served him each lunchtime), and these paintings finally brought him a degree of notice as a "real artist", with his first one-man exhibition, at a commercial gallery in Los Angeles, taking place in the summer of 1962, exactly a year before Cale came to America.

In this search for a distinctive niche he found himself linked by the media to other American artists – Lichtenstein, Claes Oldenburg, James Rosenquist, Tom Wesselmann – who were allied to an existing British movement known as pop art which both admired and critiqued American popular culture.[37] The thing about Warhol, though, was how he claimed that he – as a first-generation American – genuinely celebrated consumerism and admired the mass production of uniform goods because "All Coca-Colas are alike, and all Coca-Colas are good."[38] Yet his most radical "inversion" of abstract expressionism came in his refusal to interpret what he was doing. Unlike the prolix statements about their work made by the Barnett Newman generation, Warhol's famous blankness – his "um, gee" mumbling – certainly played on the shy provincial he had been but it was also a staged persona devised to disturb the modernist establishment for whom adroit articulation justified the worth of one's work. To an extent it was this academic-graduate-playing-dumb routine by which Warhol came close to Reed.

Looking for a way to exalt the standardization of goods that was so much feared by the abstract expressionists, Warhol chanced upon the semi-mechanical process of screen-printing. He first tried this method out with his "200 one-dollar bills" of April 1962. From then on he would discard painting in favour of this quicker, idiosyncratic system. Warhol was a hard worker and, as attention grew, he produced new ranges of items. They can be summarized in the following way:

		2-D	*Film*
1962	Early	Paintings: Campbell soup cans	
	Mid	Silkscreen multiples: Marilyn Monroe[39] 23 portraits	
	Late	Multiples: Campbell soup cans, Coca-cola bottles	
1963		Multiples: Elvis Presley with Gun, Warren Beatty	
	Mid	Society "portrait" multiples: Ethel Scull 36 Times	*Tarzan and Jane Regained, Sort of* *Sleep* *Kiss*
	Late	Multiples: "Death and Disaster": (a) Electric chair, suicides, race riot, car crash	*Haircut* *Eat*

	(b) 16-panel Jackie Kennedy[40]		*Handjob*
1964		*3-D*	
		Brillo boxes/ Del Monte Peach boxes	*Blowjob*
		2-D	
	Mid	Black and white mural: 13 Most Wanted Men[41]	*13 Most Beautiful Women*
	Late	Multiples: Flowers	*13 Most Beautiful Men* *Empire*

This summary excludes the sequence of gallery exhibitions in this period, and so it fails to show the link between production and sales, which were very slow until the success in New York and Paris of his Flower multiples, where he had been advised by a curator friend to move from the negative – death and disaster – to the positive. It also omits the most startling difference that Warhol's associates noticed, his reinvented look. Ingrid Superstar believed that at this point he gave himself an instantly recognizable black and white identity (the silver wig, striped T-shirt, black leather jacket and pants) that would be the same in the newspaper as it would be on the street.[42] But the list does show two changes taking place: firstly, in 1962 his discovery of screen-printing which enabled him to make multiples quickly where nevertheless each one of which might be slightly different in registration and colour and thus unique; secondly, in 1964 his discovery of the fad by experimental artists for making films with cheap equipment formerly the sphere of amateurs (to a degree this project corresponded to the growth of rock bands formed out of scenes of enthusiasts fond of budget technology). Suddenly Warhol became less interested in screen-prints and more interested in the screen. He also moved away from canvas work to three-dimensional objects like the Brillo boxes and later helium-filled silver pillows, in order to broaden the range of what he sold. This was the first stage of his transformation from a producer of art to a producer of people.

The New York "underground[43] film" scene had started in 1960 (at the time that LaMonte Young arrived there) through the New American Cinema Group, the result of a plan among independent film-makers for a cooperative distribution scheme which stated that, "We don't want false, polished, slick films – we prefer them rough, unpolished but alive."[44] In 1962 a Lithuanian emigré, Jonas Mekas[45] (b. 1922), helped to form The Film-makers' Cooperative to present and distribute films "with nobody ruling as to quality".[46] Artists here explored two related areas. Firstly, some of them played with abstraction but emphasized the reality of the medium. The Velvets' Tony Conrad was one of these. His 1966 *Flicker*, with its intense strobe effect, is still considered the most radical of its type.[47] Secondly, film-makers like Jack Smith recorded the staged reality of taboo subjects – sex, and especially gay sex. Their films were piquantly camp versions of Hollywood,[48] doting on the glamour that the "silver screen" provided rather than the storyboard it presented. Sensationalist media coverage got The Film-makers' Coop a reputation that fermented the (still) undecided debate of the 1960s between "art" and "porn". And it was this that first brought The Coop to the attention of the voyeuristic Warhol.

Using domestic equipment, Jack Smith had made a 50-minute film in 1962 called *Flaming Creatures*. It kept getting banned by the authorities who licensed screenings. Described as an orgy of "legs where heads should be...rage, rape and hairy paws"[49] while "the sex of the strange personages is certain only when their genitals are showing",[50] the film heralded that crusade of sexual liberation which the 1960s has since emblematized.[51] Among "the strange personages" in *Flaming Creatures* were Marian Zazeela and LaMonte Young, who also provided some of the music (bowed disc), the whole montage of which was put together on tape for Smith by Tony Conrad. *Flaming Creatures* was shown now and again at The Film-makers' Coop, which screened a range of such films at various temporary locations around mid and lower Manhattan. Warhol began to attend these screenings and, on seeing *Flaming Creatures*, decided to participate in the underground scene by making his own films in this style, as it appeared to be a satisfying vehicle in which to portray gay sex.

For this purpose he bought a Bolex 16 mm camera in July 1963. He started by filming his boyfriend, poet John Giorno, sleeping; the lack of movement, or rather, the sense of iconicity in the screen portrait, was an approach Warhol had premeditated. A locked, passive camera – with silent film – turned celluloid into print to render to the viewer a flickering canvas. The effect of *Sleep* was too similar to Young's examinations of stasis to be coincidental, and it's now known that Warhol attended performances of Young's work at this time.[52] One of Warhol's "tribe", Billy Name – who turned the Silver Factory silver by covering pipes and ducts with foil and became its "caretaker" – had played in Young's group between 1962 and 1963. When Warhol chose to add music to his "still" films for the 1967 New York Film Festival, he commissioned Young to make drones.

Yet Warhol executed two types of film, and although the other style emerged soon after the first, it did so for a contrasting set of reasons. First of all Smith was shooting his all-colour follow-up to the monochrome *Flaming*

Creatures, called *Normal Love*, during the summer of 1963 in outdoor spaces near New York which had been made available by sympathizers. Smith had a fixation on the Dominican-born Hollywood star Maria Montez (1920–51),[53] who as "The Queen of Technicolor played princesses, queens, and dancing girls who all wear colourful, erotic outfits... She was a terrible actress but she was perfect for these ridiculous escapist films. Playing two parts in *Cobra Woman* she is doubly bad."[54] In *Normal Love* a transvestite performer on the New York experimental scene, Rene Rivera, changed his name to Mario Montez in order to play his namesake for Smith, where Montez as a mermaid is threatened by a werewolf.

Warhol went to see what was happening and took along his new Bolex. What he shot of the production became his short movie *Andy Warhol Films Jack Smith Filming Normal Love*. Warhol later claimed of this experience that "I picked something up from him for my own movies – the way he just kept shooting until the actors got bored."[55] However this was not all he learnt. He saw how he could make his own camp versions of the Hollywood movies that he adored. An opportunity to do so presented itself very quickly, but there was an ulterior reason for taking it up – that of revenge.

A second art exhibition had been arranged in Los Angeles in September 1963, a year after the first. He travelled there in a station wagon driven by a playful performer on the New York underground film scene, the hyper-mincing Taylor Mead, who acted in Smith's films. Although by now Warhol had gained notice as a "real artist" on the West Coast, and despite attention from Hollywood actors who showed up for a party in his honour, the show was a flop and he sold next to nothing. An early collector of his work had been the film actor Dennis Hopper, and – in reprisal for his Hollywood defeat – Warhol used Hopper and Mead to film with his Bolex a parody of a genre that epitomized Hollywood machismo – the Tarzan film. *Tarzan and Jane Regained, Sort Of* became the first of his absurd, camp caricatures of the silver screen in the Jack Smith style where every aspect of the profession is traduced by technical ignorance. *Batman Dracula* (1964), *The Life of Juanita Castro* (1965), *Hedy* (1966, "starring" Mario Montez, with music by the Velvets) and others followed in its wake. They represent the cinematic equivalent of the garage band. This is the third connection one can make between Warhol's work and that of The Velvet Underground, and it explains how Warhol could approve of Nico's "amateur" participation in the group, in that she offered an iconic presence that the others lacked. And, after all, she really was a film star, at least in *La Dolce Vita*.[56]

Yet the "underground" connection between the Velvets and Warhol runs even closer. One link already established is that of the early Velvets member Tony Conrad, a musician and film-maker who organized the sound for Jack Smith's films. When Smith bought the tape recorder previously mentioned for *Normal Love*, Conrad and his new flatmate Cale worked on it to edit the soundtrack and to use for other projects, including eventually the Velvets' Ludlow Tapes of July 1965. On some of the "underground" films of this time, Conrad coordinates the sound and there seem to be three methods:

(i)   editing existing tapes together;
(ii)   recording (and then perhaps editing) improvisations;
(iii)   having live music during screenings, sometimes in conjunction with the film sound.

One of the film-makers most interested in using music was Piero Heliczer. Born in Rome, Heliczer became a child film actor. In 1944 his father was killed by the Nazis and soon after the end of the war his mother took the family to Washington DC. At school there he met the young Angus MacLise, with whom in 1958 he moved to Paris where he set up The Dead Language Press. Moving on to Brighton, England, he made his first film in 1961, *Autumn Feast*. Arriving in New York City in 1962 he acted in *Flaming Creatures* and began to make his own films there, adding the music to *Autumn Feast* using MacLise and Conrad to do so (Heliczer also played flute and saxophone). LaMonte Young and Marian Zazeela appear with Jack Smith and MacLise in *The Soap Opera* (1964) and the subsequent *Dirt* made in the summer of 1965 includes Warhol, Cale, Edie Sedgwick, Young and Zazeela and others alongside "the New York police department". Heliczer also appears in Warhol's 1964 film *Couch*, lying – as you might guess – on a couch and talking to Warhol's assistant Gerard Malanga.

Heliczer sometimes used recorded music – Charpentier, The Rolling Stones – but he cultivated the use of live sound. As Sterling Morrison recalled of this period, which developed between April and November 1965,

> We [Cale, Reed, MacLise, Morrison, sometimes with Heliczer on saxophone] would play live at Cinematheque showings and other screenings that took place in lofts and places like that. It was kind of a performance but also a little informal but it was arranged so that veils (transparent drapes) came at the side or in front of the screen so that the film was pro-

jected through the drapes and we would improvise. Dancers would dance (in silhouette) and there'd be incense and
people speaking poetry. It came out of the "happenings" but
at the centre of all this was the film. We were accompanying the film, even though I'm not sure I knew what the film
was or what it was about! I think this was the first time we
saw two simultaneous films being screened, really interesting things like that. We made some amazing sounds, really
experimental, and later on we carried those improvisations
into our set. I think it was this that appealed to Andy: you
know, the relation of the music to the film, to what else was
going on around the music. In fact, I think we did play to
some of Andy's films back then.[57]

Indeed they did, as they also did to showings of films by Jack Smith, Ron
Rice (for his sensuous *Chumlum*) and the 19-year-old Barbara Rubin, who
would be the one who alerted Warhol to the Velvet Underground residency
at the Café Bizarre. On the underground film scene Warhol would have come
across the musicians named as The Warlocks or as members of LaMonte
Young's set and seen them as improvisers rather than a rock group, but he
certainly had heard and seen them before his encounter in December 1965.
Cale recalls that, "Whenever we performed music for [Warhol's] films we
could do anything we wanted. And the more distance there was between
the music and the film, the better the drama created by that tension."[58] Up
to this point it was Heliczer who most exploited their creativity on the film
scene; he also used them as actors. On his website[59] can be found images
of Angus MacLise in *Satisfaction* and Maureen Tucker (being filmed by CBS
television during the making of Heliczer's *Venus in Furs* for a documentary
about the New York underground film scene, broadcast on December 31st,
1965, where the Velvets can be heard playing an extract of 'Heroin' and
'Venus In Furs', but with Heliczer on saxophone). Lou Reed's song 'Venus
In Furs' was not written for the film but his awareness of the Baron Sacher-
Masoch novel came from it.

Cinematheque mastermind Jonas Mekas naturally took an interest in
this fusion of two-dimensional film with three-dimensional action. Under
the heading "expanded cinema" he organized a festival of it in October and
November of 1965, the one at the Wurlitzer Building where Cale gave his last
performance with Young, and when Warhol saw Zazeela's *Ornamental Lightyears Tracery* that he would turn into the *Exploding Plastic Inevitable* (readers

will now also appreciate the source of Warhol's "exploding" in "expanding"). This willingness to bring improvised music into a multimedia frame is the fourth operative link between Warhol and the Velvets. Yet, while the four connective modes so far outlined help to explain Warhol's interest in the Velvets as a creative project, they don't explain why an artist would wish to take them up as a commercial operation. To explain that we must turn to Paul Morrissey, Warhol's manager.

Morrissey, a young film-maker who also had something of a business brain, is a canny, quick-talking, pro-enterprise New Yorker of Irish stock – "a cross between a New England whaling captain and Bob Dylan" according to Malanga – who tolerated rather than indulged the oddballs of Warhol's retinue. He became employed by Warhol when the artist decided to move from his small uptown studio to what soon became known as the "(Silver) Factory" at 231 East 47th Street. With his new occupation in mind, Warhol saw the Factory as a kind of film studio and so the technically adept Morrissey was helpful in running that, but at the same time Warhol was being forced by circumstance to try new projects, and Morrissey, as manager, was hired to keep tabs on those. Morrissey says that, "I really became his manager in the sense that I did all the talking; I also had to suggest what to do. Andy would get up in the morning and say, 'What do I do today?' and you had to tell him what to do. I'd say, 'Let's make a picture', and he'd say, 'Great, what shall we do it about?' He was terribly indefinite about everything."[60]

Morrissey, in interview, offered this frank account of Warhol's gradual move from art and films into music.

> We have to go back a little, I mean no more than the start of November [1965]. Andy had begun getting a fixed income from the Leo Castelli gallery. But he wasn't doing any art. He withdrew from the art world for a number of years to put his price up and make the earlier stuff more collectible. He got a thousand dollars a week from Castelli. And he didn't want to pay any taxes, so he decided to spend the leftover to make little films; an hour's worth of developed 16 mm black and white stock cost $200. Well, for $200 we weren't exactly going to compete with Hollywood. But this guy, Jonas Mekas, used to rent an off-Broadway theatre on a Monday night when it wasn't showing plays, and called it the Cinematheque. These films were truly experimental; no one in their right mind thought there'd be an audience. Now, Andy was always look-

ing for ways to keep his name in the papers, and it turned out that the film critic of the *New York Times* reviewed this stuff at the Cinematheque, and so we'd put something on there and it'd get Andy's name in the *Times*. I'd project a reel for 30 minutes and then there was no cut in it so that it just went on and on, the camera maybe zoomed in and out a couple of times, but it was pretty boring. One day I got fed up with this and put the other reel on at the same time on the other projector to see if there was anything of interest in either, and putting them on together made them better. I told Andy; he said, "Oh, gee, um, okay" and so we started showing films at the Cinematheque two reels at a time. That's how the multi-projection thing started up that we used in The Velvet Underground shows and got us all that avant-garde reputation.

Morrissey and Warhol were always keen for ways to bring new money into the Factory and get "employment for our employees". Anything would do, they said, simply anything. Nevertheless, they were amazed when an old theatre producer called Michael Myerberg phoned in November 1965 with a plan to have Warhol host a discothèque he was building. At this time the discothèque – a French word for a French concept – was a fairly novel notion, that of having a club space designed for dancing to records. The idiom was gaining ground in a transitional period where groups were beginning to think of leaving the stage for the recording studio;[61] it was also a way that white people could dance to black music with the "blackness" being consigned to invisibility. Morrissey continues:

> For some godforsaken reason [Myerberg] wanted to open up a discothèque in an aircraft hangar in the district of Queens, where nobody in the world went. There weren't many discothèques in New York and they were all small like Arthur's, Ondine's, The Scene – that was some rich kid renting a basement with a dance floor the size of a toilet seat. We went to Myerberg's office above the famous Sardi's restaurant and he said to Andy, "You go to discothèques and you've got that girl Edie Sedgwick and you both have your names in the papers all the time going to clubs. I'd like to hire you to come to this discothèque every night." Andy was always interested in people offering him money, but the problem here was that nobody would believe Andy was really going to Queens every night!

While trying to accommodate them Myerberg suggested that the club could be called "Andy Warhol's Discotheque". According to Morrissey:

> We were sitting there a bit startled by now, but Andy said, "Er...er... The Up. Andy Warhol's Up". Of course this guy had no idea that Andy was being a little naughty: "That sounds fine to me", he replied. We said we'd think about the deal. Outside, I said to Andy that we could go to this stupid discothèque and he could pay us, but it didn't make sense unless we had some financial stake. In those days discothèques had records *and* live bands. I told Andy we'll find a rock and roll band and then we'd have a reason for going there because it was our group and Andy would be like Brian Epstein. He said, "Ooh, that's great". And I told him not to worry about the arty part because Cocteau once managed a prize fighter. So suddenly Andy was sold on this idea of managing a group, and it just came from me trying to accommodate this guy Myerberg.

Morrissey phoned Myerberg that Warhol would do the deal if he'd promote their band for the opening. Myerberg said, "Fine. What's the name of the band?" Morrissey gulped. He had no band. He garbled and said he'd let him know. He sat around the Factory for a week, head in hands, trying to sort it out: "It turned out that the Factory kids didn't like to go out and hear bands," he complained. "They'd only go if it was an event like The Rolling Stones." It was then that Barbara Rubin mentioned that her Cinematheque contacts had a residency at the Café Bizarre. Gerard Malanga borrowed Warhol's Bolex camera to take to the café to film them as a screen test. Morrissey went with him in order to work the light meter. He thought they were fascinating:

> But you had to have three things to run a group: a guitar, an amplifier and a manager. Well, they didn't even have the amplifiers. Maureen was only brought along because her brother had one to lend. I asked them, "How would you like Andy Warhol to be your manager? We are looking for a band, we can guarantee employment, we can open you in a big discothèque with lots of publicity, we'll sign a contract with you and find you a record deal." If things hadn't worked out the way they had, there wouldn't have been a group a week

later. That's the power of coincidence. I brought Andy along the next night. He said, "Ooh, yeah, great. I love that word 'Underground' in their name." But he always said yes. He just wanted something to happen.

At this point the problem emerged, mentioned in Chapter 2, of Reed's lack of "stage presence" and the solution of a female singer. Morrissey's first proposal was not Nico, who had just arrived at The Factory with her "Rolling Stones" single, but the cabaret performer Tally Brown (1924–89),[62] then in her early forties, who had appeared in Warhol's *Batman Dracula* and did impressions of the uncommonly camp "Inca" soprano Yma Sumac. While the combination of Brown and the Velvets is a highly intriguing one, Nico eventually managed to gain a "guest spot" in the band in order to give it the glamour Morrissey thought it needed. He persuaded the rest by offering them some money to live on. He added:

> But you have to remember that we'd gotten hold of this group only because of Myerberg's discothèque deal. But he kept stalling, the date kept getting postponed. Finally, we got a date in April 1966. The Velvets were going to open the place on the Friday. On the Monday before, I phoned Myerberg but he said, "There's been a change of plan. I can't use your group. We're gonna open with The Young Rascals." The Rascals were a group of New York Italians managed by the kind of people who run West Village cafés [he means the Mafia]. I shouldn't really have been surprised. However, there I was, sitting in this room with a band who think they start work on Friday in a big club.

In order to manage the band on a legal basis Morrissey had set up a company called the Warvel Corporation. The War(hol) Vel(vet) directors were Warhol and Morrissey, who racked up 25 per cent of the Velvets' earnings and 25 per cent of Nico's earnings from the work that the Corporation got them. Morrissey already earned 25 per cent of Warhol's earnings, "which made it a bit complicated because I got something stupid like 15.625 per cent of Nico and Andy got 9.375 per cent – well, we never made a buck so it doesn't matter in the end!" With the contract signed in early January, the financial stake was large enough to warrant a few try-outs before their debut, then still imminent, at Myerberg's discothèque in Queens. They started with a television feature for the WNET cable station (not to be confused with the CBS *Venus in Furs* feature). The WNET crew had come to make a short item on Warhol which was subverted into a promotional item for the group then rehearsing at The Factory. Warhol taped an introduction in which he gauchely chatted for the considerable length – for him – of 30 seconds:

> We've sponsored a new band that's called The Velvet Under-
> ground, and – erm – and we're trying to – erm – and since I
> don't really believe in painting any more, I thought it'd be a
> nice way of combining – erm – and we have this chance to
> combine music and art and – er – er – films all together and
> – and – we're sort of working on that and the whole thing's
> being auditioned tomorrow at 9 o'clock and if it works out it
> might be very glamorous.[63]

The so-called audition was hardly a try-out, being the annual dinner of the New York Society for Clinical Psychiatry at the dapper Delmonico Hotel on the 10th of January. Warhol had been asked to give a lecture but instead he proposed a "performance". Ultra Violet described the event as "Andy and the Underground giving shock treatment to the 175 well-dressed shrinks and their perfumed, carefully coiffed wives".[64] The clinical psychiatrists must have seen several past and future patients posing on the stage, not only Reed but also Sedgwick. Jonas Mekas recorded a little of the occasion for his film *Walden*; Edie Sedgwick can be seen dancing the watusi next to a notably frigid Nico, who – when she wasn't singing her songs – never knew quite what to do. When she asked Reed he replied, "Nico, you can always knit". When she said he could go to hell, he shot back, "Well, where do you think we are now?" The Velvets were bemused with the event because their identity was being blurred between the rock band persona they were attempting to define and their role within the underground film scene which was being replicated on a huge scale. Warhol and Morrissey had brought in film and slide projectors. While Warhol's black and white film of a Velvets rehearsal, titled *The Velvet Underground and Nico (A Symphony of Sound)* was being projected on two simultaneous reels behind the band, Warhol was sometimes holding and moving slide projectors showing images in the manner of Marian Zazeela, but in a nascent form. More problematically for the band, Gerard Malanga, Barbara Rubin, Sedgwick and others were taking up space on the stage with their dancing (Malanga with a whip). Clearly Warhol was encouraging this to make the expanse look exciting, but it would later become more formalized and ritualesque. In any case, the night was a sensation.

Mekas was organizing an Edie Sedgwick retrospective in February 1966, and this would be the second opportunity Warhol and Morrissey had to try out what Nico called "the circus" surrounding the band's performances. As by this time Sedgwick was having an affair with Dylan, the Cinematheque had the focus of its season quietly changed. It became a week-long twice-nightly try-out for The Velvet Underground spectacle called *Andy Warhol, Up-Tight*. Warhol showed only his new film *Lupe*, where Sedgwick played the Mexican diva Lupe Velez. In its final scene she was made to retch over a toilet bowl, which was Warhol's way of saying "Ciao, Edie". At the first show Sedgwick appeared and tried to sing along with the band. Nico was there too and the group played Dylan's 'I'll Keep It With Mine' for her to sing, for, as Nico explained, "I didn't have enough to sing otherwise. Lou wanted to sing everything. I had to stand there and sing along with [him]. I had to do this every night for a week. It was the most stupid concert I have ever done."

In March they repeated the experience at Rutgers University in New Jersey and titled it the *Erupting Plastic Inevitable*. For this Warhol tried out strobe lamps, which "were magical, they went perfectly with the chaos music the Velvets played, and that long piece of Sylvania tape that Gerard was now using for his dance numbers, whipping that around, looked terrific when the strobes flashed on it".[65] An accounts book for this concert, now stored at the Warhol Archive, shows that Nico was paid $100 while the four Velvets shared $100 between them (Warvel therefore got $50 from the 25 per cent arrangement on the two payments[66]). In between the appearances Reed was working up songs and the band was providing music for Warhol's new films, including *Hedy* and *More Milk Yvette*. As Cale has put it, "With Andy work was the ethic, not sitting about taking drugs."[67]

Then, at the start of April, came the fateful morning when Morrissey learned in horror that The Young Rascals had taken the Velvets' place in Queens. He continued:

> But, coincidentally, that very same day I had to go with Andy to a coffee shop so he could have his photograph taken with Allen Ginsberg for some godforsaken reason or other. I'm sitting there telling Andy we're got a group and no gig, when a guy at the next table leans over and says, "You've got a rock'n'roll band and you need a hall to play in? We've just done a dance recital on 8th Street; it's called The Dom. It's a large hall, has a stage and a bar. If you go over there now you could probably rent it for the weekend." So I went over to St Mark's Place where it

was – not the chic area it is now – met this guy called Stanley, who was Polish, because the club was a Polish nationalist social club [Dom means "home"], and rented it.

The next day Morrissey placed an ad in *The Village Voice* for the opening on 8th of April – the only publicity – which ran:

DO YOU WANT TO DANCE AND BLOW YOUR MIND
WITH
THE EXPLODING PLASTIC INEVITABLE
live
ANDY WARHOL
THE VELVET UNDERGROUND
and
NICO
Live Music, Dancing, Ultra Sounds, Visions, Lightworks
by Daniel Williams, Color Slides by Jackie Cassen, Discotheque,
Refreshments, Ingrid Superstar, Food, Celebrities and Movies
including: Vinyl, Sleep, Kiss, Empire, Whips, Faces, Harlot, Hedy,
Butch, Banana, Etc
Etc, Etc
ALL IN THE SAME PLACE AT THE SAME TIME

The *New York Times* mentioned the event, on the women's page. "The first [ever] story about The Velvet Underground was on the women's page of the *Times* and it was all about Nico," recalled Morrissey.

> You can imagine how well that went down with Lou Reed. It was really all about Nico being the new girl of the year. Then it talked about this extraordinary event that did things that hadn't been used before – strobe lights, films, five carousel slide projectors – oh, did I tell you about that? That was Andy's one contribution, I must say. He took some coloured gels (green, I think, and red) and took a cutter for making holes in paper – he remembered this from his art school days! – and he made holes in the gel and put them in frames to sit in the slide projectors. These little things worked wonders because they went over the black and white films they were showing. The colours were just bouncing around the hall, it was so kinetic. You can see how they worked because we put them on the original [back] cover of the Velvets' first LP. Then we used them in the *Chelsea Girls* movie. Nico has these holes on her face.

Readers will remember the red and green lighting and slide projectors of Zazeela. As Cale commented,

> So much of what Andy did seemed to be a diluted version of the downtown avant-garde scene... We got the feeling that strong ideas were being recycled and thinned out by people like Andy. Yet he made it popular, and the way he formed this multimedia thing around the Velvets is an example of how this copying could work to the good.[68]

Whether, as Cale believes, the "events" (plural) decorated the Velvets' set, or whether, as Warhol saw it, the event (singular) included the Velvets as part of his rock version of a "happening", remains a matter of debate. The set-up, in general graphic form, is shown in the diagram below, with the slide projectors directed at random angles, the strobe lights directed at the stage, and – suspended in the centre of the hall – a spinning silver glitterball which, according to Cale, "splintered the strobes' powerful beams".[69]

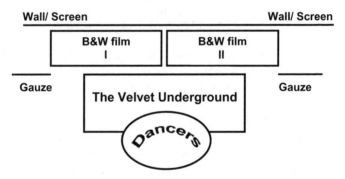

The E.P.I. finished its April season at The Dom on April 30th. During this month Morrissey paid $2,500 for the Velvets to record their debut album at the run-of-the-mill Cameo Parkway Studio on Broadway. Cale recalls that, "It only had four working microphones, and there were holes in the floor."[70] Over three days 13 songs were recorded, of which ten made the LP (but only six in the version recorded at these sessions). Morrissey had the job of selling the tapes to a record company:

> Andy produced it in the sense of paying for it, and then I tried to get Atlantic, Elektra and Columbia Records to buy the tapes. Ahmet Ertegun [Atlantic] didn't want drug songs,[71]

> blah-de-blah, but Tom Wilson at Columbia was sort of keen.
> He's a very interesting man; he was terribly tall, he'd been
> to Harvard I think, and he was a negro. He had discovered
> Simon and Garfunkel for Columbia Records and they were
> a goldmine for that company [he also produced Bob Dylan's
> 'Like A Rolling Stone']. He said, "I think that Nico is great. I'll
> buy the tape off you" – he gave us probably the cost of it. And
> he bought the record because of Nico.

But Wilson was just about to leave Columbia for a subsidiary of MGM called Verve, which was a jazz label hoping – by hiring Wilson – to get rebranded as a rock label; Frank Zappa's The Mothers of Invention from the West Coast were signed by Verve at the very same time.

Yet Wilson wasn't that happy with the recording quality of the tape or, indeed, the songs, which lacked the single he would need to promote the album. Morrissey recalls Wilson telling him, "'There's not enough Nico. Why don't we get Nico to sing another song that would be right for radio play?'" As The Velvet Underground had a month's residency with the E.P.I. booked at a Los Angeles club called The Trip throughout May, Wilson hired the superior TT&G Studios, where he produced the re-recordings with the new 'Sunday Morning' as the single, previously mentioned. This productive use of time proved helpful, as the club residency was closed down on the third night and the entourage was forced to hang around California for a month under Musicians' Union regulations in order to get paid the full fee. This was the first of a number of work disappointments which resulted in the break-up between Reed and Warhol and Reed and Cale.

A second setback was the delay in the release of the debut album, which was completed by August 1966 at the time that The Mothers of Invention's *Freak Out!* was issued by the company. Wilson was determined to sell the Velvets on Nico's voice rather than Reed's, and so Verve put out two sets of singles, the first in October of 'All Tomorrow's Parties' (with Nico's voice, capitalizing on Nico's participation in Warhol's film *Chelsea Girls* which had been very successfully premièred in September[72]) and then afterwards the album's "single" 'Sunday Morning' with Reed's voice. *The Velvet Underground & Nico* was finally released in the USA in March 1967 and in Europe in October. On the one hand, it arrived in time for the Summer of Love. On the other hand, the Summer of Love was not enamoured of what was on offer in it. The two singles and the album had to compete in the American market with albums or singles by The Beatles, Bob Dylan, The Beach Boys and others:

Year	Month	Artist	Album/Single
1966	**Aug**	Bob Dylan	*Blonde On Blonde*
		The Mothers of Invention	*Freak Out!*
		The Beatles	*Revolver*
		The Troggs	'Wild Thing'
	Sep	The Byrds	*Fifth Dimension*
	Oct	The Kinks	*Face to Face*
		The Beach Boys	'Good Vibrations'
		? & the Mysterians	'96 Tears'
		The Velvet Underground	**'All Tomorrow's Parties'**
	Nov	The Monkees	*The Monkees*
	Dec	The Who	*Happy Jack* [73]
		Tim Buckley	*Tim Buckley*
		The Velvet Underground	**'Sunday Morning'**
		The Monkees	'I'm A Believer'
1967	**Jan**	The Doors	*The Doors*
		Bob Dylan	*Greatest Hits*
	Feb	The Beatles	'Strawberry Fields Forever'
		The Grateful Dead	'The Golden Road'
	Mar	Jefferson Airplane	*Surrealistic Pillow*
		The Velvet Underground	***The Velvet Underground & Nico***
		The Rolling Stones	'Ruby Tuesday'
		Jimi Hendrix Experience	'Purple Haze'

Before the Velvets' album appeared in the UK, Jimi Hendrix's *Are You Experienced?* (May), The Beatles' *Sgt Pepper's Lonely Heart's Club Band* (June) and Pink Floyd's debut *The Piper At The Gates Of Dawn* (August) were released. It received little or no attention from the press in the USA or Britain, and the only English mention of it is to be found in the August gossip column of *Melody Maker* as a "West Coast" import being used to sell clothes:

> *Meanwhile what are the beautiful people digging?*... The voice on the phone of *Granny Takes A Trip* in King's Road told the Melody Maker that they are listening to The Incredible String Band (Elektra); The Doors (Elektra); Nico & The Velvet Underground, an American import; another American West Coast sound, the 13th Floor Elevators; a sitar record "which is really good" ... The newest rave is, of course, Moby Grape – an energetic urging group of happenness presently being dug in London.[74]

This is not to say that the album was ignored. It peaked at 197 in the US charts, which means at least that it was bought in quantity to a degree. An American student at that time, Alan Campbell, recalls that, "The group was known. Their album was talked about; it was part of the 'underground' scene. But so were The Fugs and similar alternative bands. The Velvet Underground were on that kind of level."[75] In an attempt to get better known, the band needed to tour, but while Warhol's E.P.I. gained publicity as a cross between an avant-garde spectacle and a freak show, it didn't procure much work. The dates for 1966 were limited to two nights in San Francisco in May, six nights in Chicago in June (caught on film by Ron Nemeth), the odd university booking, and on November 20th a wedding in Detroit. Warhol told the Velvets, "Other people succeed who have no talent. Here we are with you gorgeous people and we can't make it."[76] Morrissey stressed the fact that it was hard to know how to work things because:

> You have to remember that there wasn't this big rock industry structure yet. A good example was accommodation. I went to LA a few days ahead to check on dumb things like whether the club had enough sockets to plug the projectors in, and the toughest job I had was finding somewhere for the band to stay. Hotels did not take bands. I put Andy and "respectable" folk in the Tropicana Motel, but they wouldn't take the Velvets or Nico. They said bands rented houses, and

> I got put on to this wonderful guy called Jack Simmons. He
> was James Dean's best friend and now he ran this big place
> called The Castle. It really is a castle surrounded by a park.
> Nico got to love the place and later she stayed there for a time
> with Jim Morrison. So, you see, however straight you tried to
> run these operations in those days, you still ended up with
> these crazy, exotic alternatives.

By the autumn, when the singles were due to come out, Morrissey scrutinized The Dom again. The E.P.I. had been so successful an enterprise there that, while the band was on the West Coast, Dylan's manager Albert Grossman had surreptitiously taken the lease to open it up in the autumn as The Balloon Farm.[77] Morrissey was offered a residency there for the Velvets ("The son-of-a-bitch!") but instead got Nico a turn as a solo singer in Stanley's basement bar, where one of her admirers, the young Leonard Cohen, would go to listen. Morrissey put 8 mm film loops behind her of people sky-diving, a kind of mini-E.P.I. Cale, Morrison, and Reed would take turns with Tim Hardin and the 17-year-old Jackson Browne in accompanying Nico on guitar, while Nico started to learn to play an Indian harmonium. But at the same time Nico's employment as a soloist was a message to the band that Warhol's musical project could carry on without them.

It was then that the band started to prepare for the second album. They moved in communally to a West 3rd Street tenement, which they dubbed "the 'Sister Ray' house"; it lasted for a year before they split up. At the same time Reed started talking to a young Boston promoter called Steven Sesnick, part-owner of a popular club called The Boston Tea Party. In the following months Sesnick would increasingly destabilize the existing arrangements in an attempt to obtain more regular work for the band and a higher profile independent of the Warhol scene. When *The Velvet Underground & Nico* came out in March 1967 Morrissey revived the E.P.I. to help publicize the record, with the participation of Warhol and Nico. In April, Stanley's son approached him with a proposal to lease a Czech sports club on the lines of The Dom, but uptown, called The Gymnasium. Although the revival took place, it wasn't successful. Reed declared that the band shouldn't play in New York again, and indeed it didn't until 1970, by which time its membership had changed. The failure of Warhol's Gymnasium, together with the lack of media interest in the album, brought matters to a head.

In July Reed told the others that he'd sacked Warhol, and Sesnick was now managing the band. This came as a surprise, even a shock, to the others and Reed's autocracy was a major factor in the breakdown of the communal living project. In July Nico recorded her first solo album, *Chelsea Girl*, with Tom Wilson as the producer. It really looked as though the Velvets were being left behind, and so, in September, the second album – *White Light/White Heat* – was recorded under their Verve contract, with Tom Wilson producing although only in the sense of him arranging matters with the engineers.[78] The Velvets recorded over three days in an endeavour to replicate their live sound, which was in fact what Warhol had told them to do for their first album. As Cale put it, "We insisted on playing at the volume that we played on stage... because we were so good [by] that point [from touring]."[79] Morrison recalled that, "Everything was leaking and the needles were constantly hitting the red. The engineer kept warning us, and we kept ignoring him."[80] One of the tracks, 'I Heard Her Call My Name', was secretly remixed by Reed, who, according to Tucker, was "having a little ego trip at the time – there's no rhythm, no nothing. You can't hear anything but Lou."[81]

White Light/White Heat was released at the end of January 1968 (May 1968 in the UK) and it sold less well than the first album. The Reed–Sesnick axis blamed Cale's experimentalism. After some endeavours to try out new songs, a final attempt in August to record tracks for the third contracted album for Verve yielded no helpful results, and a month later Reed fired Cale. He got Morrison to do it for him. In Cale's words, "We were supposed to be going to Cleveland for a gig and Sterling showed up at my apartment and effectively told me that I was no longer in the band."[82] Given that Cale has often declared how Reed revelled in confrontation, it seems remarkable that he would depute this task to another. Perhaps it shows how far Reed was fearful of Cale, who was himself demonstrative. As Cale admits, "Things had been pushed pretty far between us and I can't say I was entirely blameless."[83]

For the next two years The Velvet Underground would be merely the convenient name for Lou Reed and his backing band.

6 Death and Transfiguration

On June 3rd, 1968, a year after he was sacked by Lou Reed, Andy Warhol faced a further disappointment. He was shot in the chest by Valerie Solanas, a radical feminist writer who felt he owed her money. At one point clinically dead, Warhol survived, but the wounded husk that finally returned to work was christened "Cardboard Andy" by Billy Name. Yet even Cardboard Andy retained Flesh Andy's fetish for celebrity and, once revived, he was eager to see how the press had covered his shooting. Imagine his disappointment to learn that, just as the news of his apparent death had been breaking, Robert Kennedy was assassinated in Los Angeles. Kennedy – brother of the President killed in Dallas in 1963 – had just won the Californian Democrat "primary" election in the contest to become the next President, which he did on an anti-war agenda. The artist had been wiped from the papers to make way for the politician.

And this is how it was for the Velvets. Whatever impact they hoped to make, events on the streets, on campuses, on the Left Bank of the Seine, in the napalmed schools of Vietnam – all conspired to make the Velvets immaterial. Consider the political and military events that took place around the release of the first three albums:

1a. April/May 1966: *Velvet Underground & Nico* – recording

Transport strike in New York; 8,000 troops in biggest Vietnam offensive to date; US renews bombing of North Vietnam and shells Cambodia; May 15th: 8,000 anti-war protesters encircle White House; major race riots in Brooklyn, Chicago and Cleveland.

1b. March 1967: *Velvet Underground & Nico* – release

United Nations and Pope call for an end to the war; April 15th: 200,000 protest in New York against Vietnam war; Central Park Be-In; anti-war hunger strikes and sit-ins at colleges; boxer Muhammad Ali faces jail after refusing to be drafted for military service in Vietnam.

2a. September 1967: *White Light/White Heat* – recording

Late July: paratroopers called to Detroit race riots; Puerto Rican shops looted in New York, two killed, 300 injured; President Johnson orders commission of inquiry; anti-war demonstra-

tors surround Pentagon, violence flares, 250 arrested including
Norman Mailer; major increase in raids by B-52 bombers and
extended use of napalm in North Vietnam.

2b. January 1968: *White Light/White Heat* – release
Tet offensive – Viet Cong invade Saigon, 30 aircraft destroyed
at Da Nang US airbase; major American and South Vietnamese
casualties; violent anti-war demonstrations around the world; by
now 486,000 US troops in Vietnam; Richard Nixon declares he
will run for President.

3a. November 1968: *The Velvet Underground* – recording
April – Martin Luther King killed, riots follow across USA;
Columbia University (NYC) strike and occupation; May: Paris
riots; June: Robert Kennedy and Warhol shot; August: violent
Yippee conflict at Chicago Democratic convention; Soviet tanks
invade Prague; October 27th: demonstrations and riots against
United States in Tokyo, London and Amsterdam; November:
Richard Nixon elected president; first wave of Catholic/Prot-
estant riots in Northern Ireland; atrocity of Biafra.

3b. March 1969: *The Velvet Underground* – release
January: Jan Palach immolation in Prague, Nixon sworn in as 37th
president; March: Viet Cong attacks throughout South Vietnam;
De Gaulle resigns; post offices bombed across Northern Ireland.

It would be naïve to expect that songs should directly reflect these events
and portents, although some did, such as Country Joe's 'Feel Like I'm Fixin'
To Die Rag'; MC5's 'The Human-Being Lawnmower'; Crosby, Stills and Nash's
'Chicago'; The Temptations' 'Message From A Black Man' and 'Cloud Nine';
Jefferson Airplane's 'Volunteers'; even Hendrix's all-guitar 'Star-Spangled
Banner'. Yet the point here is that some critics do consider that in fact the
uncontrolled, menacing, "dark" sounds of The Velvet Underground mirror
or indeed represent the wrenching episodes of the central 1960s, against
which 1967's Summer of Love was attempting to more positively confront
through "flower power". It's suggested that 'Sister Ray' and 'Heroin' offer a
soundtrack to this immensely exhilarating but fraught period. Yet, as it has
been argued in Chapter 4, those sounds derive from an entirely different
set of influences – firstly from Cale's neo-expressionistic transformation of
the "pure", meditative compositions of LaMonte Young, and secondly from

the confluence of a songwriter imbued with 1950s existentialism meeting an arranger attracted to the performative actions of neo-Dadaism.

There were four main reasons why The Velvet Underground failed to engage and sustain support for its project as it conceived it in 1965. These causes took hold despite strong and distinctive support from Warhol and Morrissey as management, and notwithstanding a record deal they obtained for the band from MGM–Verve with the backing of a prominent producer in Tom Wilson. They are:

(a) *Irrelevance*

Other people of the band's age were active in attempts to change US imperialist policy, or to improve domestic welfare systems, or to assert a libertarian or civil rights agenda in the domains of ethnicity, gender, disability, sexuality, and ecology. And, in accordance with these efforts – as music historian Anthony DeCurtis put it in a radio interview – the bands most associated with these times

> seemed to be offering a vision of a freer life... When The Grateful Dead and Jefferson Airplane came to New York they'd play at the Fillmore East, two shows a night at weekends...and it was ecstatic. There was a sense of tremendous freedom, there was a heavier vibe about that a new world is possible, that there was a new way to organize life here. It was very utopian.[1]

Meanwhile Reed's output was locked into an outmoded Beat agenda of the 1950s: unadorned, disinterested observation of idiosyncratic characters, voyeuristic description of rough sex and indulgence in hard drugs, automatic writing, a desire to bring together 1950s rock'n'roll with the "ever now" improvisational approach of 1950s jazz.[2] Cale was relatedly concerned with elitist, vanguard, performative minimalism influenced by late 1950s jazz (Coltrane, Coleman, Taylor). Neither of them "reached out" to contemporary experience, which was in a prodigious phase of transition. Cale's experiments in sound were overtaken by other artists (just as he had feared in 1965), while Reed's lyrics appeared either frivolous ('Venus In Furs', 'Lady Godiva's Operation', 'The Gift', 'The Black Angel's Death Song') or meretricious ('White Light/White Heat', 'Heroin', 'I'm Waiting For The Man', 'Sister Ray').

(b) *Absorption versus observation*

Just as Marshall McLuhan's notion of the mediated "global village" was taking hold,[3] and new avenues of communality were explored, the widely developing drugs culture simultaneously took people the other direction "into themselves". Nico was introduced to LSD[4] and she tried to get Warhol to take some. She failed but revealed:

> You read everywhere that Andy never took drugs. But it wasn't true. He took amphetamine – a type of amphetamine, I forget its name.[5] Andy took pills. He told me that pills were normal. His mother took pills, the President of the United States took pills. He didn't like anything more mysterious than a pill. This was our biggest difference. Brian [Jones] said that it was the world we had not yet discovered, a world inside. America and Russia had a fight to go to outer space, but we wanted to go into inner space; we would not be Astronauts, we would be Intranauts. Andy said, "Oh no, Nico, there's nothing inside. I wear my soul on my sleeve." Well, anyway, he took a drug so he would go faster and miss what there was inside. Maybe that's why he got so bored.[6]

While the Velvets welcomed psychedelia they sniffed at psychedelics. Cale stressed that, "We thought that the solution lay in providing hard drugs for everyone. There is already a very strong psychedelic element in sustained sound, which is what we had...so we thought that putting viola behind guitars and echo was one way of creating this enormous space...which was itself a psychedelic experience."[7] He added that by hard drugs he meant heroin: "We had little patience for flower power... We didn't fall for that sunny, Californian crap." Morrison commented, "What was annoying – among so many other things about flower power – was the way taking psychedelics was intellectualized as being 'mind-expanding' or somehow insightful, as though all those stupid hippies were on a spiritual quest instead of just taking drugs. It wasn't a question [for us] of seeing something as something else, but of seeing what it was in fact."[8]

It must be made clear here that the Velvets didn't object to West Coast ideology solely on the issue of subjectivity and self-delusion. The band was in brisk competition with this burgeoning scene, and above all it detested the encroachment onto their New York City locale of Frank Zappa and his Mothers of Invention in 1967. Zappa (1940–93) took over The Dom when it was relabelled The Balloon Farm, and later the Garrick Theatre for six months.[9] Twice nightly his resident outfit would improvise theatrical events in a sort of cabaret pastiche of Warhol's *Exploding Plastic Inevitable*. While this rankled, the Velvets especially detested Zappa's anti-drugs evangelism. Zappa, a right-wing, sexist libertarian, also desired to write finicky compositions in the style of the avant-gardist Edgard Varese, a pretension that irritated Cale. He retorted that Zappa was someone who "did nothing to make you love music".[10]

However, Morrison's more general view of "flower power" is commensurate with Reed's practical use of reportage and detachment in his construction of lyrics, using observation of real people to shape his characters. At first sight this rendering of "fact" fits in neatly with Warhol and the ideology of pop art associated with him, which was itself originally titled – as with Beat 15 years before – "The New Realism". Yet the Velvets and Warhol were passing each other from separate directions, just like AbEx and the Beats had done a decade earlier. Post-war Greenwich Village abstract expressionism ran parallel with Greenwich Village Beat literature, where both used automatism (Pollock's drips and Burroughs' scribble) and took inspiration from improvised modern jazz. But the Beats attempted "new sharp, straightforward writing" which would represent existential reality, while the severely subjective AbExes believed that the "inner reality was the only reality".[11] Both were reacting directly in their way to their predecessors – the muralists on the art side and the modernist authors of the 1920s and 1930s on the other – and therefore started in opposed positions. Yet the spirituality that ministered to AbEx ideology also took a hold of the Beats from the mid 1950s on, as Kerouac and then Ginsberg turned Buddhist ("beat – beatitude") while Burroughs devoted himself – astounding as it seems – to the Christian faith. Reality began to mean to them a report on spiritual dereliction. By then both sets, as they passed by in the night of the soul, became Ginsberg's "prophets howling in the wilderness". They remained contrasting projects because both groups had consciously fashioned encoded subcultures by which they were separately mediated and marketed. Yet, at the point where introspection was acknowledged and cultivated by the Beats, affiliations appeared, and not only through the liquor glasses of The Cedar Tavern and The Five-Spot.

So, too, with Warhol and the Velvets. What made the group's work so singular in its most dynamic period, 1966–7, was the combination of the stylistic preoccupations of the three protagonists:

January 1966–July 1967:

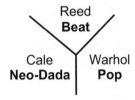

Reed
Beat

Cale   Warhol
Neo-Dada   **Pop**

Warhol supported the Velvets in ways other than finance and projects. At the aesthetic level he championed the following:

(i)   a "Factory" work ethic, an incentive to constantly invent;

(ii)   a fervour to explore the materiality of sound through repetition of fields extended by improvisations ("eternal now");

(iii)   a need to translate the live sound onto recordings;

(iv)   a compulsion to enhance the visual impact of the performance as a multimedia experience.

When Reed sacked Warhol, the *Exploding Plastic Inevitable* inevitably exploded. Yet at the same time other groups – Pink Floyd most famously, but Stockhausen and other avant-gardists too – developed audiovisual sensoria in the wake of Warhol (and, of course, his concestors Young and Zazeela). Reed filled the lacuna left by Warhol with a move to the folk-rock[12] sound that Dylan had helped to establish[13] and which was evolving rapidly on the West Coast. As an intimate, vocal-dense style it obviated visual supplement. When Reed sacked Cale, all that was left was Reed. He continued his integration of a Beat aesthetic with folk-rock delivery. When Reed walked out defeated in 1970, the band – in name only – kept going until 1973, derided by those detractors who could be bothered to note its existence as "The Velveteens". This can be represented graphically as:

July 1967–September 1968

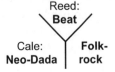

Reed:
Beat

Cale: **Folk-**
Neo-Dada   **rock**

September 1968–August 1970

Reed: $\dfrac{\text{Beat (lyrics)}}{\text{Folk-rock (music)}}$

However, while Warhol's engagement with the Velvets had been predicated on a need to construct projects other than painting or screen-printing – a policy that caused his shift to film (with The Factory as a film studio) – by mid 1967 he had handed over film-making to Morrissey, who had some success with it, and, in the wake of a subsequent demolition order, transferred the work space from the midtown Silver Factory to the new downtown Union Square Factory,[14] which – Morrissey saw to it – became more business-like than its predecessor.

At this point Warhol was not considered successful as an artist in New York. During 1967 his dealer Castelli sold only $20,000 of his work.[15] To an extent this was one sign of the New York art market reflecting an intensifying economic crisis facing city investors, but it was also a snub to Warhol whose celebrity as a media icon and socialite was at its height. He would not have another New York show until 1977; this withholding reflected a general disengagement from New York City, which was facing increasing infrastructural problems (culminating in the 1974 metropolitan bankruptcy). As a result Warhol now turned to commissioned socialite portraiture using the screen-print technique, and eventually to magazine publishing. At this level Warhol and Reed were as one in their determination to turn their projects into commercially successful enterprises. But, while the former succeeded, the man who had sacked Warhol from his own undertaking failed.

This defeat returns us to our substantive theme, that of Reed's distance from the drift of lyric writing of the period. His decision to place his lyrics at the centre of attention made this seclusion all the more apparent. As Cale saw it, "There were a lot of soft songs and I didn't want that many soft songs... I was trying to get something big and grand and Lou was fighting against that. He wanted pretty songs."[16] Yet these "soft" and "pretty" songs[17] concerned odd relationships and dissatisfying sex ('What Goes On', 'I Can't Stand It', 'Lisa Says', 'Some Kinda Love': "Put jelly on your shoulder/lie down upon the carpet"), men as women ('Candy Says', 'Stephanie Says' – about their new manager) as well as weak, half-written drafts like 'That's The Story Of My Life' or 'Ferryboat Bill', and the maudlin folly of 'Jesus'. Together these exemplify what the Texan band, The 13th Floor Elevators, had dismissed in 1966 as "old reasoning", which "involves a preoccupation with objects...and takes on a superficial aspect of the quest" which is "childishly unsane". In contrast the "new reasoning", which dealt with inner emotions, "involves a major evolutionary step for man".[18] This reproach of childishness – here spurning evolutionary progress – remained a standard criticism of "punk" as hollow and delinquent, the latter in the sense of an impairment of intellect.

Many popular songs of the same period – from, say, The Beatles' 'Tomorrow Never Knows' (1966) to Joni Mitchell's 'Both Sides Now' (1968) take up the "within you/without you" paradigm which is inspirited by the project of psychedelia, a de-centring of perception that in turn informed the "double coding" of post-modernism as defined by Charles Jencks in the 1970s, meaning here a communication between the inner and the outer.[19] That the Velvets would ideologically reject this as "navel-gazing hippy nonsense"[20] is not surprising in a contested neighbourhood market where they were trying to define a style influenced by, but distinct from, LaMonte Young's scene, which could truly be construed as "navel-gazing", and where Young was, indeed, way-to-go "West Coast".

Yet a bigger picture can be drawn in terms of spatial identity.[21] While groups such as The Beatles took an inclusive approach to musical resources at a global level (not just the sitar and the tabla, but an appropriation of many examples of music in the manner of Stockhausen's *Hymnen*), and did so with an integrative agenda, the folk-rock project moved in the "local" direction of rural representation, "country" traditions, and a critique of urbanism. It was left to the black urban genres cultivated by Motown (Detroit) and Stax (Memphis) to define a progressive urban presence; a move to lyrical sophistication and interiority soon took place in that domain too. Meanwhile it seems that The Velvet Underground could construct its own spatial frame of reference only in terms of outmoded values of the 1950s black-sweatered "underground" beatnik.

There is also an irony in this spacialization. As mentioned earlier, the Velvets' residency at The Gymnasium in 1967 failed to attract a local public. As Sesnick, their new manager, co-owned a club in Boston, they retreated there where they gained a local following among students. The Velvets were no longer a New York band but a Massachusetts one. Their terminal return to New York, a ten-week residency for the tiny Max's Kansas City bar, was recorded on a cassette in "bootleg" fashion by a Warhol staffer and released in 1972.[22] It was at the end of this residency – this misfired homecoming – that Reed quit the band and returned to live with his parents in Queens, quite the prodigal son.

The Velvet Underground in 1967:
left to right, John Cale (on chair), Maureen Tucker, Sterling Morrison, Lou Reed

(c) *Blatancy*

In April 1966, as the Velvets were recording their debut album, The Byrds released the song 'Eight Miles High'. This title alone caused a great deal of international comment, as it was assumed to be a drugs song where "high" was a reference, perhaps, to the potency of ingested cannabis. Radio stations declined to play it for this reason. Byrds' singer Roger McGuinn retorted, "If we'd wanted to write a drug song, we'd have written a drug song", and argued that the title referred to a flight to, or from, England. Yet the song can indeed be interpreted as a drugs song, and member David Crosby did later admit that the inference was fair.[23] There were many other songs of this period where the media suspected – and consumers frankly craved – references to illegal drugs, most notoriously The Beatles' 'Norwegian Wood' and 'Lucy In The Sky With Diamonds'.

One year later, what was most shocking to the media and potential consumers of *The Velvet Underground & Nico* was the cover – not Warhol's AbEx parody of the peelable banana with a naked man underneath, but the simple word 'Heroin' as track seven. It was this that led Ahmet Ertegun, owner of Atlantic Records, to decline to handle it, with his comment to Morrissey, "No drugs records".[24] While other artists encoded references within titles of songs, and around lyrics, the Velvets, supported by The Factory, took Warhol's opinion of "What you see is what you see".[25] Brave as this was, it was not impelled by astute marketing. Many consumers, especially young people still at home or in formal campus housing, lacked the environment in which to be blatant about drugs use, or even a milieu that permitted associated material to be displayed, especially as this was incriminating and drugs possession was illegal. Through necessity, a fashion was cultivated for coded references to drugs and sex, and in the mid 1960s this encoding was still desired as a valued method of intimation.[26]

While various liberation movements campaigned for concealing codes of this kind to be exposed as oppressive, especially with regard to homosexuality, a reformed vocabulary took more than a decade to get a grip. The appeal and cleverness, then, of Reed's 'I'm Waiting For The Man' lies in the very ambiguity of carrying either a drugs or a gay theme. Although Nico wanted to sing it, she agreed that "It would be only one song with a woman's voice. When Lou sings it you hear two songs, and they are both strong."[27] 'Heroin', 'Venus In Furs', and 'Sister Ray', however, hide nothing, and they were most valued and covered by young bands when subject matter was more directly handled one generation on at the end of the 1970s.

(d) *Presence*

Cale: "You can only get a flavour of what we did from the recordings. On 'Sister Ray' you can hear the cues [on the organ] I would have to move the music along, but we did more than you hear on the album. And we had no set line-up. We could swap around. One time we all played percussion. Even Nico improvised, singing without words, while Lou could improvise lyrics for himself."[28]

Morrison: "You'd have to time-travel to hear what we could do. It's not on the albums, it wasn't done in the studio. It's one of those ironies that whatever we did in the studio – prepared and redone or just worked through live like on stage – it never captured what we were, man."[29]

Tucker: "You had to hear us live. It's a crying shame that all these young people who have all the records and know everything about us never heard us!... I kept a beat going for the others and what they did was wild. It sometimes drove me mad trying to keep that beat going. There was nothing like it."[30]

Nico: "My first music was in a studio [London, 1965] and I didn't know the etiquette of performing.[31] I discovered that it was so different, it was closer to modelling. Modelling with your mouth open... There were some songs where we did what came to us from the air. It is all lost."[32]

A recording exists of The Velvet Underground with Nico performing one of their improvising pieces, 'Melody Laughter', in Columbus, Ohio, November 1966. It has been edited down to 11 minutes from 30,[33] and this editing creates an ambiguity in timing and tuning, as the opening section is centred on the axis $A^\flat$–$D^\flat$–$G^\flat$ (amplified harmonics) while, after Tucker enters with a measured tom-tom pulse and at the arrival of Nico's voice, the pitch has settled almost on G; Nico improvises on the Mixolydian mode while a related guitar solo chooses a blues-like Dorian mode on G. This fascinating recording has been released on the compilation *Peel Slowly And See* (1993). The most remarkable example of improvisation, however, was made in the studio. It can be heard on Nico's first solo album, *Chelsea Girl* (1968), produced by Tom Wilson, in a song co-authored by Nico, Cale, and Reed titled 'It Was a Pleasure Then'. Both this track and 'Melody Laughter' offer a rare example of Nico singing falsetto, in a vibrato-free soprano voice, but it is the studio recording that reveals both Reed and Cale at their most instrumentally adventurous yet least egoistic.

Improvised experimental pieces that exist on recordings somewhere or other, and as documented in discographies, are as follows:

1.	*Noise*	ESP-Disk August 6th, 1966, electronic newspaper of the East Village Other. "A loop of feedback and viola howl" by John Cale.
2.	*Loop*	Flexidisc on *Aspen* magazine, December 1966. 15 mins. Cale improvisation using "guitar and feedback".
3.	*The Nothing Song*	(Perhaps a reference to The Fugs' song of the same name?)
4.	*Melody Laughter*	Both *The Nothing Song* (3) and *Melody Laughter* (4) were on recording of show at Cincinnati (presumably *Melody Laughter* is different from that recorded at Columbus).
5.	(a) *Hedy* (b) *The Gerard Malanga Story*	1965. Soundtracks for Warhol's films.

These improvisations generally include four elements which may or may not take place simultaneously:

(i)   de-tuned strings on guitars and viola, generally lower, sometimes all to same pitch class (e.g. E) to nourish feedback;

(ii) harmonics and feedback, sometimes in combination;

(iii) drones that get overshadowed by the feedback tones;

(iv) structural junctions where the soundframe could be moved into new territory (addition of pulse from the drums, introduction of bass guitar or voice, and so forth).

Morrison: "We would practise the beginning and end of a song. As we never played it the same way twice, it didn't matter if we practised the middle."[34]

However, the most extended of these experimental works was made a decade later as a solo studio piece by Reed and titled *Metal Machine Music*.[35] Clearly a prolongation of 'Loop' of 1966, and four times as long, it comprised tape manipulation (that is, octave displacement and accelerated or decelerated fusions creatively edited by Reed) of two guitars each placed close to a speaker to generate feedback in two monaural images simultaneously, as did 'Loop'. *Metal Machine Music* was considered by some media reviewers, and thus their public, to be little more than fulfilling in the most sardonic manner a contractual obligation to RCA Records.[36] Yet it was successfully promoted on RCA's classical Red Label imprint as an experimental work, one intended to position Reed as a "serious" artist by reminding followers of the Velvets' remarkable contribution to an exploratory scene of the mid 1960s. He made *Metal Machine Music* shortly following the release in 1974 and 1975 of three live albums: Reed's *Rock'n'Roll Animal* (February 1974), *Lou Reed Live* (March 1975) and *The Velvet Underground Live 1969* (September 1974) which provided a very limited impression of lineage, influences, and genres. It was also the follow-up to his most successful LP to date, *Sally Can't Dance* (August 1974). At this time, too, Reed was in competition with Cale and Nico as solo artists and with a new generation of punk performers.

Reed called it "an electronic instrumental composition" in reference to the contemporaneous modernist work of Stockhausen and Cale's Tanglewood tutor Xenakis (which it most resembles[37]) and he divided it into four equal sections determined by clock time in the manner of Cage, doing so in order to site the work on vinyl. On the one hand, it could be a parody, in the style of Warhol's send-ups of abstract expressionism. Yet Warhol made his game jokingly clear to insiders, while *Metal Machine Music* is anything but funny.

On the other hand it fits squarely alongside the experimentation of which all the Velvets partook between 1965 and 1968. In either case, the work remains controversial in that it is an attempt to transfer, to an epic degree, an improvisational sound world of performance onto record through the medium of not performing (the feedback performs). In this, like the Velvets' attempts to capture presence, there remain the regrets of the Velvets themselves, noted above, that it was a band to be experienced in the flesh rather than through a flat disc. In its inability to negotiate the demands of these distinct spheres,[38] The Velvet Underground failed – firstly against its more adept market competition, and secondly in underestimating the need to maintain consumer support by combining concert performances with more frequent releases of records.

The Velvet Underground failed but ultimately thrived. In conventional accounts of popular music history the story runs as follows. From 1968 onwards a number of disparate bohemians on the art and music scene – Richard Hell (b. 1949, Kentucky), Iggy Pop (b. 1947, Michigan), Jonathan Richman (b. 1951, Boston), Patti Smith (b. 1946, Chicago), Johnny Thunders (1954, Florida – 1991), Tom Verlaine (b. 1949, New Jersey)[39] – cultivated their interest in garage rock to which the two-chord Cale/Reed Velvets were now associated. Yet these artists took a different turn. Back in the early 1960s Young and Warhol, among others, had helped to evolve multimedia actions with a focus on simultaneity, a pursuit that ran in parallel with a general social demand for equal rights. With 1967's "Summer of Love" now seen as a culmination of democratic hopes, against the devastating events of 1968 as its nemesis in asserting conservatism (the election of Nixon, complicated by the realization that the Vietnam War was a lost and costly cause), the East Side scene of the late 1960s splintered in the face of growing economic tensions. Those stresses not only led to the consequent insolvency of the New York City authority but also informed the artistic shift of interest away from objects and constructions towards concepts and the artists' own bodies in order to confirm that, as nothing was being bought, there was nothing to buy.

Within the competing factions were those who were attracted to simple sex-and-drugs music-making as a means to gain cultural capital and, let's be frank, monetary capital. Most of these artists had prioritized literature (Verlaine and Hell – out of Rimbaud – making this clear to insiders in their choice of names), and, following Dylan by prioritizing words in a folk/blues narrative frame, they had wanted to present sophisticated lyrics over unaffected music. Yet they took this on within a more cynical dynamic than hitherto, one that still recognized ties with the bohemian/Beat/punk scene most recently exemplified by the Velvets, with the difference that these new artists were fervid performers, keen to strut and rile the crowd,[40] eager to show, as Nico said of Patti Smith that "she means business [while] Lou looks like he couldn't care less".[41]

This style of assertiveness had been influenced on the one side by the development of performance art, and on the other by the posturing and theatrical dressing-up of "glam rock" (as in "glamour"), a mannerist development of the very late 1960s[42] – again, a consequence of a utopia that wasn't delivered – concerned with camp flamboyance and a play on gender conventions which resulted in a desire to project blatantly constructed, vain personas in the manner of film and rock stars, where ostentatious wealth is represented by cheap glitter. If garage rock considered itself authentic and reductive, glam was artificial and exaggerated. Both, however, dealt with undiluted expression enacted through the directness of the post-war rock'n' roll style, which was what drew the rats and the peacocks onto the same Lower East Side stages.[43] Between them The Ramones (garage) and The New York Dolls (glam) were influences on the short-lived British punk scene and its more significant successor, post-punk.[44]

Lou Reed as a soloist, 1973

But so was Lou Reed. His revival in late 1971 as a solo artist had been advanced by entrepreneurs putting him in touch with David Bowie in London, where Reed – recognizing a resemblance with Warhol's Factory – now joined in with the glam scene as something to do rather than to watch, even though he was nearly 30. In view of his apparent stand against the prevailing virtuosity and fantasies of programme rock – although he relied on exceptionally fine session musicians for his recordings – the cartoon punks (from 1976) and the more musically literate post-punks (from 1978) traced a heritage back from Reed to The Velvet Underground in order to keep Reed in view but to denude him of his glam persona, which had become passé. The Velvets became iconic figures by having presented existentialist views and deadpan observation in a simple but epic and deranged musical style. Songs from the first two albums were covered by a large number of successful or failed bands,[45] often as training exercises.

It was no coincidence that this canonization took place in similar social conditions to those a decade earlier when the Velvets were dissolving – now with Europe and the USA at the end of the 1970s reacting to major cultural collisions and economic grief[46] by retreating to political conservatism (Reagan and Thatcher). That several of the key bands who most claimed affinity with the Velvets held reactionary principles – such as the Warsaw/Joy Division/New Order cadre and the "Goth" (neo-Gothic) artists who revered Nico[47] – was not surprising either. Nevertheless, in 1982, for the first time ever and due to this interest, The Velvet Underground, which no longer formally existed, came "into the black" and finally made money from record sales which were split as royalties among the separated members, including Nico (and, after her death in July 1988, her estate), a fair-minded situation which still applies at the time of writing.

Nico's ghastly demise – left to die from a brain haemorrhage in a hospital on Ibiza because she looked to the duty doctor like just another stoned hippie – followed that of Andy Warhol, who, in February 1987, had also died of medical negligence following a routine gallstone operation in New York. His unexpected death brought Cale and Reed together to compose a sequence they called *Songs for Drella* (their nickname for Warhol, mixing Dracula with Cinderella). That Cale and Reed could still bear to work together, although in exceptional circumstances, led to hopes from promoters and new fans that they might reform the band with Morrison and Tucker. A business meeting regarding royalties in November 1992 did indeed bring the quartet together, and, following a couple of days jamming as a band in February 1993, a reunion tour of Europe was arranged for the summer of that year. But the four weeks of rehearsals for this led to tensions so deep that following this desultory tour, collaboration ceased. Soon after, Morrison died.

So much, anyway, for the customary chronology. There is another way to view this, and one more complicit with recognizing how bands in an increasingly congested market – such as that between 1978 and 1984[48] – must not only make themselves distinct but also need to identify themselves with a pedigree through which the market can best place them as being beyond genre. They gain media exposure and sales by doing so because both of these outlets (media, sales) work most effectively by communicating and applying patterns and types. It is also through declarations of dissimilarity in the present, together with allusions of similarity to the past, that the artists' claim to authenticity is measured. While this intricate orienting manoeuvre turns into an awkward contradiction – defining uniqueness and affinity to the same degree – no artist cares to be a lost cause.

Categorizing bands by reference to previous bands is often resolved with ease, thanks at times to the clear aural influences from which the artists derive their sound world, very often through the direct need of bands with little training to drill themselves into shape by copying the recordings of existing or past acts, which was certainly what united punk and post-punk practice. Nevertheless, generally speaking, this simple process has to be camouflaged in order to protect an equal obligation to the band's "uniqueness", even though this also has to be traceable (to a point) for the sake of certifying authenticity. For this reason two qualities control the means by which affinity is disclosed and mediated. Firstly, the antecedent has to be *mythologized* in its ontology – its being, its essence – to a degree that diffuses hard, decisive connections and makes this source an attractive one for a variety of latent artists. To their potential successors an artist's value is determined by his or her capacity to accept this role in league with their suitability to effect it. Secondly, specific derivations must be *mystified*, so that practical influence is transformed into disembodied "inspiration" – nothing you can put your finger on.

In the case of the rediscovery of The Velvet Underground, the fact that Reed, Cale, and Nico had managed to keep solo careers going, in a rather dishevelled fashion, through the 1970s, maintained for them a certain alternative authority, especially when Reed was able to provide a personal mythology through statements such as, "My week beats your year".[49] Nevertheless, they remained shadowy; the group existed solely on vinyl which was often out of circulation. This situation enhanced their credentials with young bands for whom mythologies could be better constructed through absence of information. More crucially, when biographies of the Velvets began to be published, from 1982 onwards, the members' propensity for fabrication[50] was passed on in print, helped greatly by the method Bockris used in 1983 for *Up-Tight*, the first history of the Velvets – that of uncritical blocks of direct quotation.[51] In terms of mystification, the appeal of 'Sister Ray', as an exemplar to copy or imitate, lay in its moderate tempo and its I/IV simplicity against its seemingly endless length filled with competing layers of activity; it had already mystified itself. Joy Division's producer Martin Hannett described the Velvets as, "Primitive and complex at the same time, and just a fantastic, moody atmosphere. It was the atmosphere that interested us."[52] In other words, nothing you could put your finger on.

The legitimation of The Velvet Underground as a concestor, to borrow Dawkins' term again, came from defining it as a group ahead of its time, hence its frequent designation as "proto-punk". However, this book has proposed the opposite – that the reason for the Velvets' lack of success was to do with it facing away from its present, or at least not being pertinent to the times. Reed had worked on a manifesto in 1965 which read, "Western music is based on death, violence and the pursuit of progress... Our band is the Western equivalent to the cosmic dance of Shiva. Playing as Babylon goes up in flames."[53] To see this in more general terms, the need to mythologize, for the reasons mentioned above, demands a degree of historicization – of viewing the past from the present – which reshapes its trajectory in order to render it as being aware of its future. In the specific case of The Velvet Underground, here is apparently under these conditions a band that suffered for its vision, died (rather than fizzled out in 1973) and whose sound world was revived by a new generation. This exercise reorientates the group towards its future, and as a by-product obscures its relation to the past. Let us call this practice *anteriority*, a term to describe a condition of anticipating, envisioning or even precluding, but especially in this case indicating how something from the past, looking to the past within its own present, or facing laterally to it, can be reorientated – in retrospect – to face the future, in order that those responsible for, or complicit with, this operation will benefit in terms of reputation, that is, social status. In this case study The Velvet Underground produced a sound world that failed in its time to find support, but eventually found eminence through other artists influenced by it who then, by indicating the source of their inspiration, gave it new life as an influence to address all futures; in this case it is the Velvets' foresight that is ultimately rewarded, but also in equal measure their successors' judgment.

The opposite of anteriority is surely *posteriority*. However, this term relates to those who follow, who succeed, who are descendants (and the application of anteriority makes them so whether they are or not). A more appropriate term, then, to account for the position by which this book identifies The Velvet Underground, is *preterity*. Referring to the past as immanence, of the ultimate having already been fulfilled, of origins being present in meaning, this expression allows us in general terms to identify something as remaining in the position it had established for itself, while recognizing how others – in order to gain status from identification with it – will use strategies of disorientation. In this specific case, the preter- itative view of The Velvet Underground identifies it in terms of its own influences – and its representation of those influences in its own work – as well as acknowledging its historicized/mythologized, almost biblical posi- tion in popular consciousness. The Velvets' preterite view of the world, of the present as an assemblage of recent pasts, fusing dimly connected ele- ments (modern jazz, doo-wop, rockabilly – "Put it all together and you end up with me" – Reed[54]), will remain influential whenever crises in periods of transition lead listeners to dwell in a dark space, a velvet undergound perhaps, for the sake of stasis.

The band's regard for an ideology rooted in existentialism – with its concern for individual freedom and its awareness of the alienated condi- tion through which we isolated individuals take on the absurdity of choice – locks it into a position that will always be examined by those who are out of kilter with contemporary life, and who reject communal counteraction. They will seek solace in this idiosyncratic clash of creative individuals who only half comprehended their own influences – Reed's Beat poetry, Cale's fusion of Young and Spector, Morrison's rock'n'roll, Tucker's African drum- ming. The Velvet Underground is existential proof that four halves make a whole.

As Nico pointed out, "After all, it was just my backing band. I left it and it fell apart. That is the story you could put about it. That will do just as well as all the stories I read about it now. They are all incredible. You could say they were a group of aliens who landed [in order] to entertain all the other aliens in the world. That would explain the record sales, at least."[55]

Notes

1 New York City

1. Victor Bockris, *Lou Reed: The Biography* (London: Hutchinson, 1994), p. 144.
2. *America*, trans. C. Turner (London: Verso, 1988), p. 15.
3. 1960: 7,781,984; 1970: 7,894,862. Source: US Bureau of Censuses.
4. US Bureau of Censuses.
5. See David Brown, *Tchaikovsky: Biographical and Critical Study. IV. The Final Years* (London: Gollancz, 1991).
6. Charles R. Morris, *The Cost of Good Intentions* (New York: Norton & Co., 1980), p. 58.
7. Barry Gottehrer, *New York, City of Crisis* (New York: David McKay Co., 1965), p. 130.
8. See 'I'm Waiting For The Man' on *The Velvet Underground & Nico* (1965), lyrics to first verse.
9. Caroline Jones, *Machine in the Studio: Constructing the Post War American Artist* (Chicago: University of Chicago Press, 1996), p. 144.
10. Interview, *Fusion* magazine (USA) 6.3 (1970), p. 14.
11. Other such places had names like "Café Wha?", "The Why Not?", "Hip Bagel" and "The Bitter End."
12. 161 W4th St., 1961–3, then 92 MacDougal Street until 1966 when he moved upstate to Woodstock. See Bill Morgan, *The Beat Generation in New York* (San Francisco: City Light Books, 1997).
13. Morris, *op. cit.*, p. 95.
14. In the baby-boom period up to 1956, the average annual US birth rate was 4 million. In 1960 college student enrolment increased to 3.6 million, double the number enrolled in the years just before World War II. By 1960 just under half the population was under 23 years of age. Source: Maurice Isserman and Michael Kazin, *America Divided: The Civil War of the 1960s* (New York: Oxford University Press, 2004), pp. 12, 16.
15. *Strange Brew*, BBC Radio 3. Phil Lesh interviewed by Richard Witts, recorded May 5th, 1993, transmission June 5th, 1993.
16. Alice Echols, "Nothing Distant About It: Women's Liberation and 1960s Radicalism", in David Farber, ed., *The Sixties: From Memory to History* (Berkeley: University of California Press, 1994), p. 152.
17. Federal arts subsidy began only in 1965 when the National Endowment for the Arts was authorized as part of President Johnson's "Great Society" programme. Up to then artists were reliant on commerce and private charity.
18. In 1945 Barnett Newman wrote in an unpublished article, "The New Sense of Fate," "The war, as the Surrealists predicted, has robbed us of our hidden terror... We know now the terror to expect. Hiroshima showed it to us...

After all, wasn't it an American boy who did it? The terror has become as real as life." Quoted in Thomas Hess, introduction to the Barnett Newman catalogue (London: Tate Gallery, 1972).

19. Cage (1912–92) arrived in New York in 1942, settling in the Village at Sutton Place from 1946, but from 1954 he lived out of town at Stony Point, returning in 1970 to live at 107 Brook Street in the West Village. Therefore he was absent from New York City during the essential period of The Velvet Underground's existence. See David Revil, *The Roaring Silence: John Cage, A Life* (New York: Arcade Publishing, 1992).

20. 4' 33", first performed on August 29th, 1952 by David Tudor at the piano, Maverick Concert Hall, New York City.

21. Interview with A. Berman (Part 1, p. 1, *Archives of American Art*), quoted in James A. Breslin, *Mark Rothko: A Biography* (Chicago: University of Chicago Press, 1993), p. 283.

22. "[At Syracuse 1960–4] I was very into Hegel, Sartre, Kierkegaard. After you finish reading Kierkegaard you feel like something horrible has happened to you – Fear and Nothing. That's where I was coming from." Lou Reed quoted in Bockris, *op. cit.*, p. 22.

23. Still, letter, July 1950, in John P. O'Neill, ed., *J.P. Clyfford Still* (New York: Metropolitan Museum of Art, 1979), p. 21.

24. Barnett Newman, "The First Man Was An Artist," article, 1949, quoted in Charles Harrison, "Abstract Expressionism," in Nikos Stangos, ed., *Concepts of Modern Art* (London: Thames & Hudson, 3rd ed., 1994), p. 197.

25. See Eric Hobsbawm, *Age of Extremes: The Short Twentieth Century 1914–1991* (London: Michael Joseph, 1994), pp. 241–2.

26. Starting with *Life* magazine, August 8th, 1949: "Jackson Pollock – is he the greatest living painter in the United States?" See reproduction in Steven Naifeh and Gregory White Smith, *Jackson Pollock: An American Saga* (London: Barrie & Jenkins, 1990), p. 595.

27. Jackson Pollock lived in Greenwich Village from 1930 to 1945, when he moved to East Hampton on Long Island. He continued to socialize in the Village; there are many anecdotes of his brawling there.

28. John Cage, who socialized almost nightly at the Cedar Tavern, talked of "the *climate* of being together... Each had absolute confidence in our work." See Mary Lynn Kotz, *Robert Rauschenberg: Art and Life* (New York: Harry N. Abrams Inc., 1990), p. 89.

29. Edward Lucie-Smith, *Movements in Art Since 1945* (London: Thames & Hudson, 2000), p. 37. See also George Cotkin, "The spontaneity that had originally been part of Abstract Expressionism had hardened into a style, transformed into objects of veneration and commercial value," in *Existential America* (Baltimore: Johns Hopkins University Press, 2003), p. 133.

30. Quoted in Leonard Wallock, ed., *New York: Cultural Capital of the World 1940–1965* (New York: Rizzoli, 1988), p. 154.

31. Kaprow, *The Legacy of Jackson Pollock* (1958), quoted in David Joselit, *American Art Since 1945* (London: Thames & Hudson, 2003), pp. 50–1.

32. See RoseLee Goldberg, *Performance Art: From Futurism to the Present* (London: Thames & Hudson, 1979, rev. ed. 1988), p. 126.

33. See Goldberg, *op. cit.*, pp. 128–30.

34. Kaprow, article in *It Is* journal, No. 4 (1959), quoted in Wallock, *op. cit.*, p. 149.

35. Sally Banes, *Greenwich Village 1963* (Durham, NC: Duke University Press, 1993), p. 14.

36. "Monogram" (1955–9), Collection Moderna Museet, Stockholm.

37. Quoted in Kotz, *op. cit.*, p. 90. The artist had a pet goat as a child, and so there is an argument around "Monogram" as to whether it relates to urban collage or to nostalgia.

38. Kotz, *op. cit.*, p. 87.

39. Seitz, "Introduction to the catalogue" (*The Art of Assemblage*, MOMA, 1961), quoted in Lucie-Smith, *op. cit.*, p. 97.

40. "Rauschenberg's and [Jasper] John's images of coffee cans, flags, targets and jet fighters, created under the influence of the beat poets, returned New York painting to the details of daily life, making the content of their work obvious." W. B. Scott and P. M. Rutkoff, *New York Modern: The Arts and the City* (Baltimore: Johns Hopkins University Press, 1999), p. 319.

2 The Band

1. Richard Dawkins, *The Ancestor's Tale: A Pilgrimage to the Dawn of Life* (London: Weidenfeld & Nicolson, 2005), p. 10.

2. "Throughout the whole time I was in The Velvet Underground we never sorted out any set line-up. Sometimes we'd even get Moe to play bass, it was that unstructured." John Cale in John Cale and Victor Bockris, *What's Welsh for Zen?* (London: Bloomsbury Press, 1999), p. 106.

3. Richard Witts, Nico interview, London, February 12th, 1986.

4. Bockris, *op. cit.*, p. 2.

5. Paul Morrissey declared in a January 1991 interview with this author, "He married a man. He married a woman. What the hell's wrong with him?"

6. Cale and Bockris, *op. cit.*, p. 69. Reed has often made the observation that a number of personalities inhabit him ("up to eight"); this merely conforms to a popular and coarse rationalization of schizophrenia as "split personality."

7. A brand name of Ethchlorvynol. See William Martindale, *The Complete Drug Reference* (London: Pharmaceutical Press, 32nd ed., 1999).

8. On February 3rd, 1959 Buddy Holly, Richie Valens and the Big Bopper were killed together in a plane crash. In 1958 Elvis Presley was called up for his two-year national service, and in the same year the House of Representatives set up a committee to scrutinize the independent record companies most associated with rock and rhythm & blues music, while in 1960 rock DJ Alan Freed was arrested for violating New York's commercial bribery laws, the so-called "payola scandal." These signalled the end of rock'n'roll as a primary commercial market and in its place the revival of Brill Building pop song writing.

9. See Peter Doggett, *Lou Reed: Growing Up in Public* (London: Omnibus Press, 1992), p. 16.

10. Doggett, *op. cit.*, p. 17.
11. "So Blue": 165 bpm/G major; "Leave Her": 72 bpm/G major.
12. Until 1962 located at E4th Street but in that year it moved to 2 St Mark's Place. See Morgan, *op. cit.*, p. 116. For an account of the club, see Martin Williams, "A Night at the Five Spot," in R. Gottlieb, ed., *Reading Jazz* (London: Bloomsbury, 1997), pp. 679–85.
13. Bockris, *op. cit.*, p. 14. Jack Kerouac, "If you know the proprietor you sit down at the table free with a beer, but if you don't know him you can sneak in and stand by the ventilator and listen." From *Lonesome Traveler*, quoted in Morgan, *loc. cit.*
14. Cecil Taylor, public interview with Richard Witts, Royal Festival Hall, London, May 15th, 1988.
15. Bockris, *op. cit.*, p. 20.
16. According to a girlfriend of that time, he consumed drugs "to take a break from his brain". Bockris, *op. cit.*, p. 39.
17. Richard Witts, Nico interview, London, February 12th, 1986.
18. Bockris, *op. cit.*, p. 61.
19. McCarthy's vehicle was The House [of Representatives] Un-American Activities Committee (HUAC).
20. Finally recorded in 1975 on a Lou Reed solo LP titled *Coney Island Baby*.
21. "[Reed] was a terrible guy to work with. He was impossible. He was always late, he would always find fault with everything." Band member Richard Mishkin quoted in Bockris, *op. cit.*, p. 45.
22. Janet Maslin, "Bob Dylan," in Jim Miller, ed., *The Rolling Stone Illustrated History of Rock & Roll* (New York: Random House, 1976), pp. 220–1.
23. "Prominent Men" on *Peel Slowly And See*, PolyGram, 1995.
24. Reed quoted in Bockris, *op. cit.*, p. 75.
25. According to Doggett (*op. cit.*, p. 28) Reed sang on Pickwick-produced records accredited to The Roughnecks (a supposed English band) and The Beachnuts (West Coast Surfing parody).
26. Reed: "They would say, 'Write ten Californian songs, ten Detroit songs'." Bockris, *op. cit.*, p. 77.
27. "If you want a picture of the future, imagine a boot stamping on a human face – forever." George Orwell, *1984*.
28. A chart hit for The Crystals in 1963.
29. The recording is in a slightly flat B flat major, which suggests it was speeded up from A major (therefore the chords are A and D), making the opening reiterated treble D flat a more conventional C.
30. Doggett (*op. cit.*, p. 29) claims it was *American Bandstand*, but Bockris (*op. cit.*, p. 80) is unspecific.
31. Churchill's address to Harrow School, December 1940. Quoted in Peter Hennessy, *Never Again: Britain 1945–1951* (London: Jonathan Cape, 1992), p. 155.
32. Sir Toby Weaver, quoted in Hennessy, *op. cit.*, pp. 157–8.
33. *Ready Teddy*, BBC Radio 4, October 9th, 2004. Written by Ray Gosling.
34. It was kick-started in Britain by the film *Blackboard Jungle*, September 1955,

which featured Bill Haley and his Comets' song 'Rock Around The Clock'. Cale was then 13 years old.

35. "The ted was uncompromisingly proletarian and xenophobic...and the teds' shamelessly fabricated aesthetic – an aggressive combination of sartorial exotica (suede shoes, velvet and moleskin collars, and bootlace ties) – existed in stark contrast to the beatniks." Dick Hebdige, *Subculture: The Meaning of Style* (London: Routledge, 1979), p. 51.

36. Cardew earned his living in London mainly as a graphic designer. His scores such as *The Great Learning* (1968–70) comprise elegant graphics. Cardew later abjured Stockhausen in his Maoist treatise *Stockhausen Serves Imperialism* (1974).

37. Composed 1952–4. The British première took place in 1959.

38. Essay by Kaprow in Geoffrey Hendricks, ed., *Critical Mass: Happenings, Fluxus, Performance, Intermedia and Rutgers University 1958–1972* (Piscataway, NJ: Rutgers University Press, 2003), p. 7.

39. No details of this performance survive at Goldsmiths College, but a copy of the programme is held in the "Happening und Fluxus" collection of the Koelnerische Kunstverein, Cologne, Germany, which was reprinted in the catalogue on the subject of 1970.

40. Jon Hendricks, ed., *Fluxus Codex* (Detroit: Gilbert & Lila Silverman Fluxus Collection, 1988), p. 221.

41. *Fluxus Codex*, *op. cit.*, pp. 61-3; see also Hannah Higgins, *Fluxus Experience* (Berkeley: University of California Press, 2002).

42. For an account of Tanglewood and Bernstein's close relationship to it, see Humphrey Burton, *Leonard Bernstein* (London: Faber & Faber, 1994), pp. 73–83.

43. Copland visited London to conduct the European première, by the London Symphony Orchestra, of his new work *Connotations for Orchestra* (1962) which had been commissioned by Bernstein's New York Philharmonic Orchestra to inaugurate the Avery Fisher Hall at the Lincoln Center in New York City, première September 23rd, 1962. See Howard Pollock, *Aaron Copland: The Life and Work of an Uncommon Man* (New York: Henry Holt, 1999; London: Faber & Faber, 2000), p. 501.

44. Cale and Bockris, *op. cit.*, p. 57.

45. *Strange Brew*, BBC Radio 3. LaMonte Young interviewed by Richard Witts, May 11, 1993. "And when John came over he had this Leonard Bernstein scholarship and he went to Tanglewood and I guess he got a little bored with the academic situation and he asked John Cage, you know, what should he do, and John Cage said, 'Well why don't you go and work with LaMonte Young?' and John came and I immediately recognized he was very talented and I asked him to play viola in my group."

46. September 9th–10th, 1963, 6 pm–12:40 pm the next afternoon, at the Pocket Theatre (100 3rd Avenue).

47. Cale and Bockris, *op. cit.*, p. 30.

48. Birthdate unknown.

49. On June 22nd, 1963.
50. A scholarship to study electronic music with Richard Maxfield. "They gave me the travelling scholarship to get rid of me, so that I wouldn't be there any more. They were afraid I was going to take over the department or something." Young to Richard Witts, *Strange Brew*, *op. cit.*
51. 112 Chambers Street.
52. Keith Potter, *Four Musical Minimalists: La Monte Young, Terry Riley, Steve Reich, Philip Glass* (Cambridge: Cambridge University Press, 2000), p. 61.
53. Modal playing came out of a dissatisfaction with Western (white) chord progressions and instead an interest in African musics. At the same time Western folk music also developed its use of modality. In both cases this exploration of modality (unlike tonality, not a universalizing system, as each mode has its own formulation) was eventually seen as a manifestation of the shift from modernism to post-modernism.
54. "Everybody I knew and worked with was very much into drugs as a creative tool." Young quoted in Potter, *op. cit.*, p. 66.
55. Cale and Bockris, *op. cit.*, p. 59.
56. Paul Cumming interview with De Maria on http://www.aaa.si.edu/oralhist/demari72.htm.
57. Cale and Bockris, *op. cit.*, p. 64.
58. But see Chapter 4 about this Dream Syndicate.
59. Cale and Bockris, *op. cit.*, p. 70.
60. Cale: "Jack Smith acquired a new state-of-the-art Ferrograph tape machine – Revere 2-track machine." Cale and Bockris, *op. cit.*, p. 63.
61. These are the so-called "Ludlow Tapes" which can be found on the Velvet Underground CD collection *Peel Slowly And See* (PolyGram, 1995).
62. Paul McCartney: "That's me, including the guitar lick with the first feedback ever recorded. I defy anybody to find an earlier record – unless it is some old blues record from the twenties – with feedback on it." Interview in Playboy (n.d.), quoted in Fred Bronson, *The Billboard Book of Number One Hits* (New York: Billboard, 3rd ed., 1993), p. 164.
63. Source: A.C. Nielsen ratings; 73 million viewers estimated.
64. See Mark Lewisohn, *The Complete Beatles Chronicle* (London: Pyramid Books, 1992), pp. 136–45.
65. Cale and Bockris, *op. cit.*, p. 73.
66. "I was in a record store when I suddenly saw a record by The Warlocks. As we hadn't made one, I phoned the guys and said, 'We need to change our name – now'." Phil Lesh to Richard Witts, *Strange Brew, op. cit.*
67. Victor Bockris and Gerard Malanga, *Up-Tight: The Velvet Underground Story* (London: Omnibus Press, 2002), p. 27.
68. Bockris and Malanga, *op. cit.*, p. 29.
69. Bockris and Malanga have it as Bayport, while one website also mentions his birthplace as Westport. Tucker once said he came, like her, from Levittown. However, these and East Meadow are all small towns close to each other, and to Freeport, at the west end of Long Island.
70. Richard Witts interview with Sterling Morrison, London, September 8th, 1994.

71. See Bill Bentley, "Sterling Morrison: Appreciation," *Austin Chronicle* 15.2 (September 1995).

72. Interview with Nick Modern for *Slugg* fanzine (1980?), reprinted in *NYRocker* fanzine July/August 1980. It is this interview from which the Morrison quotes are taken for Bockris and Malanga (*op. cit.*), although the source is not credited there.

73. Modern, *op. cit.*

74. Modern, *op. cit.*

75. Richard Witts interview with Morrison, 1994.

76. Bockris and Malanga, *op. cit.*, p. 43.

77. Bockris and Malanga, *op. cit.*, p. 23.

78. Bockris and Malanga, *op. cit.*, p. 40.

79. Richard Witts interview with Morrison, *op. cit.*

80. Quoted in Karen O'Brien, *Hymn To Her: Women Musicians Talk* (London: Virago, 1995), p. 109.

81. Quoted on http://www.velvetunderground.co.uk/index/Tucker (accessed April 10th, 2005).

82. Richard Witts interview with Nico, 1986.

83. In another interview she says she was aged ten: http://www.spearedpeanut. com/tajmoehal (accessed February 7th, 2006).

84. *Ibid.*

85. O'Brien, *op. cit.*, p. 100.

86. O'Brien, *op. cit.*, pp. 97–9.

87. Cale claims that at these rehearsals the band would ingest blue tranquillizers, four quarts of beer and a joint. Cale and Bockris, *op. cit.*, p. 78.

88. Cumming, *op. cit.*

89. Source: Mela Foundation, New York. See http://www.melafoundation.org.

90. Marian Zazeela: "[Angus] was really a great poet, and one of his inventions was the poem called 'Year'... The name of the day that [LaMonte and I] met is called Day of Wages. So we thought, 'We're getting our due here!' and then it went on to Day of the Heart's Release and some certain various things that seemed terribly poignant." *Strange Brew*, BBC Radio 3. Zazeela interviewed by Richard Witts, May 11, 1993.

91. Story quoted by René van der Vort in *Blastitude* webzine 13 (August 2002), p. 8.

92. Richard Witts, *Nico: The Life and Lies of an Icon* (London: Virgin Books, 1993), p. 20. All of the information in this section is a summarized version of that to be found in this biography.

93. *Un chant d'amour* (1950).

94. Richard Witts, interview with Nico Papatakis, Paris, March 4th, 1991.

95. Nevertheless, Delon's mother did formally recognize Ari and adopt him. He's known as Ari Boulogne, from the surname of Delon's mother by her second marriage.

96. "Hip is hip, and groove is groovy/life's a wild Fellini movie" – lyric from *Far Out Munsters*, The Munsters TV series, transmitted USA, March 18th, 1965.

97. Morrissey to Richard Witts, January 1991.

3 Reed

1. *Chuck Berry* documentary, Programme 1, School's Out production for BBC Radio 2, broadcast May 21st, 2003.
2. Quoted in Chris Roberts, *Lou Reed – Walk on the Wild Side: The Stories Behind the Songs* (London: Carlton Books, 2004), p. 9.
3. See Doggett, *op. cit.*, p. 60. He couldn't make this claim for the debut album, as Nico sang some of the songs.
4. For example, on the sleeve note to *Metal Machine Music* (1975).
5. Press release for *Street Hassle* (Arista, 1978), quoted in Bockris, *op. cit.*, p. 322.
6. Unattributed quote in Bockris, *op. cit.*, p. 219.
7. Bockris, *op. cit.*, p. 68.
8. Victor Bockris, interview in *The Independent*, July 22nd, 2004, Review section, p. 6.
9. See Music Example 3(d) in Chapter 4.
10. Roberts, *op. cit.*, p. 34.
11. Sleeve note to *Metal Machine Music*.
12. Bockris, *op. cit.*, p. 130.
13. Morrissey interview with Richard Witts, January 1991.
14. Bockris, *op. cit.*, p. 326.
15. Bockris, *op. cit.*, p. 155.
16. Reed's song was commissioned for the film but it was not ready in time. It appeared on Nico's first solo album, *Chelsea Girl* (1968). Chelsea is a neighbourhood north of Greenwich Village, but in both cases here it refers to the Chelsea Hotel, 222 W23rd Street, where some Warhol associates lived for a time (it is mainly a residential hotel), including John Cale, Viva, and, later, Nico.
17. Bockris, *op. cit.*, p. 155.
18. Bockris, *op. cit.*, p. 91.
19. Bockris, *op. cit.*, p. 61.
20. Nico interview with Richard Witts, February 12th, 1986.
21. Paul Morrissey: "Then Tom [Wilson, the producer of the debut LP] said, 'Listen. The only thing I don't like about the record is, there's not enough Nico. You've got to get another song for Nico...' So, Lou comes up with this song which is terribly insipid, called 'Sunday Morning': 'Suuunday Mor-ning, Withooout a warning.' Yech, it's so dopey... Somehow at the last minute he wouldn't let her sing it. He sang it! The little creep." Interview with Richard Witts, January 1991.
22. Lesh to Richard Witts, *Strange Brew, op. cit.*, 1993.
23. Bockris, *op. cit.*, p. 145.
24. "Beyond The Teacup" or "Déjeuner en fourroure" (1936) – cup, saucer and spoon using the fur of a Chinese gazelle. See Bice Curiger, *Meret Oppenheim: Defiance in the Face of Freedom* (Zurich: Parkett Publishers Inc., 1989).
25. Man Ray (Emmanuel Rudnitsky), 1890–1976.
26. See William Plank, *Sartre and Surrealism* (Ann Arbor: Michigan University Press, 1981).

27. John Cale said that he hated Dylan's songs "because they were full of questions." Interview with Richard Witts, January 1991.

28. Richard Witts interview, February 12th, 1986.

29. There is a short story by Delmore Schwarz from 1958 titled *The Gift*. This appears to be a coincidence, however, as the stories are not related.

30. Lenny Bruce, *Obscenity, Busts and Trials* (Sheffield: Pirate Press, 1992), p. 22.

31. According to record producer Phil Spector, "Bruce died of an overdose – of police."

32. *The Village Fugs: Ballads of Contemporary Protest, Points of View and General Dissatisfaction*, Folkways Records, 1965. Re-released on CD, Fugs Records (UK), 1993.

33. In "Poetry, Violence and the Trembling Lambs," *San Francisco Chronicle*, July 26th, 1959. Quoted in James Campbell, *This Is The Beat Generation* (London: Secker & Warburg, 1999), p. 252.

34. A set of norms, values, and stylistic traits consciously adopted by a class-derived group in order to distinguish themselves, in terms of a collective identity, from the most common cultural order and from other competing subcultures. See Dick Hebdige, *Subculture: The Meaning of Style* (London: Routledge, 1979). But see also Sarah Thornton, *Club Cultures: Music, Media and Subcultural Capital* (London: Polity Press, 1995), pp. 8–12.

35. "Lifestyles are patterns of action that differentiate people... Dependent on cultural forms, each is a style, a manner, a way of using certain goods, places and times that is characteristic of a group but is not that totality of their social experience." David Chaney, *Lifestyles* (London: Routledge, 1996), pp. 4–5.

36. Elias Wilentz, ed., *The Beat Scene* (New York: Corinth Books, 1960), p. 8.

37. Cecil Taylor, interview with Richard Witts, Royal Festival Hall, May 4th, 1985.

38. Preston Whaley Jr states that, "The Beats certainly trafficked in primitivisms", defining the "vogue of the Negro" as a desire by artists and intellectuals to return to the alienated personality "what machine-age modernity had taken away – nature". See *Blows Like A Horn: Beat Writing, Jazz, Style, and Markets in the Transformation of US Culture* (Cambridge, MA: Harvard University Press, 2004), p. 29.

39. Jack Kerouac, *On The Road*, written 1950, published 1957.

40. In line with the religious shifts outlined in Chapter 1.

41. Herb Caen in the *San Francisco Chronicle*, April 2nd, 1958.

42. Campbell, *op. cit.*, p. 245.

43. See Ned Polsky, *Hustlers, Beats and Others* (London: Penguin, 1967). See also C. R. Starr: "I Want To Be With My Own Kind – Individual Resistance and Collective Action in the Beat Counterculture," in Jennie Skerl, ed., *Reconstructing the Beats* (London: Palgrave, 2004).

44. The poet Kenneth Rexroth, father figure to Beat poets, wrote about the "utter nihilism of the emptied-out hipster" in 1957. See Campbell, *op. cit.*, p. 206.

45. Quoted in James J. Farrell, *The Spirit of the Sixties: Making Postwar Radicalism* (London: Routledge, 1997), p. 69.

46. Of course there are exceptions of the period, such as Gil Evans and Bill Evans in jazz, Odetta and Richie Havens in folk music.

47. A term used in Campbell, *op. cit.*, p. 12, as is much of this information (pp. 5–9), which can be also verified in the standard biographies of these writers.

48. See Whaley, *op. cit.*, pp. 47, 83, 85.

49. In March 1959 Ginsberg told the New York Port Authorities (trying to hold back distribution of *Howl*) that the Beat Generation "is prophets howling in the wilderness against a crazy civilisation".

50. *Howl*, Part II, in *Collected Poems 1947–1980* (London: HarperCollins, 1984).

51. Barry Miles, *Ginsberg: A Biography* (London: Penguin, 1990), p. 25.

52. Nico interviewed by Richard Witts, February 12th, 1986.

53. Ginsberg quoted in Jesse Monteagudo, *The Death of the Beat Generation* (1997) at http://gaytoday.com/garchive/viewpoint/102797vi.htm (accessed February 13th, 2006).

54. John D'Emilio, *Sexual Politics, Sexual Communities: The Making of a Homosexual Minority in the United States, 1940–1970* (Chicago: University of Chicago Press, 1983), p. 181.

55. See D'Emilio, *op. cit.*, p. 181.

56. Lower case was her chosen spelling.

57. Whaley, *op. cit.*, p. 12.

58. Kenneth Rexroth, "Jazz Poetry" (from *The Nation*, March 29th, 1958) in B. Morrow, ed., *World Outside The Window: The Selected Essays of Kenneth Rexroth* (New York: New Directions, 1987).

59. Miles, *op. cit.*, pp. 424–5.

60. Cale and Bockris, *op. cit.*, p. 106.

61. Cale and Bockris, *op. cit.*, p. 70.

62. Bockris, *op. cit.*, p. 158.

63. Seeing the need for reflection, the Beat poet Brion Gysin introduced the "cut-up" method of reassembling in chance ways words and phrases and by this "finding the truth". This technique was taken up by Burroughs in 1960 when he was working on *The Naked Lunch*. Some songwriters subsequently used the method, including Nico, who said she was introduced to it by Jim Morrison of The Doors.

64. Stereophonic discs for the domestic market were first issued in 1958. Throughout The Velvet Underground's period of activity, monophonic discs were still manufactured.

65. Bockris, *op. cit.*, p. 244.

66. Introduction to *Between Thought and Expression: Selected Lyrics of Lou Reed* (New York: Hyperion Books, 1991; London: Viking, 1992).

67. Whaley, *op. cit.*, p. 29.

68. There is a theory, expounded by broadcaster Tony Wilson among others, that popular music runs on 13-year cycles, possible related to the arrival of a new teenage market (13 being the start of the "teen").

69. Track on *Street Hassle* (Arista, 1978).

70. In Cale and Bockris, *op. cit.*, p. 102.

71. Originally printed in *Dissent* (1957), later published as a pamphlet (San Francisco: City Light Books, 4th ed., 1970).

72. Thomas Newhouse, *The Beat Generation and the Popular Novel in the United States 1945–1970* (Jefferson, NC: McFarland & Co., 2000), p. 169.

73. Dashiell Hammett, *The Maltese Falcon* (London: Orion, 2002), p. 103.

74. Chandler created Philip Marlowe, Hammett Sam Spade, both of whom were portrayed by Humphrey Bogart in films.

75. Hammett's first success was *The Maltese Falcon* of 1930, Chandler's *The Big Sleep* of 1939. Hammett, a communist, was driven out of a career by the post-war McCarthy "witch hunt". Chandler's last novel was *The Long Goodbye* of 1953.

76. See James Atlas, *Delmore Schwartz: The Life of an American Poet* (New York: Farrar Straus Giroux, 1977), pp. 342–3.

77. "Existentialism: The Inside Story," in R. Phillips (ed.), *The Ego is Always at the Wheel: Bagatelles by Delmore Schwarz* (Manchester: Carcanet Press, 1987), pp. 7–8.

78. Doggett, *op. cit.*, p. 22.

79. Atlas, *op. cit.*, p. 3.

80. Atlas, *op. cit.*, p. 272.

81. Reed's 'Sunday Morning' follows this pattern, although it is not a rock song.

82. First and third stanza lines of 5 syllables (7 lines), second and fourth of 9 (5 lines).

83. Interview with Allan Jones, *Melody Maker*, 1978. Quoted in Bockris, *op. cit.*, p. 326.

4 Cale

1. Cale and Bockris, *op. cit.*, p. 70.

2. First performance, May 14th, 1961, New York City.

3. Young: "The work that allows members of the audience to sit on the stage and look at the audience, reversing the roles, this was getting into a very conceptual level. It was geared towards making people really think about what is this experience that we allow ourselves to walk into and be hand-fed, and are we going to put up with it or are we going to do something about it?" Young to Richard Witts, *Strange Brew*, *op. cit.*

4. Wim Mertens, *American Minimal Music* (London: Kahn & Averill; New York: Broude, 1983).

5. Young: "Probably I started to work on the way that became LaMonte Young in 1957 when I first composed long, sustained tones in the middle of a work for brass and then in 1958 when I composed the trio for strings which was the first work composed of sustained tones. And this led through a series of works to a work called *Composition 1960 no. 7* which was just B and F sharp sustained for a long time." Young to Richard Witts, *Strange Brew*, *op. cit.*

6. Dave Smith, "Following a Straight Line: LaMonte Young," in *Contact* magazine 18 (Winter 1977–8), pp. 4–9. This article remains a ground-breaking source of information on Young. An updated version of this article can be found at the JEMS – the online Journal of Experimental Music.

7. Young: "[*Compositions 1960*] were a very strong social statement about what we'd been having in our concert halls, and what does it mean, and what could be happening in our concert halls. At the same time poetry was within the works." Young to Richard Witts, *Strange Brew, op. cit.*

8. However, the audience had been invited to bring sounds with them, although inaudible ones.

9. Cornelius Cardew, "On the Role of the Instructions in the Interpretation of Indeterminate Music," in *Treatise Handbook* (London: Peters, 1971), p. xiv. See also Cardew, "One Sound: LaMonte Young," *Musical Times* 107.11 (1966), p. 959.

10. Quoted in *Fluxshoe* (Devon: Beau Geste Press, 1972).

11. Smith, *op. cit.*

12. Smith, *op. cit.*

13. Indica Gallery, October 9th, 1966. Lennon offered Ono an imaginary five shillings to knock an imaginary nail into one of her exhibits.

14. Young: "You have fluxus and you have statis. I really was not very interested in fluxus. I was interested in concept art, but I was interested in statis." Young to Richard Witts, *Strange Brew, op cit.*

15. Potter, *op. cit.*, pp. 21–76, and Smith, *op. cit.*

16. Potter reports that a big influence on Young was John Coltrane's recorded improvising to Rodgers' and Hammerstein's song 'My Favourite Things'. Potter, *op. cit.*, p. 63.

17. Potter, *op. cit.*, p. 57 (unpublished material in composer's archive, p. 348).

18. His connection with modern jazz is stronger. For example, at school Young shared with Eric Dolphy (1928–64) the saxophone desk and the clarinet desk in the dance band and the orchestra respectively. Dolphy became a leading modern-jazz virtuoso, playing on Ornette Coleman's *Free Jazz* LP and also performing with John Coltrane and Charles Mingus.

19. J.S. Bach, *Das wohltemperirte Clavier, oder Praeludia, und Fugen durch all Tone und Semitonia* ("24 Preludes and Fugues in all keys") BWV 846-69 (1722). But see Malcolm Boyd, *Bach* (London: J.M. Dent, 1983), pp. 97–9 on the relationship between "well tempered" and "equal temperament."

20. Première, Rome 1974, New York 1975.

21. First performance, outdoors at George Segal's farm, May 19th, 1963.

22. Readers of Chapter 1 will recognize here the "American pioneer" parable being asserted through this, and the link with Rauschenberg's stuffed goat, in something exceptional being related to something much more ordinary in childhood. Young: "You have to remember I was a hillbilly. I was born in Idaho, in a log cabin. My dad was up in the hills herding sheep, living in a tepee, then coming down and staying at the cabin." Young to Richard Witts, *Strange Brew, op. cit.*

23. Young: "I remember that we composed some of the first titles together as a kind of group stream of consciousness." Young to Richard Witts, *Strange Brew, op cit.* This connects with the mid-1960s, drug-related revival of surrealism mentioned in Chapter 2.

24. Potter, *op. cit.*, p. 76.

25. Cale: "The music has a beat-poet quality, these interesting, pitter and pat-ter rhythmic patterns behind the drone." David Fricke, liner notes to Velvet Underground, *Peel Slowly & See* (USA: PolyGram, 1995), p. 17.

26. I labour the point about saxophones in B flat and E flat because Coltrane moved from tenor to soprano which are both in B flat, while Young took the corresponding move, but, as his first instrument was the alto sax in E flat, he took up the sopranino, also in E flat.

27. See Chapter 2.

28. Zazeela to Richard Witts, *Strange Brew, op. cit.*

29. Herz = cycles per second.

30. Cale and Bockris, *op. cit.*, p. 58.

31. Young used no notation between 1962 (*Death Chant*) and 1990 (a commission for the Kronos Quartet). Potter shows a one-page "complete score" of one version of a section of *Tortoise* (example 1.9, p. 75) where Cale's viola part and voice part can be clearly made out. But this "score" was constructed as part of a grant application to the Guggenheim Foundation, which stipulated that a score must be submitted.

32. Cale: "To this day he refuses to acknowledge our contribution." Cale and Bockris, *op. cit.*, p. 61.

33. Potter, *op. cit.*, p. 76.

34. See Ann Harrison, *Music – The Business: The Essential Guide to the Law and the Deals* (London: Virgin Books, 2003). See also Michael F. Flint, Nicholas Fitz-patrick and Clive D. Thorne, *A User's Guide to Copyright* (London: Butterworth, 5th ed., 2000).

35. Smith, *op. cit.*, ex. 3.

36. Cale and Bockris, *op. cit.*, p. 60.

37. Adolphe Sax 1814–94. Sax invented the saxophone in 1846 as a military band instrument. Its carrying power made it a favourite instrument in the dance hall, which was the origin of its use in jazz, and it was ultimately Young's cho-sen instrument. Young: "I started playing saxophone when I was seven years old. My father taught me. He had learned from his uncle who was my Great Uncle Thornton. My Uncle Thornton had a swing band in Los Angeles." Young to Richard Witts, *Strange Brew, op cit.*

38. They were soon developed by the firm Barcus-Berry directly for string instru-ments.

39. Cale and Bockris, *op. cit.*, p. 60.

40. This may be why Reed adopted Dylan's nasal style in order to get his voice to "carry".

41. Zazeela to Richard Witts, *Strange Brew, op. cit.*

42. Cale and Bockris, *op. cit.*, p. 58.

43. Smith, *op. cit.*

44. Cale: "I could just pick two notes on the viola that really fit for the whole songs. It would give a dream-like quality to the whole thing." Fricke, *op. cit.*, p. 11.

45. As the chord in aggregate is B–D#–F#–A, the D natural conjoins with F#–A to make a D major/B major composite.

46. Cale uses his viola on four tracks out of the eleven on the debut album, the fourth being 'Sunday Morning', where it's used in the traditional context of backing harmonies; see Example 3a.

47. R–L–R–R L–R–L–L.

48. Reed otherwise uses *Sprechgesang*, a vocal technique halfway between singing and speaking, throughout 'Sister Ray'.

49. Young to Richard Witts, *Strange Brew*, *op. cit.*

50. Smith, *op. cit.*, para. 23.

51. Young to Richard Witts, *Strange Brew*, *op. cit.*

52. Cale and Bockris, *op. cit.*, p. 91.

53. Cale and Bockris, *op. cit.*, p. 113.

54. Richard Witts: "Looking at this language, to me it's...almost the vocabulary of the hippie." Zazeela: "Yes!" Young: "Absolutely, completely." Zazeela to Richard Witts, *Strange Brew*, *op. cit.*

55. Cale and Bockris, *op. cit.*, p. 93.

56. Further performances were given there on the weekend of November 20th, 1965. Potter, *op. cit.*, has the chronology.

57. Zazeela to Richard Witts, *op. cit.*

58. Young: "I think we all know from an historical point of view that, if we look back at Baroque times, Bach and others, and even Mozart, were great improvisers. But this aspect of our classical tradition began to get lost as printing improved... We began to lose our improvisation skills, so that being involved in jazz was very exciting for me." Young to Richard Witts, *Strange Brew*, *op. cit.*

59. Richard Kostelanetz, *The Theatre of Mixed Means* (New York: Dial Press, 1968), p. 183. Quoted in Potter, *op. cit.*, p. 72.

60. Cale would later wear masks.

61. See Nik Cohn, "Phil Spector," in *The Rolling Stone Illustrated History of Rock & Roll* (New York: Rolling Stone Press, 1980), p. 153.

62. There are thousands of examples, from Doris Day's 'Whatever Will Be Will Be (Che Sera, Sera)' of 1956 to Ben E. King's 'Stand By Me' (1961).

63. Camp in the sense of self-consciously underdone or overblown – that is, missing the target. See Susan Sontag, "Notes on Camp (1964)," in *A Susan Sontag Reader* (London: Penguin Books, 1983), pp. 105–19.

64. Spector became marginally involved with both The Beatles and The Rolling Stones, though in neither case successfully. His "Wall of Sound" records, especially "Be My Baby," were a key influence on Brian Wilson of The Beach Boys.

65. The American guitarist Les Paul started multi-tracking as an idiosyncratic novelty in 1948. RCA had started 3-track recording experiments in 1954, and the 4-track machine had been quickly developed, but it was only in the middle 1960s that the 4-track (and fairly soon after multiples of it, usually up to 32-track) were used, the most famous example being The Beatles' *Sgt. Pepper's Lonely Heart's Club Band*, which they started to record (with 'Strawberry Fields Forever') in November 1966, eventually using two 4-track machines.

66. Cale and Bockris, *op. cit.*, p. 73.

67. Yet the description is closer to the "sonoral" group of Polish composers which sprang up from the late 1950s, in particular Penderecki (b. 1933) and Górecki (b. 1933). The 2nd Symphony of Lutoslawski (1913–94) famously opens with an increasingly chaotic stream of fanfares (1966).
68. Bockris, *op. cit.*, p. 158.
69. Bowing near the bridge to produce a glassy tone saturated with harmonics.
70. Starting at 1:21 with an arpeggiated drone, G–D–G.
71. Bockris and Malanga, *op. cit.*, p. 115.
72. Cale to Richard Witts, January 1991.
73. This enlarges Reed's persistent tendency to place the opening of a verse halfway through the bar (e.g. 'Sunday Morning', 'I'm Waiting For The Man', etc.).
74. Cole, interview with Richard Witts, January 1991.
75. See, for example, Dave Thompson, *Wall of Pain: The Biography of Phil Spector* (London: Sanctuary, 2003), p. 74.
76. Cale and Bockris, *op. cit.*, p. 74.
77. Vocals at I 2:55–3:56; II 6:35–7:25; III 9:04–9:38; IV 10:21–11:53; V 12:26–13:11; VI 16:06–16:48.
78. In fact 13 tracks in total were recorded.
79. See Thompson, *op. cit.*, pp. 48–9.
80. Untuned or, at least, de-tuned. The "Ostrich" guitar was the one used for "Do The Ostrich" in early 1965. From Cale's account (Cale to Richard Witts, 1991), it seems that this guitar (where the six strings were tuned to the same pitch class) was eventually left to be played without being tuned, so that it produced for The Velvet Underground a twanging texture as the six strings clashed against each other.
81. Roger McGuinn of The Byrds: "The Beatles were a strong influence. They kept us moving... They were going from one direction to another, not wanting to be locked in a box, and we didn't either." Quoted in Robert Palmer, *Dancing in the Street* (London: BBC Books, 1996), p. 99.
82. A European-wide interest brought about in part by the presence (through the post-war occupation of the USA military) of American Forces network radio stations playing, sometimes on segregated shows, a range of rhythm & blues and urban blues records. This helps to explain the knowledge of, and interest in, the American blues tradition to be found throughout Germany.
83. Morrison to Richard Witts, *op. cit.* Because of Morrison's aversion, even Tucker was known to play bass guitar in performances.
84. This raises the issue of how far it matters quite what pitches bass guitarists play in performance or when recording conditions are poor. In the late 1970s it became considered appropriate by some musicians (most usually male) for females to play bass guitars in punk and post-punk bands on the understanding that it was easier to play than a guitar and it didn't really matter what notes they played as long as they kept in time.
85. Beats per minute.
86. T. W. Adorno, "On Popular Music," in Simon Frith and Andrew Goodwin, eds., *On Record: Rock, Pop and the Written Word* (London: Routledge, 1990), pp. 301-14.

87. Cale played organ in the recording of the former album.

88. I'm aware that in inverse configuration these spell fifths and therefore can imply (as spelt) dominant-to-tonic or (in retrograde) tonic-to-dominant, but functionally they are substantively tonic-to-subdominant.

5 The Factory

1. Keir Keightley in his essay "Reconsidering Rock" writes of the concept "teen" music (its opposite being "adult" music) being replaced by "youth" from 1964–5 onwards, admitting that "youth" is a more complex term. See Simon Frith, Will Straw and John Street, eds., *The Cambridge Companion to Pop and Rock* (Cambridge: Cambridge University Press, 2001), pp. 122–5.

2. The system of two people writing one song, or a number of songs, together has a long history and stems from the practice of one composer writing the music and one lyricist writing the words. Although solo song writers such as Cole Porter existed, Richard Rodgers and Lorenz Hart in the 1920s and 1930s were exemplars (they often started with the music, Hart adding words), followed by Leiber and Stoller in the 1950s. In the early 1960s the Brill Building and Aldon company nearby employed female/male pairs of songwriters such as Carole King and Gerry Goffin, Cynthia Weil and Barry Mann, Ellie Greenwich and Jeff Barry. The solo female singer-songwriter genre grew very slowly out of the folk movement. Odetta, Joan Baez and Judy Collins sang traditional works and those of contemporary writers, but from this background emerged Joni Mitchell in the late 1960s. Rock groups were exclusively all male in membership (with the exceptions noted in the main text) and so in consequence male writing partnerships were the norm.

3. Their manager locked them in a room until they came up with something of their own.

4. Cale and Bockris, *op. cit.*, p. 73.

5. The Doors, 'Light My Fire' (lyrics by Robby Krieger and Jim Morrison), 1967.

6. Bockris and Malanga, *op. cit.*, p. 96.

7. 'White Light/White Heat'.

8. Quoted in Robert Hughes, *American Visions* (London: Harvill Press, 1997), p. 563. Warhol also wrote: "Love and sex can go together. And sex and unlove can go together. And love and unsex can go together. But personal love and personal sex is bad", in Andy Warhol, *The Philosophy of Andy Warhol: From A to B and Back Again* (New York: Harcourt Brace Jovanovich, 1975).

9. Morrissey to Richard Witts, January 1991. Possibly a reference to Oscar Levant's droll comment on Day, "I knew her before she was a virgin".

10. Nico to Richard Witts, February 12th, 1986.

11. As a Maoist – a revolutionary communist – which he became at that time.

12. The MC5 (Motor City 5) from Detroit came to be known around 1968, hence its exclusion from the 1966/7 list.

13. A fourth category could be added, that of "mainstream", to cover the most economically successful bands; The Beatles were "activist", at least in relation

to "non-activist" The Rolling Stones. Jimi Hendrix was activist in contrast to Cream. Both The Beatles and Hendrix may be considered musically "experimental" but lyrically "reflexive" in the same manner.

14. Cale to Richard Witts, *Strange Brew*, *op. cit.*

15. Robert Hughes, *New York Review of Books* 1982, quoted in Robert Hughes, *Nothing If Not Critical* (London: Harvill Press, 1990), pp. 245–6. Also Holly Woodlawn: "If it wasn't for Andy, these lunatics, these mental defectives, would have no place to go." *Andy Warhol: The Complete Picture*, directed by Chris Rodley (USA: World of Wonder, 2002) Programme II (20:20).

16. Thanks to the gay liberation movements of the late 1960s and 1970s.

17. Morrison to Richard Witts, September 1994. Also Nat Finkelstein: The hatred "[of V.U.] had nothing to do with their music; a lot of it had to do with the gay image", in Bockris and Malanga, *op. cit.*, p. 127.

18. Ingrid Superstar: "Some people mistake [Nico's voice] for a boy's voice." Quoted in Bockris and Malanga, *op. cit.*, p. 62.

19. Nico, interview with Richard Witts, February 12th, 1986.

20. See Jean Stein, *Edie: An American Biography* (New York: Knopf, 1982).

21. Richard Witts, *op. cit.*, p. 133.

22. Richard Witts, *op. cit.*, p. 133.

23. In fact a Slovakian dialect rather than the Czech language: "a language is a dialect with an army and a navy" (with thanks to Alex Bellem).

24. Warhol gained a degree in pictorial design from the Carnegie in 1949.

25. Paul Warhola in *Andy Warhol: The Complete Picture*, Programme 1: "Leader of the Brand" (14:30).

26. For example, the young British "pop" artist Peter Blake collected these illustrations at the time: "What attracted me was a fluid, broken line. It was a searching line. I collected his work." *Andy Warhol: The Complete Picture* (16:30). These lines were also described as "blotchy" or "scratchy", as he copied the original line onto blotting paper to achieve the effect, discarding the original in the process, leading – it's been suggested more than once – to Warhol's later interest in multiples and screen-printing.

27. He was good at his job. For his shoe ads he was awarded the 1957 Art Directors' Club Medal.

28. Cultural critic Dwight MacDonald: "Western culture has been about two cultures: the traditional kind – let us call it 'High Culture' – that is chronicled in the textbooks, and a 'Mass Culture' manufactured wholesale for the market... like chewing gum." "A Theory of Mass Culture," from *Diogenes* 3 (Summer 1953), reprinted in Bernard Rosenberg and David Manning White, eds., *Mass Culture: The Popular Arts in America* (New York: Free Press, 1957), p. 46.

29. Post-war American culture was otherwise considered to be the Hollywood film, popular music, and the "horror comic".

30. Warhol, *The Philosophy of Andy Warhol*, p. 229.

31. Capote interviewed in Stein, *op. cit.*, pp. 196–7.

32. Mark Rothko and Ashile Gorky committed suicide, while Jackson Pollock and David Smith were killed in car crashes.

33. Unlike Warhol they chose a pseudonym of "Matson Jones" to hide their trade from other artists.

34. Poet John Giorno: "[The art world was] completely homophobic and that's what had always terrified Andy and Bob Rauschenberg and Jasper. Having grown up in the fifties, coming into the sixties was like punching out of a paper bag." Quoted in Bockris, *op. cit.*, p. 203.

35. Kenneth E. Silver, "Andy Warhol 1928–1987," *Art in America* 75.5 (1987).

36. See Chapter 1 on hard-edged abstraction.

37. See David E. Brauer *et al.*, *Pop Art: US/UK Connections 1956–1966* (Houston, TX: Hatje Cantz, 2001).

38. Quoted in Rodley, *op. cit.* (41:00).

39. Begun a week after Monroe's suicide.

40. From press photographs taken before and after the shooting of her husband, and also at the funeral.

41. Commissioned through architect Philip Johnson for the 1964 New York World's Fair, but rejected. Warhol had it painted over in silver.

42. Quoted in *Andy Warhol: The Complete Picture* (51:00). Additionally Warhol desired to alter his name, partly to reverse the decreased circulation of his existing work. Sam Green: "He decided not to sign his name that year [1965]. In fact that was the year he applied to the Library of Congress to have his name officially changed to John Doe." In *Warhol Denied*, dir. Chris Rodley, BBC1 TV, transmission January 24th, 2006.

43. "Underground" was a term taken from the French, where it had first been descriptive of the World War II anti-Nazi resistance movement, but post-war came to epitomize the cultural underground, a modish subculture associated with the Left Bank of Paris, where existentialist-inspired youths would gather in "caves" – underground bars – to listen to singer-songwriters. Nico Papatakis owned one of the first and most famous of these, La Rose Rouge, where singer Juliette Greco was "discovered".

44. Quoted in Sheldon Renan, *The Underground Film: An Introduction to its Development in America* (London: Studio Vista, 1968), p. 100.

45. Warhol's Slovakian background, Nico's German, Maciunas' Estonian, Cale's Welsh and Mekas' Lithuanian backgrounds, illustrates the notion of New York City as a city of immigrants.

46. Renan, *op. cit.*, p. 101.

47. Conrad: "My principal motivation was to explore the possibilities for harmonic expression using a sensory mode other than sound.... I was interested to see whether there might be combination-frequency effects that would occur with flicker, analogous to the combination-tone effects that are responsible for consonance in music." Brian Duguid interview with Tony Conrad, *Table of the Elements* 1996, at http://media.hyperreal.org/zines/intervs/conrad (accessed August 8th, 2005).

48. "What the comic book and the soup can were for painters, Hollywood and home movies were for some film-makers." Stephen Dworkin, *Film Is: The International Free Cinema* (London: Peter Owen, 1975), p. 50.

49. Dworkin, *op. cit.*, p. 129.

50. See Renan, *op. cit.*, pp. 181–3.

51. It was used in a campaign by reactionary politicians who opposed President Johnson's appointment of a liberal judge to the Supreme Court in 1968. The Congressional Record for September 4th, 1968 registered an account of the film: "[*Flaming Creatures*] presents homosexual acts between a man dressed as a female who emerges from a casket, and other males, including masturbation of the visible male organ."

52. For instance, Warhol attended the New York première in 1962 of Young's *Trio for Strings* (of 1958). See Potter, *op. cit.*, p. 91.

53. The daughter of Montez and the French film star Jean-Pierre Aumont, Tina Aumont, coincidentally, became one of Nico's best friends after she left the Velvets. Tina starred opposite Donald Sutherland in Fellini's *Casanova*, but, like Nico, became a regular heroin user.

54. Danny Peary, *Cult Movie Stars* (New York: Simon & Schuster, 1991), p. 387.

55. Quoted on http://www.warholstars.org/warhol/warhol1b/jacksmith.html.

56. Nico would make 18 films in total, including eight for Warhol/Morrissey. See Richard Witts, *op. cit.*, pp. 319–21.

57. Morrison to Richard Witts, September 1994.

58. Cale and Bockris, *op. cit.*, p. 224.

59. http://mujweb.cz/www/heliczer

60. Morrissey to Richard Witts, January 1991.

61. See, for example, comments by Paul McCartney and Ringo Starr on the South Bank Show, *The Making of Sgt Pepper* (London Weekend TV, 1992).

62. There is a documentary about Tally Brown by the German transvestite director Rosa von Praunheim (1979).

63. Warhol feature, WNET, New York, January 8th, 1966.

64. Ultra Violet, *Famous for Fifteen Minutes: My Years with Andy Warhol* (New York: Harcourt Brace Jovanovich; London: Methuen, 1988), p. 107.

65. Andy Warhol and Pat Hackett, *POPism: The Warhol Sixties* (New York: Harcourt, Brace & Co., 1980), p. 147.

66. See *Andy Warhol: The Complete Picture*, Programme II (36:00).

67. *Desert Island Discs*, February 2004, BBC Radio 4. In fact Warhol was addicted from 1963 to Obetrol, a prescription amphetamine drug that gave the user energy to do a lot of work.

68. Cale to Richard Witts, January 1991.

69. Cale and Bockris, *op. cit.*, p. 90.

70. Cale to Richard Witts, January 1991.

71. Ertegun did sign The Young Rascals, however.

72. *Chelsea Girls* earned $300,000 in the first six months. By November 1966 it was playing daily in two Manhattan cinemas.

73. Titled *A Quick One* in the UK.

74. *Melody Maker* (London), August 19th, 1967, p. 9.

75. Alan Campbell interviewed by Richard Witts, May 2004.

76. Morrissey interview with Richard Witts, January 1991.

77. It was sold on in 1967 to a man who wanted to promote coffee to teenagers as a coffee-shop-cum-discothèque called The Electric Circus.
78. Cale: "He spent all the time on the phone, talking to various girlfriends." Cale interview with Richard Witts, January 1991.
79. Cale and Bockris, *op. cit.*, p. 108.
80. Morrison interview with Richard Witts, September 1994.
81. Quoted in Bockris, *op. cit.*, p. 157.
82. Bockris, *op. cit.*, p. 168.
83. Bockris, *op. cit.*, p. 168.

6 Death and Transfiguration

1. De Curtis to Richard Witts, *Strange Brew, op. cit.*
2. Ralph Gleason, *San Francisco Chronicle*, May 1966: "If this is what America's waiting for, we are going to die of boredom because this is a celebration of the silliness of a café society, way out in left field, instead of far out – and joyless." Quoted in Bockris, *op. cit.*, p. 136.
3. See Marshall McLuhan (1911–80), *The Gutenberg Galaxy* (London: Routledge & Kegan Paul, 1962) and *Understanding Media* (New York: McGraw-Hill, 1964). His *The Medium Is The Massage* (New York: Random House, 1967) includes a photograph of The Velvet Underground playing at The Trip in Los Angeles, May 1966.
4. Lysergic acid diethylamide (first synthesized in Switzerland, 1943). Outlawed only in 1966. Nico was later introduced to peyote buttons by Jim Morrison.
5. Obetrol. See Chapter 5.
6. Richard Witts, *op. cit.*, p. 165.
7. Cale to Richard Witts, *Strange Brew, op. cit.*
8. Morrison to Richard Witts, September 1994.
9. See Frank Zappa with Peter Occhiogrosso, *The Real Frank Zappa Book* (London: Pan, 1989), pp. 91–9.
10. Cale and Bockris, *op. cit.*, p. 96.
11. Lucie-Smith, *op. cit.*, p. 24.
12. The Velvets' producer Tom Wilson began this when he put electric guitars, electric bass and drums on Simon and Garfunkel's hit 'The Sounds of Silence' in 1965. By folk-rock is meant the addition of electric instruments and even a rhythm & blues backing style to established numbers of the folk song repertory, or to new songs in that style, or to the folk-style songs that Dylan described in 1964 as coming "from the inside of me" in contrast to his protest, "finger-pointing" songs.
13. A motorcycle accident in July 1966 took Dylan out of commission. He left a space which others attempted to fill. He returned in 1968 with *John Wesley Harding*, which seemed to effortlessly consolidate the explorations of those others to gain him a "smoother" sound. Reed, influenced by Dylan, endeavoured to produce his version of that stylistic shift, but fitted around his established subject matter.

14. From 231 E 47th Street to the fifth floor of 33 Union Square West, February 1968.

15. Victor Bockris, *Warhol* (London: Penguin, 1989), p. 337.

16. Peter Hogan, *The Complete Guide to the Music of the Velvet Underground* (London: Omnibus Press), p. 25.

17. Here I'm including the songs released not only on the third and fourth albums, *The Velvet Underground* (1968/1969) and *Loaded* (1969/1970), but also those songs recorded in 1968 and 1969 yet only released in the 1980s on *VU* (1985) and *Another View* (1986).

18. Liner notes to *The Psychedelic Sounds of the 13th Floor Elevators* (1966), quoted in Palmer, *op. cit.*, p. 163.

19. Charles Jencks, *The Language of Post-Modern Architecture* (London: Rizzoli, 1978). See also Jencks, *What is Post-Modernism?* (London: Academy Editions, 1986), p. 14.

20. Cale to Richard Witts, January 1991.

21. See Michael Keith and Steve Pile, *Place and the Politics of Identity* (London: Routledge, 1993).

22. LP *Cotillon*, May 1972; CD on Atlantic. It's supposedly recorded on Reed's last night with the band (August 23rd, 1970), though there is nothing to confirm this. Morrison was certainly sceptical of the claim that this was the recording's date.

23. Palmer, *op. cit.*, p. 166.

24. Morrissey to Richard Witts, January 1991.

25. Originally a quote from 1961 by painter Frank Stella.

26. Even in 1997 the discography of the fan-focused *Velvet Underground Companion* (ed. Albin Zak; London: Omnibus Press) mentions "Heroin" consistently as "H."

27. Nico to Richard Witts, 1986.

28. Cale to Richard Witts, *Strange Brew*, *op. cit.*

29. Morrison to Richard Witts, September 1994.

30. Tucker to Richard Witts, September 1994.

31. Morrison complained that, in between her songs, Nico would wander off-stage and talk to friends in the audience, because that's what she'd seen Marlene Dietrich do during cabaret scenes in films.

32. Nico to Richard Witts, February 1986.

33. According to Hogan, *op. cit.*, p. 92.

34. Bockris and Malanga, *op. cit.*, p. 142.

35. Lou Reed, *Metal Machine Music* (Double LP on RCA, 1975; CD on Buddha Records, 2000).

36. In fact his final contractual commitment to RCA was realized with *Coney Island Baby* released January 1976, his sixth solo album. He had provided four albums of a five-album deal prior to *Metal Machine Music*. This surely accounts for the press comment that *Metal Machine Music* was a cynical, effortless "spoiler" to discharge his legal obligation.

37. It is rather close in sound to Xenakis' *Persepolis* of 1971.

38. The general move from the stage to the studio has already been noted. However, from 1968 onward there came a reaction by artists considering the studio an inauthentic environment.

39. Their given names were Tom Miller (Verlaine), Richard Meyers (Hell), John Gezale (Thunders), James Osterberg (Pop). Osterberg was one of Nico's lovers.

40. Ron Ashton of The Stooges: "Our audiences were the opposite of fans." They threw eggs, cigarette butts and whiskey bottles at the stage. Iggy Pop: "I had to quit. It's hard to beat yourself up every night." In *Punk Rock USA*, BBC Radio 2, March 13th, 2004.

41. Nico to Richard Witts, February 12th, 1986. When Nico lost her Indian harmonium, Patti Smith bought her a new one.

42. Most conspicuously brought together by the British singer David Bowie (David Jones, b. 1947) who trained as a mime artist and worked in an arts centre.

43. While popular bands moved into large arenas and stadiums, the alternative scene lost the wide range of performance spaces available in the 1960s and moved into small bars and clubs, the most well-known New York club of this kind being CBGBs ("Country, Blue Grass and Blues") which could be hired on an otherwise empty Monday night.

44. Also known as New Wave, both terms being music-industry constructs.

45. Perhaps with the exception of "Run Run Run". I'm grateful to Graham Duff for pointing this out.

46. Brought on by the Yom Kippur War of 1973 between Israel, and both Egypt and Syria, and the subsequent global rise in the price of oil.

47. See Paul Hodkinson, *Goth: Identity, Style and Subculture* (Oxford: Berg, 2002).

48. Congested not only by artists but also by the burgeoning number of small, independent record companies. It was also a period of recession; the market itself was small.

49. Liner notes to *Metal Machine Music*, 1975.

50. As previously noted, Reed, Cale, and Nico each had felt the need to hide some facts about age, drugs, or relationships. The exception has been Tucker whose accounts of events have been convincingly straightforward.

51. However, his later books surpassed this.

52. Hannett to Richard Witts, *New Manchester Review*, April 1980.

53. Bockris (1994), *op. cit.*, p. 98.

54. Bockris (1994), *op. cit.*, p. 21.

55. Nico to Richard Witts, February 12th, 1986.

References

Adorno, T. W. "On Popular Music." In *On Record: Rock, Pop and the Written Word*, eds Simon Frith and Andrew Goodwin. London: Routledge, 1990.

Atlas, James. *Delmore Schwarz: The Life of an American Poet*. New York: Farrar Straus Giroux, 1977.

Banes, Sally. *Greenwich Village 1963*. Durham, NC: Duke University Press, 1993.

Bentley, Bill. "Sterling Morrison: Appreciation." *Austin Chronicle* 15.2 (September 1995).

Boyd, Malcolm. *Bach*. London: J.M. Dent, 1983.

Brauer, David E., *et al. Pop Art: US/UK Connections 1956–1966*. Houston, TX: Hatje Cantz, 2001.

Breslin, James A. *Mark Rothko: A Biography*. Chicago: University of Chicago Press, 1993.

Brown, David. *Tchaikovsky: Biographical and Critical Study. IV. The Final Years*. London: Gollancz, 1991.

Bruce, Lenny. *Obscenity, Busts and Trials*. Sheffield: Pirate Press, 1992.

Burton, Humphrey. *Leonard Bernstein*. London: Faber & Faber, 1994.

Campbell, James. *This Is The Beat Generation*. London: Secker & Warburg, 1999.

Cardew, Cornelius. "One Sound: LaMonte Young." *Musical Times* 107.11 (1966).

———"On the Role of the Instructions in the Interpretation of Indeterminate Music." In *Treatise Handbook*. London: Peters, 1971.

Chaney, David. *Lifestyles*. London: Routledge, 1996.

Cohn, Nik. "Phil Spector." In *The Rolling Stone Illustrated History of Rock & Roll*. New York: Rolling Stone Press, 1980.

Conrad, Tony. *Table of the Elements* 1996, at http://media.hyperreal.org/zines/intervs/conrad. Accessed August 8th, 2005.

Cotkin, George. *Existential America*. Baltimore: The Johns Hopkins University Press, 2003.

Curiger, Bice. *Meret Oppenheim: Defiance in the Face of Freedom*. Zurich: Parkett Publishers Inc., 1989.

D'Emilio, John. *Sexual Politics, Sexual Communities: The Making of a Homosexual Minority in the United States, 1940–1970*. Chicago: University of Chicago Press, 1983.

Dawkins, Richard. *The Ancestor's Tale: A Pilgrimage to the Dawn of Life*. London: Weidenfeld & Nicolson, 2005.

Dworkin, Stephen. *Film Is: The International Free Cinema*. London: Peter Owen, 1975.

Echols, Alice. "Nothing Distant About It: Women's Liberation and 1960s Radicalism." In *The Sixties: From Memory to History*, ed. David Farber. Berkeley: University of California Press, 1994.

Farrell, James J. *The Spirit of the Sixties: Making Postwar Radicalism*. London: Routledge, 1997.

Flint, Michael F. Nicholas Fitzpatrick and Clive D. Thorne. *A User's Guide to Copyright*. London: Butterworth, 5th ed., 2000.

Fluxshoe (Devon: Beau Geste Press, 1972).

Frith, Simon, Will Straw and John Street, eds. *The Cambridge Companion to Pop and Rock*. Cambridge: Cambridge University Press, 2001.

Frith, Simon, and Andrew Goodwin, eds. *On Record: Rock, Pop and the Written Word*. London: Routledge, 1990.

Ginsberg, A. *Howl*, Part II, in *Collected Poems 1947–1980*. London: HarperCollins, 1984.

Goldberg, RoseLee. *Performance Art: From Futurism to the Present*. London: Thames & Hudson, 1979, rev. ed. 1988.

Gottehrer, Barry. *New York, City of Crisis*. New York: David McKay Co., 1965.

Gottlieb, R., ed. *Reading Jazz*. London: Bloomsbury, 1997.

Hammett, Dashiell. *The Maltese Falcon*. London: Orion, 2002.

Harrison, Ann. *Music – The Business: The Essential Guide to the Law and the Deals*. London: Virgin Books, 2003.

Hebdige, Dick. *Subculture: The Meaning of Style*. London: Routledge, 1979.

Hendricks, Geoffrey, ed. *Critical Mass: Happenings, Fluxus, Performance, Intermedia and Rutgers University 1958–1972*. Piscataway, NJ: Rutgers University Press, 2003.

Hendricks, Jon, ed. *Fluxus Codex*. Detroit: Gilbert & Lila Silverman Fluxus Collection, 1988.

Hennessy, Peter. *Never Again: Britain 1945–1951*. London: Jonathan Cape, 1992.

Hess, Thomas. Introduction to the Barnett Newman catalogue. London: Tate Gallery, 1972.

Higgins, Hannah. *Fluxus Experience*. Berkeley: University of California Press, 2002.

Hobsbawm, Eric. *Age of Extremes: The Short Twentieth Century 1914–1991*. London: Michael Joseph, 1994.

Hodkinson, Paul. *Goth: Identity, Style and Subculture*. Oxford: Berg, 2002.

Hughes, Robert. *Nothing If Not Critical*. London: Harvill Press, 1990.

——*American Visions*. London: Harvill Press, 1997.

Isserman, Maurice, and Michael Kazin. *America Divided: The Civil War of the 1960s*. New York: Oxford University Press, 2004.

Jencks, Charles. *The Language of Post-Modern Architecture*. London: Rizzoli, 1978.

——*What is Post-Modernism?* London: Academy Editions, 1986.

Jones, Caroline. *Machine in the Studio: Constructing the Post War American Artist*. Chicago: University of Chicago Press, 1996.

Joselit, David. *American Art Since 1945*. London: Thames & Hudson, 2003.

Keith, Michael, and Steve Pile. *Place and the Politics of Identity*. London: Routledge, 1993.

Kostelanetz, Richard. *The Theatre of Mixed Means*. New York: Dial Press, 1968.

Kotz, Mary Lynn. *Robert Rauschenberg: Art and Life*. New York: Harry N. Abrams Inc., 1990.

Lewisohn, Mark. *The Complete Beatles Chronicle*. London: Pyramid Books, 1992.

Lucie-Smith, Edward. *Movements in Art Since 1945*. London: Thames & Hudson, 2000.

Martindale, William. *The Complete Drug Reference*. London: Pharmaceutical Press, 32nd ed., 1999.

McLuhan, Marshall. *The Gutenberg Galaxy*. London: Routledge & Kegan Paul, 1962.

——*Understanding Media*. New York: McGraw-Hill, 1964.

——*The Medium Is The Massage*. New York: Random House, 1967.

Mertens, Wim. *American Minimal Music*. London: Kahn & Averill; New York: Broude, 1983.

Miles, Barry. *Ginsberg: A Biography*. London: Penguin, 1990.

Miller, Jim, ed. *The Rolling Stone Illustrated History of Rock & Roll*. New York: Random House, 1976.

Monteagudo, Jesse. *The Death of the Beat Generation*, 1997, at http://gaytoday.com/garchive/viewpoint/102797vi.htm. Accessed February 13th, 2006.

Morgan, Bill. *The Beat Generation in New York*. San Francisco: City Light Books, 1997.

Morris, Charles R. *The Cost of Good Intentions*. New York: Norton & Co., 1980.

Morrow, B., ed. *World Outside The Window: The Selected Essays of Kenneth Rexroth*. New York: New Directions, 1987.

Naifeh, Steven, and Gregory White Smith. *Jackson Pollock: An American Saga*. London: Barrie & Jenkins, 1990.

Newhouse, Thomas. *The Beat Generation and the Popular Novel in the United States 1945–1970*. Jefferson, NC: McFarland & Co., 2000.

O'Neill, John P., ed. *J. P. Clyfford Still*. New York: Metropolitan Museum of Art, 1979.

Palmer, Robert. *Dancing in the Street*. London: BBC Books, 1996.

Peary, Danny. *Cult Movie Stars*. New York: Simon & Schuster, 1991.

Phillips, R., ed. *The Ego is Always at the Wheel: Bagatelles by Delmore Schwarz*. Manchester: Carcanet Press, 1987.

Plank, William. *Sartre and Surrealism*. Ann Arbor: Michigan University Press, 1981.

Pollock, Howard. *Aaron Copland: The Life and Work of an Uncommon Man*. New York: Henry Holt, 1999; London: Faber & Faber, 2000.

Polsky, Ned. *Hustlers, Beats and Others*. London: Penguin, 1967.

Potter, Keith. *Four Musical Minimalists: La Monte Young, Terry Riley, Steve Reich, Philip Glass*. Cambridge: Cambridge University Press, 2000.

Renan, Sheldon. *The Underground Film: An Introduction to its Development in America*. London: Studio Vista, 1968.

Revil, David. *The Roaring Silence: John Cage, A Life*. New York: Arcade Publishing, 1992.

Rexroth, Kenneth. "Jazz Poetry." In *World Outside The Window: The Selected Essays of Kenneth Rexroth*, ed. B. Morrow. New York: New Directions, 1987.

Rosenberg, Bernard, and David Manning White, eds. *Mass Culture: The Popular Arts in America*. New York: Free Press, 1957.

Scott, W. B., and P. M. Rutkoff. *New York Modern: The Arts and the City*. Baltimore: The Johns Hopkins University Press, 1999.

Silver, Kenneth E. "Andy Warhol 1928–1987." *Art in America* 75.5 (1987).

Skerl, Jennie, ed. *Reconstructing the Beats*. London: Palgrave, 2004.

Sontag, Susan. "Notes on Camp (1964)." In *A Susan Sontag Reader*. London: Penguin Books, 1983.

Stangos, Nikos, ed. *Concepts of Modern Art*. London: Thames & Hudson, 3rd ed., 1994.

Starr, C. R. "I Want To Be With My Own Kind – Individual Resistance and Collective Action in the Beat Counterculture." In *Reconstructing the Beats*, ed. Jennie Skerl. London: Palgrave, 2004.

Stein, Jean. *Edie: An American Biography*. New York: Knopf, 1982.

Thompson, Dave. *Wall of Pain: The Biography of Phil Spector*. London: Sanctuary, 2003.

Thornton, Sarah. *Club Cultures: Music, Media and Subcultural Capital*. London: Polity Press, 1995.

Turner, C., trans. *America*. London: Verso, 1988.

Wallock, Leonard, ed. *New York: Cultural Capital of the World 1940–1965*. New York: Rizzoli, 1988.

Warhol, Andy. *The Philosophy of Andy Warhol: From A to B and Back Again*. New York: Harcourt Brace Jovanovich, 1975.

Warhol, Andy, and Pat Hackett. *POPism: The Warhol Sixties*. New York: Harcourt, Brace & Co., 1980.

Whaley, Preston, Jr. *Blows Like A Horn: Beat Writing, Jazz, Style, and Markets in the Transformation of US Culture*. Cambridge, MA: Harvard University Press, 2004.

Wilentz, Elias, ed. *The Beat Scene*. New York: Corinth Books, 1960.

Williams, Martin. "A Night at the Five Spot." In *Reading Jazz*, ed. R. Gottlieb. London: Bloomsbury, 1997.

Zappa, Frank, with Peter Occhiogrosso. *The Real Frank Zappa Book*. London: Pan, 1989.

Bibliography of The Velvet Underground

Bockris, Victor. *Warhol*. London: Penguin, 1989.

——*Lou Reed: The Biography*. London: Hutchinson, 1994.

Bockris, Victor, and Gerard Malanga. *Up-Tight: The Velvet Underground Story*. London: Omnibus Press, 1983 (updated 1994, republished 2002).

Cale, John, and Victor Bockris. *What's Welsh for Zen?* London: Bloomsbury Press, 1999.

Clapton, Diana. *Lou Reed and The Velvet Underground*. London: Omnibus Press, 1982.

Doggett, Peter. *Lou Reed: Growing Up in Public*. London: Omnibus Press, 1992.

Finkelstein, Nat. *Andy Warhol: The Factory Years 1964–1967*. New York: St Martin's Press; London: Sidgwick & Jackson, 1989.

Fricke, David. Liner-note booklet to *Peel Slowly & See* compilation. USA: Polygram, 1995.

Griffiths, Dai. " 'Home is like a man on the run': John Cale's Welsh Atlantic." *Welsh Music History Journal*. Bangor, University of Wales Press, vol. IV (2000): 159–85.

Guiles, Fred Lawrence. *Loner At The Ball: The Life of Andy Warhol*. London: Bantam Press, 1989.

Harvard, Joe. *33 1/3 : The Velvet Underground & Nico*. London: Continuum Books, 2004.

Hogan, Peter. *The Complete Guide to the Music of The Velvet Underground*. London: Omnibus Press, 1997.

Kostek, M. C. *The Velvet Underground Handbook*. London: Black Spring Press, 1992.

Miles, Barry. *Words and Music: Lou Reed*. London: Wise Publications, 1980.

O'Brien, Karen. *Hymn To Her: Women Musicians Talk* (chapter on Moe Tucker). London: Virago Press, 1995.

Reed, Lou. *Between Thought and Expression: Selected Lyrics of Lou Reed*. New York: Hyperion Books, 1991; London: Viking Press, 1992.

Roberts, Chris. *Lou Reed – Walk on the Wild Side: The Stories Behind the Songs*. London: Carlton Books, 2004.

Thompson, Dave. *Beyond The Velvet Underground*. London: Omnibus Press, 1989.

Ultra Violet (Isabelle Collin Dufresne). *Famous for Fifteen Minutes: My Years with Andy Warhol*. New York: Harcourt Brace Jovanovich; London: Methuen, 1988.

Viva. *Superstar*. n.p.: Putnam Press, 1970.

Witts, Richard. *Nico: The Life and Lies of an Icon*. London: Virgin Books, 1993.

Zak, Albin, III, ed. *The Velvet Underground Companion: Four Decades of Commentary*. London: Omnibus Press, 1997.

Index